AF881429

Emile Zola and the Artistry of Adaptation

LEGENDA

LEGENDA, founded in 1995 by the European Humanities Research Centre of the University of Oxford, is now a joint imprint of the Modern Humanities Research Association and Maney Publishing. Titles range from medieval texts to contemporary cinema and form a widely comparative view of the modern humanities, including works on Arabic, Catalan, English, French, German, Greek, Italian, Portuguese, Russian, Spanish, and Yiddish literature. An Editorial Board of distinguished academic specialists works in collaboration with leading scholarly bodies such as the Society for French Studies and the British Comparative Literature Association.

MHRA

The Modern Humanities Research Association (MHRA) encourages and promotes advanced study and research in the field of the modern humanities, especially modern European languages and literature, including English, and also cinema. It also aims to break down the barriers between scholars working in different disciplines and to maintain the unity of humanistic scholarship in the face of increasing specialization. The Association fulfils this purpose primarily through the publication of journals, bibliographies, monographs and other aids to research.

Maney Publishing

Maney Publishing is one of the few remaining independent British academic publishers. Founded in 1900 the company has offices both in the UK, in Leeds and London, and in North America, in Boston. Since 1945 Maney Publishing has worked closely with learned societies, their editors, authors, and members, in publishing academic books and journals to the highest traditional standards of materials and production.

Emile Zola and the Artistry of Adaptation

❖

Kate Griffiths

LEGENDA

Modern Humanities Research Association and Maney Publishing
2009

Published by the
Modern Humanities Research Association and Maney Publishing
1 Carlton House Terrace
London SW1Y 5AF
United Kingdom

LEGENDA is an imprint of the
Modern Humanities Research Association and Maney Publishing

Maney Publishing is the trading name of W. S. Maney & Son Ltd,
whose registered office is at Suite 1C, Joseph's Well, Hanover Walk, Leeds LS3 1AB

ISBN 9-781-906540-27-2

First published 2009

Printed in Great Britain

Cover: 875 Design

Copy-Editor: Richard Correll

CONTENTS

ACKNOWLEDGEMENTS

I would first like to thank the Arts and Humanities Research Council and the British Academy for the research leave and conference funding which made this monograph possible. Thanks are also due to the University of Wales, Bangor for the period of research leave granted to commence the project.

Many friends and colleagues in Swansea and elsewhere have helped this project in its various stages. I am immensely grateful for their time, patience and insight. Particular thanks are owed to Michèle Hannoosh, Susan Harrow, Hannah Thompson, Glynnis Cropp, Derek Connon, Nigel Harkness, Larry Duffy, Graeme Harper, Rob Stone, Elaine Canning, Nick White, Andrew Counter and Owen Evans for their guidance, feedback, suggestions and leads. David Evans and Floriane Place-Verghnes provided valuable opportunities to test-drive aspects of the project. I thank Robert Singer for his advice and assistance in tracking down rare Zola adaptations and Katie Halsey for her help on so many occasions.

Finally, I am grateful to be able to record in print my warmest thanks to John, Margaret, David, Matthew and Daniel Griffiths, and, last but certainly not least, to Richard Sheppard.

EDITIONS CITED

Unless otherwise stated, the source for the five main novels by Zola discussed in each successive chapter of this book is *Les Rougon-Macquart*, ed. by Henri Mitterand, 5 vols (Paris: Gallimard, 1960–67). Page numbers are given in the text. They are to be found as follows:

La Terre (Chapter 1) — vol. IV
L'Œuvre (Chapter 2) — vol. IV
Nana (Chapter 3) — vol. II
La Curée (Chapter 4) — vol. I
La Bête humaine (Chapter 5) — vol. IV

Editions of other works by Zola are indicated in the notes.

INTRODUCTION

Adaptations of the novels of Emile Zola are habitually approached as imperfect reproductions of a superior textual original, or, as Millicent Marcus puts it in a different context, as 'an inferior version [...] of a formally pure source'.[1] In 2006, one of the most recent adaptations of Zola's work appeared at the National Theatre. Marianne Elliott staged Nicholas Wright's adaptation of Zola's own theatrical adaptation of his 1867 novel *Thérèse Raquin*. Critical responses to her production are revealing. Writing in *The Daily Telegraph*, Charles Spencer is damning in his assessment of Elliott's production: 'Zola's original novel will haunt my memory far more potently than this disappointingly pallid and laborious stage version'.[2] Whilst Michael Billington in *The Guardian* writes far more positively of Elliott's version, deeming it 'a miracle of sound and light, music and movement', his criticism is instead reserved for Zola's own theatrical adaptation: 'The play, in short, is nothing like as powerful as the novel.'[3] Zola's novel is implicitly positioned as a potent original text whose lustre cannot be captured by adapting hands — even if those hands belong to Zola himself.

Such reactions, far from being reserved for theatrical adaptations of Zola's novels, are comparably rife in relation to cinematic adaptations of this nineteenth-century novelist's works. Whilst some critics have even gone so far as to hail specific cinematic adaptations as improvements on the novel, their voices are few and far between. Writing on the cinematic adaptation of *Thérèse Raquin* released by Marcel Carné in 1953, François Vinneuil claims: 'Le problème de l'adaptation littéraire est résolu, cette fois, par l'éclatante supériorité, en richesse humaine, en vigueur artistique, de l'œuvre cinématographique sur le roman.'[4] Far more frequent, however, are those who borrow from the vocabulary of inferiority, incapacity and betrayal in their assessments of the films drawn from Zola's texts. David Baguley, reviewing the 'bad press' that cinematic adaptations of Zola's novels have received, almost habitually, cites Michel Capdenac's anger at the alterations made by Roger Vadim in his 1965 adaptation of *La Curée*: 'Pourquoi diable, dans ce cas, avoir conservé le titre, alors que justement ils ont édulcoré ou esquivé ce qui lui donne sens, c'est-à-dire l'essentiel, l'arrière-plan politique et social.'[5]

These fulminations and their counterparts have done nothing to put off those with an urge to adapt Zola's texts into film. Cinema's love affair with Zola's novels and short stories is an abiding one. Some eighty cinematic adaptations of Zola's works have been created and he is, as Robert Singer points out, 'one of the most adapted authors in world literature'.[6] The first known cinematic adaptation of Zola dates from as early as 1902, the year of the author's death, when Ferdinand Zecca's *Les Victimes de l'alcoolisme* appeared. Zecca's five-minute film is made up of five tableaux apparently based on *L'Assommoir.* The link between early cinema and literature is a well-established one. As soon as film technology had advanced far enough in terms of possible film length and complexity to allow the production of narrative works, filmmakers began to adapt established literary texts. Such adaptations not only enabled them to exploit the notoriety of blockbusting works for commercial gain, but also simultaneously permitted the nascent medium of film to claim some sort of cultural legitimacy for itself. However, the link between early cinema and Zola's novels in particular is pronounced. A consideration of just one of his novels, *L'Assommoir,* is revealing. Following Zecca's 1902 adaptation, a further three French adaptations were made before the outbreak of World War I: Albert Capellani's *L'Assommoir* (1909), Gérard Bourgeois's *Les Victimes de l'alcool* (1911) and Emile Chautard's *Le Poison de l'humanité* (1912). D. W. Griffith adapted *L'Assommoir* in America to create *The Drunkard's Reformation* which appeared in 1909. Moreover, Griffith's film underlines the complex processes of filtration which often lie behind certain adaptations of Zola's texts. As Diane Smith and Robert Singer point out, Griffith's film stems from the New York revival, in 1903, of the play *Drink,* which was the British theatrical version, created by Charles Reade in 1879, of Gastineau and Busnach's French theatrical adaptation of *L'Assommoir.*[7]

The reasons for early French cinema's interest in Zola's texts specifically are open to debate. A variety of responses have been suggested. Leo Braudy parallels the technical possibilities and ambitions of the new medium with Zola's naturalist aesthetic ideal. He claims:

> The young French film-makers of this period believed that the essence of the new medium was its ability to record and immerse itself in authentic detail. Their theories of film were usually parallel to the precepts of Emile Zola in his *Le Naturalisme au théâtre,* a polemical blast at the artificialities and limited social viewpoint of nineteenth-century French popular drama.[8]

Sergei Eisenstein offers a slightly different explanation for the popularity of Zola's texts as subject matter for the early years of film: what he deems their pre-cinematic qualities. Eisenstein, a life-long admirer of Zola's novels, cites the nineteenth-century novelist as being 'in the methodological sense the greatest school for a filmmaker (his pages read like complete cue sheets)'. Whilst never adapting Zola's texts, Eisenstein makes the following claim of Zola's work:

> I reread him. Before each new project I reread the appropriate volume of his works. Before *The Strike*: *Germinal.* Before *The General Line*: *Earth.* Before *October*: *The Débâcle* for the attack on 18 June 1917 and *The Happiness of Women* for the rape... of the Winter Palace.[9]

Jean Chothia, in contrast, suggests that some of Zola's influence on film stems from André Antoine, a key name in the theatre and the cinema to whom this book will return, and whom Chothia sees as a conduit carrying some of Zola's texts and ideas into the spheres of theatre and subsequently film. Whilst Antoine's output as a filmmaker was comparatively small, his impact was not. Chothia explains this impact in the following terms:

> His influence in cinema derives partly from the presence in the new industry of actors and régisseurs — de Max, Joubé, Tourneur, Capellani, Gémier — whose theatrical training had been with Antoine, and partly from the recurrence among the early scripts of the French cinema of works that had inspired or had figured in the repertoire of Antoine's theatres.[10]

Cinema's attraction to Zola's texts is not limited to its nascent years. Filmmakers from a variety of eras and countries, with affiliations to very different cinematic schools of thought, have, throughout the twentieth century, turned to create versions of Zola's texts. In order to attempt to do some justice to the variety of Zolas that exist in celluloid form, this current volume incorporates readings of two silent adaptations of the novelist's work (André Antoine's *La Terre* of 1921 and Jean Renoir's *Nana* of 1926) as well as more modern sound versions of Zola's novels. Jean Renoir's 1938 French adaptation of *La Bête humaine* is evaluated alongside Fritz Lang's 1954 film noir Hollywood remake of the same text, entitled *Human Desire.* Whilst Renoir's *La Bête humaine* was hailed, as Chapter 5 will make clear, as an exemplar of Zola adaptation, this monograph also turns to analyse the reputedly 'bad' adaptation which, as we have seen, infuriated Capdenac amongst others: Roger Vadim's 1965 version of *La Curée.* Moving into the twenty-first century, the adaptation of Zola's text into the medium of television will also be considered via an analysis of Edouard Molinaro's 2001 *Nadia Coupeau, dite Nana.* Small screen adaptations of Zola's novels have largely been neglected in the well-trodden field of Zola studies,[11] but Molinaro's self-reflexive approach to the artistry of adaptation, and the interaction of this two-part televisual offering with its cinematic predecessors, make a clear case for its inclusion in this volume.

Whilst my opening paragraphs have attempted to suggest the sheer breadth of adaptations which Zola's work has triggered, it is not the intention of the current book to detail and encompass this range — such an attempt would run to several volumes. Moreover, whilst clearly influenced by them, this piece will not retrace the steps of the body of scholars such as Leo Braudy, Tom Conley, Russell Cousins and Robert Singer, to name but a few, scholars who have valuably and persuasively focused on Zolian adaptation from the perspective of specific films, key directors or delimited historic eras. Rather, the central aim is to reconsider the critical framework according to which cinematic adaptations of Zola's texts are most often assessed in a work that spans a variety of directors, eras and films. 'Under most literary lenses', an adaptation is, according to Kamilla Elliott, considered as 'an inferior reproduction of a superior original'.[12] However, both Zola's approach to his texts and a significant selection of his works resist and destabilize the terminology of copy and original so central to conventional approaches to adaptation. Three factors are of key importance here and will be sketched out in subsequent paragraphs. First, adaptation is not something to which Zola is passively subject, it is a process in which he is actively and thoughtfully involved as he transforms and monitors the transformation of his own texts into other media in his lifetime. Secondly, at the level of plot, specific novels question the possibility of origin at a personal level in their exploration of characters' ability to author their own destiny. Finally, as Zola renders the personal origins of his characters problematic, so too, in certain texts, he explores the origin of his own authorship, playing with the status of his works as textual originals, dramatizing adaptation as a narrative theme.

Zola's involvement in the theatrical adaptation of his own work is well known. His own adaptation of the novel *Thérèse Raquin*, the adaptation from which the Nicholas Wright version mentioned above is drawn, was staged in 1873. In 1879 William Busnach and Octave Gastineau's adaptation of Zola's *L'Assommoir* opened at the Ambigu. Busnach subsequently, and with Zola's permission, adapted *Nana*, *Pot-Bouille*, *Germinal* and *Le Ventre de Paris*, as well as *La Bête humaine*, though this last script was not produced. Zola signed *Renée*, his own adaptation of *La Curée* written between 1880 and 1881, but he distanced himself to an extent from the adaptations undertaken by Busnach. Responding to criticism that the adaptation of *Nana* did not uphold his theatrical naturalist theories, Zola playfully distances himself from the work by underlining that it does not appear under his signature:

> Reste la grosse question de savoir si j'ai collaboré à la pièce et dans quelle mesure. [...] J'estime que je n'ai pas à répondre. On ne m'a pas nommé, cela doit suffire. Cherchez les causes, dites que j'ai juré de ne jamais rien signer en collaboration, ajoutez bien que *Nana* pourrait bien être une expérience et un acheminement, imaginez encore que je veux un autre terrain. Et il y a de grandes chances pour que vous soyez dans la vérité. Mais ce sont là des suppositions. Un seul fait demeure: on ne m'a pas nommé, je ne suis pas de la pièce.[13]

Busnach's correspondence reveals, however, the active participation of Zola in the creation of this adaptation.[14] Zola also collaborated with Alfred Bruneau to create 'théâtre lyrique'.[15] Moreover, as Lawson A. Carter points out, a consideration of *Madeleine Férat* reveals that Zola also engaged in the adaptation of theatre into novel form.[16] This novel first existed as a play. Having had it refused by the Gymnase and the Vaudeville theatres in 1866, Zola subsequently adapted it into a novel published under the title *La Honte* in *L'Evénement* in 1868 and then in book form with the title of *Madeleine Férat*.

Not only are textual origins blurred as Zola's original works are transformed, often by their creator's hand, into different media, but origins at times prove equally problematic, as I have suggested, at the level of characterization. Zola's interest in questions of *race* is well known. It forms the very backbone of the *Rougon-Macquart* series and finds expression in the family tree offered in accompaniment to the collection. However, using characters such as Nana, Jacques and Buteau as case studies, the chapters of this book underline that genetics often do not fix the origins of the Zolian character — rather, they more frequently testify to the very difficulty of so doing. Jacques and Buteau inherit the adapted genetic texts of an endless series of forebears, a series to which there is no true origin. Origins prove as problematic in relation to Nana. Whilst the novel which bears her name devotes textual space to her genetic inheritance, Nana, as Chapter 3 of this volume suggests, ultimately points to a genetic origin which is not her own.

No consideration of concepts of origin in Zola's text can be approached without reference to Naomi Schor's persuasive analysis of the topic in relation to *La Fortune des Rougon*.[17] Schor's book not only testifies to what she deems 'Zola's obsession with origins', it also points out the way in which such origins prove to be impossible to pinpoint in the novelist's fiction.[18] Analysing *La Fortune des Rougon*, the founding volume of the *Rougon-Macquart* series, a volume tellingly bearing the subtitle *Les Origines*, Schor focuses on the shifting position of the cemetery, the Aire Saint-Mittre, containing the grave stone upon which 'all of the *Rougon-Macquart* rests'.[19] However, the contents lying beneath this grave cannot be discovered by reading the inscription on it. Schor writes: '[...] the origins of the Rougon-Macquart are encoded in a half-erased message, at the same time revealed and concealed, thus literally indecipherable'.[20] And, perhaps even more importantly for this volume, this apparent point of origin points elsewhere, for the grave's contents have been transported from a cemetery that no longer exists. Schor is not, as she herself points out, the only critic to testify to the problematic nature of origins in Zola. She harnesses aspects of Jean Borie's reading of Zola to her fiction, in particular his claim that the genetic torments of the Rougon-Macquart family have no locatable origin, no founding event: 'Jamais, pas même dans *Le Docteur Pascal* lorsque Zola résume et passe en revue le cycle tout entier, il ne précise quel est ce premier crime qui accablera la famille'.[21] And, just as the general origins of the family Zola's novelistic series depicts are intriguingly problematic, so too, as other critics in the sphere of Zola studies make clear, are the personal presences of many of its individual members. The eye may devour the seemingly omnipresent body of the courtesan Nana, but it can never truly locate, fix or uncover her.[22] Similarly in *La Terre* Buteau may seek to assert his self-possession and originality, but his identity ultimately proves to be the latest replica in a seemingly endless series of forebears who deny him originality.[23]

Zola's exploration of the problematic nature of personal origins in his texts at the level of characterization runs alongside an examination of the origins of certain of his own texts. Zola offers a self-conscious and probing assessment of his fiction's ability to realize its stated desire to capture the reality which is the origin behind its pages. And, as characters' authorship of their own destiny is mediated by the inherited, adapted genetic texts of a series of their forebears, so Zola points to the way in which his own authorship is at times inherited and adapted from a series of earlier authors and other genres. As Russell Cousins puts it:

> The author was no stranger [...] to transposing material from one literary medium to another, or indeed to emulating the techniques initiated in other art forms. [...] Several of his atmospheric descriptions were a conscious attempt to extend the techniques of the impressionists to the world of literature.[24]

Fidelity discourses revolve around notions of an 'original' novel (or work) of which a subsequent cinematic adaptation is a copy. However, texts such as *La Terre*, *L'Œuvre* and *La Curée*, to cite but a few examples, destabilize their status as textual original. They point to their position as adaptations, and often adulterated, problematic ones at that, of earlier texts, other genres and external reality. Put simply, Zola destabilizes origins, be they those of his characters or indeed those of his own artistry.

Thus, harnessing and adding to the existing body of critical work in the sphere of Zola studies on the problematic nature of origins in Zola's texts, this volume seeks to remobilize such work in the sphere of adaptation. It does so both to underline the particular and perhaps unexpected resonances of such work when re-contextualized in the sphere of Zola and cinema and to make clear the key case study Zola offers scholars of adaptation. In a highly original manner, his texts frustrate those who would view them solely through the lens of fidelity criticism. Fidelity critics have in some ways become straw men, their approaches persuasively undercut by a growing number of cinema scholars. Brian McFarlane states, and goes on to demonstrate, that 'No critical line is in greater need of re-examination — and devaluation'.[25] Julie Sanders seeks to valorize notions of infidelity in creative terms: 'Fidelity to the original? [...] It is usually at the very point of infidelity that the most creative acts of adaptation and appropriation take place'.[26] Millicent Marcus points out that the very terms of the debate on the transformation of the novel into a cinematic copy are problematic since novels, like adaptations, constitute something of a shifting, adapted source: 'The novel is itself a mixed form whose mongrel status has often made it suspect among the apostles of generic homogeneity in literature.'[27]

This current volume is deeply indebted to and influenced by such revisionist voices, voices which will recur in its text. Yet it recognizes that fidelity, as an issue, will not quite go away. Robert Giddings and Erica Sheen in their 2000 work *The Classic Novel: From Page to Screen* acknowledge McFarlane's belief in the need to move beyond fidelity as an all-encompassing critical framework, whilst making clear that all the essays in their edited volume 'take the question of fidelity as their critical point of reference'.[28] Fidelity is, and should be, an issue for those who adapt. Instead of using it as the sole means to judge adaptations of Zola's texts, this monograph instead explores the way in which specific cinematic adaptations themselves consider the question of fidelity. They dramatize it as one of their central narrative themes, acknowledging Zola's own text in their images, assessing their own act of authorship in relation to that text. Specific adaptations of Zola's texts consider their status as adaptations, as copies, albeit in altered form. They consider their own authorial act, pointing to the borrowed origins of their work, to what they have altered, to what they have changed. In so doing, they echo in part the self-conscious authorial stance of Zola as he points to the texts from which he has borrowed, the texts which he has adapted into his own pages. Writing in the context of Italian film, Millicent Marcus has identified in specific films what she calls allegories of adaptation or umbilical scenes, moments 'in which the film reveals the traces of its derivation from the parent text and discloses its interpretive strategy'.[29] Such scenes feature in a number of the adaptations to be studied in the course of this volume as filmmakers consider their own authorial act, as well as that of the source text they copy. I do not make this claim for all cinematic adaptations of Zola's work, and consequently not all of Zola's adaptations and the adaptations springing from them find a space in this monograph. Instead this volume is structured around specific pairings of works, literary and cinematic, which actively engage in a dialogue about authorship, origin and adaptation.

My reading of the interaction of the work of Zola and various filmmakers with notions of textual origin and adaptation is informed at various points by certain theoreticians of textual relations. Harold Bloom's Freudian reading of textual relations and literary property in terms of anxiety and parricide in *The Anxiety of*

Influence resonates in relation to *La Terre*, a novel in which Zola portrays paternal relations and the inheritance of property precisely in terms of usurpation, anguish and the repeated murder of the father.[30] It is arguable that Zola did at times express anxiety in relation to notions of influence. In *L'Œuvre*, his character Claude bemoans the fact that he cannot remove the trace of Delacroix from his works.[31] And Zola himself uses the term anxiety when wondering what future readers will make of him:

> Voici, hélas! que j'arrive à un âge où le regret de n'être plus jeune commence, où l'on se préoccupe de la poussée des jeunes hommes qu'on sent monter derrière soi. Ce sont eux qui vont nous juger et nous continuer. J'écoute en eux naître l'avenir, et je me demande parfois, avec une certaine anxiété, ce qu'ils rejetteront de nous et ce qu'ils en garderont, ce que deviendra notre œuvre entre leurs mains, car elle ne peut être définitivement que par eux, elle n'existera que s'ils l'acceptent.[32]

However, in *La Terre* and elsewhere, Zola explores his own textual inheritance from his literary fathers in a manner more joyful than anguished. Zola's intricate exploration of the borrowed layers of other works in his texts could be paralleled with Gérard Genette's image of the palimpsest. Discussing the shifting and multiple relations between hypotexts and hypertexts, Genette evokes 'la vieille image du *palimpseste*, où l'on voit, sur le même parchemin, un texte se superposer à un autre qu'il ne dissimule pas tout à fait, mais qu'il laisse voir par transparence'.[33] Genette does not explicitly address the question of cinematic adaptation in much depth. He acknowledges it only in passing.[34] However, his image of the palimpsest is key to my reading both of Zola's novels which playfully point to the receding series of texts from which they have borrowed and to the adaptations of Zola's novels which acknowledge Zola's text as a source but also, at times, earlier cinematic versions of that text. Via the image of the palimpsest this monograph will explore the accreted authorial identities both in Zola's texts and in the adaptations made of them.

However, in this book about the shifting traces of earlier authors, the importance of the traces of Jacques Lacan in my reading of Zola and adaptation must also be acknowledged. Whilst Genette may explore the concept of the textual palimpsest, Lacan enacts it, exploring and questioning his own authorship in a manner which is compelling in relation to Zola's text. Lacan invokes earlier authors to facilitate his own points. Their identities are initially acknowledged and their texts remain distinct: 'Elle [la découverte freudienne] s'exprime assez bien par la fulgurante formule de Rimbaud [...] *Je est un autre*'.[35] However, Lacan blurs the citational nameplates of the sources from which he borrows, teasingly erasing them: 'La vie ne songe qu'à mourir — *Mourir, dormir, rêver peut-être*, comme a dit un certain monsieur, au moment précisément où il s'agissait de ça — *to be or not to be*.'[36] Ultimately he rewrites any number of earlier sources, subsuming them into his own authorial voice. Descartes's 'je pense, donc je suis', for example, becomes Lacan's 'je pense où je ne suis pas, donc je suis où je ne pense pas'.[37] Lacan scripts himself over the text of the seventeenth-century thinker but alerts his reader to the palimpsest-like nature of his textual act by choosing not only one of the most canonical writers of all time, but one of his most celebrated lines. Descartes's 'cogito ergo sum' has become a cliché in its own right, a fragment of text whose provenance can never fully be erased. Lacan undertakes a similar action in relation to other lines whose earlier author can never truly be erased: Shakespeare's 'to be or not to be' and Molière's 'tarte à la crème' from *L'Ecole des femmes*.[38] Lacan performs the way in which his own speech always points to someone else, someone earlier, leading his reader back in time, space and text. The texts from which Lacan borrows, themselves borrow from earlier texts and so on, seemingly ad infinitum: 'Vous connaissez tous le thème de *l'Anneau de Hans Carvel*, bonne histoire du Moyen Age, dont La Fontaine a fait un conte et que Balzac a reprise dans ses *Contes drôlatiques*.'[39]

The theories of Genette and Lacan offer a useful starting point for an exploration of the way in which certain Zola texts and specific films made from them playfully explore the palimpsest of their own artistic identity, revelling in notions of textual mobility. Mobility is, Julie Sanders suggests, a feature of the study and terminology of adaptation. In support of such a claim she cites the following list from Adrian Poole which attempts to define the Victorian era's interest in reworking the artistic past: '[...] borrowing, stealing, appropriating, inheriting, assimilating; [...] being influenced, inspired, dependent, indebted, haunted, possessed; [...] homage, mimicry, travesty, echo, allusion, and intertextuality'.[40] Sanders multiplies this mobility of terminology by offering additional suggestions of her own: 'We could continue the linguistic riff, adding into the mix: variation, version, interpretation, imitation, proximation, supplement, increment, improvisation, prequel, sequel, continuation, addition, paratext, hypertext, palimpsest, graft, rewriting, reworking, refashioning, re-vision, re-evaluation.'[41] Whilst recognizing the mobility of possible terms to describe the processes of adaptation, this monograph will structure itself around the following selection of its many variants since they are dramatized by Zola as narrative themes: inheritance, translation, imitation, the pull of texts past, the processes of replacement and displacement.

Chapter 1 explores the theme of inheritance on three levels in relation to *La Terre*. First, at the level of narrative, characters inherit from their fathers, constructing and reinforcing their identity through the property and money they receive by means fair and foul. This exploration of inheritance runs alongside a textual variety of the same phenomenon as Zola's novel about inheritance itself makes use of aspects of the literary property and riches of Shakespeare's *King Lear*. Moreover, Zola's novel was subsequently staged at the theatre in 1904 and adapted in a film by André Antoine released in 1921. The impact of each of these acts of inheritance is assessed in relation to authorship, be it personal (at the level of characterization), textual (that of Zola) or cinematic (that of Antoine).

Chapter 2 turns to consider the question of translation, a theme prominent in Zola's *L'Œuvre*. Not only does Zola present his work as the translation of the impressionists into novelistic form, he also explores the novel's status as a translation of the reality the naturalist school seeks to render. However, origins in *L'Œuvre* prove just as thorny a concept as they were in *La Terre*. Zola may proffer reality as the source behind his textual translation, but it is a reality, *L'Œuvre* makes clear, which cannot be accessed. Characters' identity cannot be unlocked in this *roman à clef* and, via the character of Christine and the portraits painted of her, Zola destabilizes the relationship between source and its artistic reproduction.

Notions of imitation lie at the heart of Chapter 3 and its exploration of the novel *Nana*. Imitation is a key narrative theme as society ladies turn to imitate the novel's heroine. However, Zola will not allow Nana to be considered as a point of origin. He not only denies the reader access to his heroine as a point of origin, mediating her constantly through a series of artistic screens, parts, images and *idées reçues*, he also examines her genetic background to reveal that in terms of heredity she points to an origin which is not her own. Questions of origin are key to a variety of the adaptations derived from *Nana*. This chapter explores Jean Renoir's 1926 silent adaptation of Nana and Edouard Molinaro's 2001 version of the same text. Whilst these versions destined for the large and small screen are very different, both engage with Zola's unpicking of the dialectic between copy and original, assessing their own status as textual copies, evaluating their own authorial act in self-reflexive acts of adaptation.

Adaptation is the focus of Chapter 4. Roger Vadim's 1965 adaptation of Zola's *La Curée* has, as this introduction has already suggested, received a largely critical reception, being frequently denounced as an unfaithful copy of Zola's original text. However, Zola's novel not only plays with notions of origin, it revels in its status as an adaptation of Racine's *Phèdre*, making explicit, at the level of narrative, a hypotextual presence which was only implicit in *La Terre*. Moreover, Racine's *Phèdre* offers no more stable a point of origin than Zola's text, for it lies at the end of a series of earlier adaptations of the original Phaedra myth. And, as Lévi-Strauss points out, 'Comme les rites, les mythes sont *in-terminables*'.[42] Zola's play on the labyrinthine series of texts and adapted images forming the pages of his novel finds an echo in Vadim's film. Vadim, like Zola, in a self-conscious manner, considers his own cinematic act of adaptation, entering into Zola's exploration of the palimpsest at the heart of his authorial act.

If Chapter 4 considers the pull of texts past on Zola's corpus, Chapter 5 assesses that of texts future, turning as it does to assess the issues of replacement and displacement in relation to *La Bête humaine*. Such issues are narrative themes in Zola's novel, themes taken up and enacted by the long line of adaptations made from that novel. Working with Jean Renoir's 1938 French adaptation of Zola's text and Fritz Lang's 1954 Hollywood remake, this chapter analyses the accretion of traces of ghostly authorial identities as successive filmmakers remake not only Zola's text, but adapt the cinematic adaptations which have preceded theirs. These ghostly authorial identities find a compelling parallel in the text itself as the protagonist's own criminal act is authored by the whispering ghostly voices of a seemingly endless series of forebears.

To suggest that origins are problematic in Zola's fiction is not necessarily new. However, to offer a portrait of Zola as an author destabilizing origins in terms of genetics and textuality and to explore the subsequent implications of this destabilization of origin for cinematic adaptation is perhaps more so. Adaptations of Zola's texts are, as has been suggested, often written off as inferior copies of a textual original. However, if certain Zola novels destabilize their status as textual originals and instead play with their own status as adaptations of other works and genres, then the cinematic versions of these novels might be seen as adaptations of adaptations, remakes of what was already a remake. Indeed, some of the adaptations assessed in this volume appear precisely to consider their own status in these terms. Such a notion complicates the dialectical discourse of original and copy, subsuming such terms into a messier and arguably more fertile vision of a shifting series of palimpsest-like works.

Notes to the Introduction

1. Millicent Marcus, *Filmmaking by the Book: Italian Cinema and Literary Adaptation* (Baltimore/London: Johns Hopkins University Press, 1993), p. 22.
2. Charles Spencer, 'Dim Shadows of Zola's Hellish Vision', *Daily Telegraph*, 15 November 2006, <www.telegraph.co.uk> [accessed 24 July 2007].
3. Michael Billington, '*Thérèse Raquin*', *Guardian*, 15 November 2006, <arts.guardian.co.uk> [accessed 24 July 2007].
4. François Vinneuil, 'Résurrection de Marcel Carné: *Thérèse Raquin*', *Dimanche Matin*, 15 November 1953. Also cited in Russell Cousins, *Zola: Thérèse Raquin* (London: Grant & Cutler, 1992), p. 79.
5. Michel Capdenac, *Les Lettres françaises*, 30 June 1966. Also cited in David Baguley, '*Riduttore, Traditore*? On Screening Zola', *Excavatio*, 21 (2006), 198–212 (p. 206).
6. Robert Singer, 'Introduction', in Gural-Migdal and Singer, eds, *Zola and Film* (Jefferson, NC: McFarland, 2005), pp. 5–14 (p. 5).
7. Diane Smith and Robert Singer, 'A Drunkard's Representation: The Appropriation of Naturalism in D. W. Griffith's Biograph Films', *Griffithiana*, 65 (1999), 96–125 (p. 109). Griffith perhaps acknowledges the partly theatrical origins of his adaptation in the fabric of his film, which employs the device of a play within the film. A young man neglects his wife and daughter by drinking too much in a tavern. After a violent scene, his daughter persuades him to take her to the theatre where they watch a dramatization of Zola's *L'Assommoir*. The young man sees his own reflection in the play: a man falling prey to drink, neglecting his family and subsequently dying of madness. He vows never to drink again and the film closes with the family reunited. For an analysis of the reasons behind the alterations to Zola's text, see Tom Gunning, 'From the Opium Den to the Theatre of Morality: Moral Discourse and the Film Process in Early American Cinema', in *The Silent Cinema Reader*, ed. by Lee Grieveson and Peter Krämer (London/New York: Routledge, 2004), pp. 145–54.
8. Leo Braudy, *Jean Renoir: The World of His Films* (London: Robson, 1977), p. 25.
9. S. M. Eisenstein, 'Literature and Cinema: Reply to a Questionnaire' in *S. M. Eisenstein. Selected Works, Volume One: Writings, 1922–1934*, ed. and trans. by Richard Taylor (London: British Film Institute, 1988), pp. 95–99 (p. 95). See also Tony Williams, 'Eisenstein and Zola: Naturalism, Cinema and Mythography', in Gural-Migdal and Singer, eds, *Zola and Film*, pp. 27–44.
10. Jean Chothia, *André Antoine* (Cambridge: Cambridge University Press, 1991), p. 186. The Capellani mentioned in this quotation is the actor Paul Capellani and not the filmmaker Albert Capellani who made a version of Zola's *L'Assommoir* (1909).
11. Notable exceptions include the following article: Russell Cousins, 'Adapting Zola for TV: The Example of Jacques Rouffio's *L'Argent*', *Excavatio*, 12 (1999), 153–61.
12. Kamilla Elliott, *Rethinking the Novel/Film Debate* (Cambridge/New York: Cambridge University Press, 2003), p. 128. Also cited in Baguley, '*Riduttore, Traditore*? On Screening Zola', p. 200.
13. Emile Zola, *Œuvres complètes*, ed. by Henri Mitterand, 15 vols (Paris: Cercle du Livre Précieux, 1966–69), XV: *Théâtre et poèmes* (1969), p. 803.
14. In a letter of 4 July 1880, Busnach writes: 'Je vous propose ceci: aller à Médan le lundi 12 avec 2 tableaux. Faire le scénario avec vous des 7e, 8e, et 9e et repartir le 13 à 5 heures du soir. Puis vous porter les 6e, 7e, 8e et 9e à la fin du mois. Dès que vous aurez mis sur pied les 5 premiers, vous remettrez sur pied les 4 derniers de 1er au 15 août. Du 20 au 25 ou 26 août j'irai à Médan

revoir le tout avec vous et nous l'enverrons à Chabrillat le 1er 7bre.' Cited in Lawson A. Carter, *Zola and the Theater* (New Haven, CT: Yale University Press; Paris: Presses Universitaires de France, 1963), p. 118.
15. See Jean-Max Guieu, *Le Théâtre Lyrique d'Emile Zola* (Paris: Fischbacher, 1983).
16. Carter, *Zola and the Theater*, p. 33.
17. Naomi Schor, *Zola's Crowds* (Baltimore/London: Johns Hopkins University Press, 1978).
18. Ibid., p. xi.
19. Ibid., p. 19.
20. Ibid., p. 19.
21. Jean Borie, *Zola et les mythes* (Paris: Seuil, 1971), p. 43. Also cited in Naomi Schor, 'Mythe des origines, origines des mythes: *La Fortune des Rougon*', *Cahiers naturalistes*, 52 (1978), 124–34 (p. 124).
22. On this point, see, *inter alia*, Janet Beizer 'Uncovering *Nana*: The Courtesan's New Clothes', *L'Esprit créateur*, 25 (1985), 45–56; Peter Brooks, *Body Work: Objects of Desire in Modern Narrative* (Cambridge, MA: Harvard University Press, 1993), p. 155; Eléonore Roy-Reverzy, 'Nana, ou l'inexistence: d'une écriture allégorique', *Cahiers Naturalistes*, 73 (1999), 167–80; Auguste Dezalay, *L'Opéra des Rougon-Macquart: essai de rythmologie romanesque* (Paris: Klincksieck, 1983).
23. See, for example, Guy Robert, *La Terre d'Emile Zola: étude historique et critique* (Paris: Les Belles Lettres, 1952), p. 311.
24. Russell Cousins, 'Zola and the Cinema: Early Screen Versions of *Germinal*', in *Emile Zola Centenary Colloquium, 1893–1993*, ed. by Patrick Pollard (London: Emile Zola Society, 1995), pp. 113–26 (p. 113).
25. Brian McFarlane, *Novel to Film: An Introduction to the Theory of Adaptation* (Oxford: Clarendon Press, 1996), p. 8.
26. Julie Sanders, *Adaptation and Appropriation* (London/New York: Routledge, 2006), p. 20.
27. Marcus, *Filmmaking by the Book*, p. 22. George Bluestone makes a similar point: 'If the film is protean because it has assimilated photography, music, dialogue, the dance, the novel is protean because it has assimilated essays, letters, memoirs, histories, religious tracts, and manifestos. There is no such thing as *the* novel.' George Bluestone, *Novels into Film* (Berkeley/London: University of California Press, 1957), pp. 7–8.
28. *The Classic Novel: From Page to Screen*, ed. by Robert Giddings and Erica Sheen (Manchester: Manchester University Press, 2000), p. 2.
29. Marcus, *Filmmaking by the Book*, p. 140.
30. Harold Bloom, *The Anxiety of Influence: A Theory of Poetry* (Oxford: Oxford University Press, 1973).
31. 'J'ai ce sacré Delacroix dans l'œil.' Emile Zola, *Les Rougon-Macquart*, ed. by Henri Mitterand, 5 vols (Paris: Gallimard, 1960–67), IV: *L'Œuvre* (1966), p. 47.
32. Zola, *Œuvres complètes*, XII: *Œuvres critiques III* (1969), p. 677.
33. Gérard Genette, *Palimpsestes: la littérature au second degré* (Paris: Seuil, 1982), p. 451.
34. Ibid., p. 218.
35. Jacques Lacan, *Le Séminaire. Livre 2* (Paris: Seuil, 1978), p. 16.
36. Ibid., p. 272.
37. Jacques Lacan, *Ecrits* (Paris: Seuil, 1966), p. 517.
38. See Kate Griffiths, 'Descartes and Lacan: Print and the Subject of Citation', *New Zealand Journal of French Studies*, 27 (2006), 16–28.
39. Jacques Lacan, *Le Séminaire. Livre 3* (Paris: Seuil, 1981), p. 356.
40. Adrian Poole, *Shakespeare and the Victorians* (London: Thomson Learning/Arden Shakespeare, 2004), p. 2.
41. Sanders, *Adaptation and Appropriation*, p. 3.
42. Claude Lévi-Strauss, *Mythologiques. Le Cru et le cuit* (Paris: Plon, 1964), p. 14.

CHAPTER 1

❖

La Terre and the Art of Inheritance

Inheritance is key to Zola's 1887 novel *La Terre* both at the level of narrative and that of characterization. As a theme it acquires increased significance when one considers the ancestry of Zola's novel itself since the work interacts with the textual property and riches of Shakespeare's *King Lear.* Prominent critics have characterized textual relations precisely in terms of inheritance. J. B. Broadbent and Harold Bloom both use the terminology of inheritance, albeit whilst conceptualizing its impact in very different ways. For Broadbent, textual inheritance has positive possibilities: 'Literary allusion can be a lesson in the abuse of authority, as well as in the generous spending of an inheritance. We need an essay on "The Poet as Heir".'[1] Harold Bloom, offering a Freudian inspired 'description of poetic influence, or the story of intra-poetic relationships', situates inheritance in far more negative terms, positing the poet as 'the inheritor of a melancholy'.[2] He suggests that 'the covert subject of most poetry for the last three centuries has been the anxiety of influence, each poet's fear that no proper work remains for him to perform'.[3]

Bloom's account of influence thus depicts the relationship between creative minds as antagonistic, as poets wrangle with their forefathers over textual property. This familial wrangle may resonate with the territorial disputes undertaken in the name of inheritance by successive generations in Zola's novel, but a consideration both of Zola's evaluation of the textual property of *King Lear* in his own pages and the author's own cinematic treatment in the hands of the filmmaker André Antoine offer a far more positive vision of textual relations. Whilst the terminology of inheritance cannot be applied wholesale to the process of adaptation, it is highly useful in assessing Antoine's cinematic adaptation of *La Terre*, an adaptation released in 1921 and widely hailed to be one of the most important early adaptations of Zola.[4] Antoine may be considered to be something of an heir to Zola's ideas on dramatic performance, ideas Antoine developed and interpreted in pioneering and distinctive stage techniques in his theatrical productions. The presence of such techniques in his 1921 adaptation underlines the way in which Antoine's authorial identity peacefully cohabits with and indeed furthers that of Zola in a symbiosis of artistic interests perhaps unparalleled in the Zola adaptations considered in this book. This chapter will thus proceed by examining inheritance on three interlinked levels: the constructive role of fiscal and territorial inheritance at the level of characters, Zola's use of aspects of the riches of Shakespeare's *King Lear* and, finally, Antoine's role as heir to Zola's text. It will use the latter to suggest that, while adaptation is at times approached as the theft of a previous author's textual property,[5] Zola is robbed of nothing by Antoine. Christopher Ricks's words on Byron's relationship with Shakespeare, in an essay whose exploration of monetary inheritance, debts and coins resonates with the concerns of this chapter, might be used to describe Antoine's link with Zola. Ricks writes: 'Shakespeare is robbed of nothing by Byron, for Shakespeare's works remain his; tribute is paid. And that which Byron filches does not make Shakespeare poor indeed, but on the contrary bears witness yet once more to the treasury that is Shakespeare; this, even while the filching, stealing, or robbery [...] does enrich Byron's art.'[6]

At the level of plot, inheritance, in its most literal sense, is explored across character and time. Inheritance, real or anticipated, touches the present of the majority of the novel's central characters. The plotline in which Fouan hands over his land to his children is intertwined both with Françoise and Lise inheriting on the death of their father and Elodie's more metaphorical assumption of her ancestral legacy as she takes the reins of the family brothel. Moreover, Zola interweaves this interlinked web of present inheritances with the layers and legacies of the testaments of the past via an exploration of the history of an area of land. As Guy Robert puts it, 'Zola retrace avec précision les vicissitudes de ce petit domaine pendant un siècle: les héritages démembrent, les mariages remembrent.'[7] The twenty one *arpents* of Fouan's father are divided equally between each of his three children. Fouan's *arpents* increase to nineteen following his marriage to Rose and are subsequently divided between his three offspring.[8] The Fouan family history can be traced via a series of inheritances related to this land:

> Ces Fouan avaient poussé et grandi là, depuis des siècles [...]. Anciens serfs des Rognes-Bouqueval, dont il ne restait aucun vestige [...] ils avaient dû être affranchis sous Philippe le Bel; et, dès lors, ils étaient devenus propriétaires [...]. Puis, avait commencé la longue lutte, une lutte de quatre cents ans, pour défendre et arrondir ce bien, dans un acharnement de passion que les pères léguaient aux fils: lopins perdus et rachetés, propriété dérisoire sans cesse remise en question, héritages écrasés de tels impôts qu'ils semblaient fondre, prairies et pièces de labour peu à peu élargies pourtant, par ce besoin de posséder, d'une ténacité lentement victorieuse. Des générations y succombèrent.[9]

The act of inheritance lies at the core of Zola's novel as well as at the heart of the Fouan family it describes.[10]

Zola's interest in the theme of inheritance extends beyond *La Terre*. *Les Héritiers Rabourdin* (1874), a comedy indebted in part to Ben Jonson's *Volpone*, revolves around the fate of an old man whose prospective heirs, mistakenly believing him to be rich, greedily wait for his death.[11] Monsieur Vabre dies intestate in *Pot-Bouille* and his would-be inheritors mourn not his loss, but their lack of inheritance: 'Les Duveyrier se montraient inconsolables de l'avoir nourri douze années, sans lui réclamer une seule fois les quatre-vingt mille francs de la dot de Clotilde.'[12] Zola's work can be seen to be tapping into the contemporary interest in this theme. As Guy Robert points out in relation to *La Terre*:

> [...] il est fréquemment question dans des nouvelles et dans des romans, voire dans l'enquête officielle menée par le gouvernement impérial de 1866 à 1870,

> du sort pitoyable réservé dans les campagnes aux vieux parents qui ont partagé leurs biens entre leurs enfants et dont ceux-ci vont parfois jusqu'à hâter la fin.[13]

Zola both hints at the prevalence of such events and predicts the course of his novel's action when he places the following warning to Fouan in the mouth of the *notaire* presiding over the division of Fouan's land:

> Beaucoup de bons esprits blâment la démission de biens, qu'ils regardent comme immorale, car ils l'accusent de détruire les liens de famille... On pourrait en effet citer des faits déplorables, les enfants se conduisent des fois très mal, lorsque les parents se sont dépouillés... (p. 384)

Zola not only situates inheritance at the core of his novel, he explores, in a manner highly resonant with critical debates on adaptation, the relationship between the property at the heart of such acts of inheritance and the identities between which it is passed. Adaptations of Zola's novels are frequently attacked for dismembering and dispossessing Zola of some of his textual property as they, at times simultaneously, at times exclusively, come to reflect the artistic identity and vision of the director who adapts them. Zola's novel explores at the level of plot not only the sense of self which may be gleaned from literal property inherited from a forebear, it also engages with the notion of bodily loss for that forebear as his/her land and the ratification it promises passes into the hands of his/her heirs.

Inheritance and the property it conveys clearly play a constitutive, constructive function in relation to individual identities. Zola underlines that the possession of land augments the familial standing of individuals. Fouan is a prime example. Zola writes, 'Pendant un demi-siècle, on avait tremblé sous lui, la femme, les enfants, les bêtes, lorsqu'il détenait la fortune avec le pouvoir' (p. 633). Territorial power also equates directly with social respect. Fouan is ignored when he divests himself of his property and only acknowledged when he reinvests in a piece of land: '[...] lui qu'on ne regardait plus dans les chemins, depuis qu'il n'avait que sa peau à traîner au soleil, il fut de nouveau salué et considéré, lorsqu'on le sut rentier et propriétaire' (p. 654). Literal property reinforces the metaphorical property of identity. Buteau is not just metaphorically reinforced by the land he inherits from his father; strikingly, his physical body appears to be literally augmented by it:

> Le fils, depuis le partage des biens, s'était élargi, carré sur les jambes, avec ses mâchoires qui avançaient davantage, dans sa tête de dogue, au crâne resserré et fuyant; tandis que le père, exterminé par ses soixante ans de travail, séché encore, la taille cassée, n'avait gardé de son visage réduit que le nez immense. (p. 632)

Body mass seems to pass from father to son concurrent with the transfer of land.

As textual property reflects the identity of its author, so, in *La Terre*, the land is a mirror which reflects the identity of individual characters. Such a notion is consonant with Zola's concept of *milieu* as one of the three factors fashioning individual identity, a notion which will receive further exploration in relation to *La Curée* in Chapter 4 of this book. A number of landscapes in a variety of Zola's novels contain metaphorical mirrors. In *La Fortune des Rougon*, the reader finds a body of water 'dont la lune faisait un clair miroir'.[14] The narrative of *Le Ventre de Paris* describes the countryside in the following terms: '[...] c'était de vastes plaines grasses, des lieues couvertes d'une végétation drue, bleuies de loin en loin du miroir clair d'un petit lac'.[15] The landscape of La Beauce in *La Terre*, repeatedly described in aquatic terms, does not contain a metaphorical mirror but instead appears to become one: '[...] et la Beauce, à l'infini, se déroulait, toute blanche, plate et immobile comme une mer de glace' (p. 438). The relationship between Buteau and the land is a reflective, narcissistic one. He suffers physically with the wheat during a period of drought: 'Il en souffrait positivement, comme les blés eux-mêmes, l'estomac rétréci, les membres noués de crampes, rapetissé, desséché de malaise et de colère' (p. 535). The onset of rain brings physical relief both to the crops and to Buteau: 'Le blé reprenait une santé de jeunesse, ferme et droit, portant haut l'épi, qui allait se gonfler, énorme, crevant de farine. Et lui, comme la terre, comme le blé, buvait par tous ses pores, détendu, rafraîchi, guéri' (pp. 535–36). A comparable symbiosis appears to link Fouan to the land: 'On le rencontrait toujours rôdant autour d'elles [his former properties] s'intéressant, triste ou gai selon l'état des récoltes [...]. Cette pluie le ragaillardissait, lui aussi' (p. 536).

If property and the act of inheriting it promise self-possession and ratification, the loss of land in *La Terre* is directly equated with the loss of limbs as Zola moves to use highly visceral terms. Buteau fears 'ce partage de biens [between Lise and Françoise], dont il s'épouvantait, comme si on l'avait menacé de lui couper un membre' (p. 622). The narrative states of his fields: '[...] et il les garderait, on lui arracherait plutôt un membre' (p. 530). Parallel links between the land and the limbs of Fouan's body are underlined. He feels dismembered when he passes his land over to his children: 'Mais ce qu'il ne disait pas, ce qui sortait de l'émotion refoulée dans sa gorge, c'était la tristesse infinie, la rancune sourde, le déchirement de tout son corps, à se séparer de ces biens si chaudement convoités avant la mort de son père' (p. 383). When Jésus-Christ allows land to pass out of family possession, Fouan enunciates the loss in personal and physical terms: '[...] t'es un assassin, c'est comme si tu prenais un couteau, vois-tu, et tu m'enlèves un morceau de viande' (p. 645). The physical reaction he experiences as he is forced to sign away this land is equally powerful: 'Ça lui avait tellement coûté, qu'il en suait, hébété, grelottant, regardant autour de lui, comme après une opération, quand on vous a coupé la jambe et qu'on la cherche' (p. 648). Fouan invests in land again precisely to save his own skin: '[...] il ne pouvait vivre ainsi, il y aurait perdu la peau' (p. 653). The relationship between property and identity is a reflective one and both Buteau and Fouan glean a very physical sense of self from their land.

Zola's novel reflects still further on the relationship between property, inheritance and identity at the level of plot. Whilst the Beaucerons state that 'l'homme fait la terre', the inverse also appears true (p. 394). Characters are repeatedly presented as plants grown and sustained by the earth. Delphin is a case in point: 'Et il semblait en tirer un orgueil, d'avoir ainsi poussé dans sa terre, avec l'entêtement borné et vivace d'un arbre' (p. 426). He is 'attaché à la terre comme un jeune chêne' (p. 661). The Fouans in general are described in similar terms: 'Ces Fouan avaient poussé et grandi là, depuis des siècles, comme une végétation entêtée et vivace' (p. 391).

However, Zola's descriptions move, at times, to blur the boundary between land and individual. Property no longer just sustains individual bodies, it also appears to infiltrate them. Thus, the viewer is presented with Delhomme and 'sa large face de terre cuite' (p. 378). Soulas is described in the following terms: 'Il était toujours droit, résistant et noueux ainsi qu'un bâton d'épine, la face creusée davantage, pareille à une trogne d'arbre, sous l'emmêlement de ses cheveux déteints, couleur de terre' (p. 609). Similarly, Rose Fouan has 'le visage couleur d'avoine' (p. 381).

As humans take on certain of the characteristics of the land from which their body is metaphorically fashioned, so the land, in turn, is personified. Zola describes a land with blood pulsing, albeit feebly, through its veins: '[...] la Beauce plate et sans eau, qui n'avait que son blé, se mourait peu à peu d'épuisement, lasse d'être saignée aux quatre veines et de nourrir un peuple imbécile' (p. 491). The leech-like vocabulary used to describe the relationship of Fouan's children to their father's possessions serves to link Fouan once more with this land: '[...] une colère grandissait en lui [Fouan] devant l'enragement de cette chair, qui était la sienne, à s'engraisser de sa chair, à lui sucer le sang, vivant encore' (p. 389). The land is personified as it is being divided between Fouan's offspring and the pain it appears to experience echoes that of its soon-to-be former owner: '[...] et la Beauce, flagellée, s'étendait, d'une tristesse morne' (p. 395). However, Zola repeatedly personifies the land in feminine terms. He states his intention to do so in his notes: 'LA TERRE. C'est l'héroïne de mon livre. [...] Un personnage énorme, toujours présent, emplissant le livre'.[16] The land, at times, appears closely linked to the character Françoise. Buteau's passion for the two become indissociable: 'Ces deux passions arrivaient même à se confondre' (p. 621). She owns the land he desires and her body offers the means to retain it. Buteau struggles to undress Françoise's body as he repeatedly attempts to sleep with her. The labourers' harvesting of the land is described in comparable terms of undressing, though the metaphorical clothes the landscape wears are more glorious than the literal variety worn by Françoise:

> Et, en tous sens, des trouées s'ouvraient, comme dans une étoffe mangée, cédant de partout. La Beauce, lambeau à lambeau [...] perdait son manteau de richesse, cette unique parure de son été, qui la laissait d'un coup désolée et nue. (p. 566)

Moreover, as Buteau brutalizes and marks Françoise's body, the harvesters inflict a similar violence on the body of the land: '[...] chaque coup de faux mordait, emportait une entaille ronde' (p. 566). However, the land is also associated metaphorically with la Cognette. Hourdequin walks across his land, land as sensual as his mistress can be: 'la terre collait à ses pieds, il la sentait grasse, fertile, comme si elle eût voulu le retenir d'une étreinte' (p. 452). Moreover, the land's repeated infidelities, passing as it does from one man to another further link it to la Cognette. Jésus-Christ's words on the land are equally applicable to la Cognette: 'La terre, [...] mais elle se fout de toi, la terre! [...] Elle est à moi, elle est à toi, elle n'est à personne. Est-ce qu'elle n'était pas au vieux?' (p. 561). The land in Zola's novel both assumes a variety of human characteristics and offers individuals the chance to reinforce and ratify their own identity.[17]

As Zola's textual property passes from adaptation to adaptation so Fouan's literal property also passes into new hands. Whilst Zola was active in enabling this process of transfer, for Fouan such movement is merely the subject of lament:

> Il ne lui restait qu'une sensation vive, persistante: la terre, la terre qu'il avait tant désirée, tant possédée, la terre à qui, pendant soixante ans, il avait tout donné, ses membres, son cœur, sa vie, la terre ingrate, passée aux bras d'un autre mâle, et qui continuait de produire sans lui réserver sa part! (p. 733)

The metaphorical mirror of the land no longer reflects his identity, no longer offers him an image of himself, it reflects, instead, another. The land does not, will not know him: 'Une grande tristesse le poignait, à cette idée qu'elle ne le connaissait plus, qu'il n'avait rien gardé d'elle, ni un sou, ni une bouchée de pain, qu'il lui fallait mourir, pourrir en elle, l'indifférente' (pp. 733–34). Without the ratification provided by the land Fouan becomes an empty identity. In a manner which will become more significant once this chapter moves to consider *King Lear*, Zola's narrative repeatedly underlines Fouan's ultimate nothingness: 'Ça se comprenait, il retombait dans le mépris de tous, maintenant qu'il n'avait plus rien' (p. 722). The word 'rien' is repeatedly applied to him: '[...] il ne réfléchissait point, c'était comme ça: quand on n'avait ni enfants, ni maison, ni rien, on se serrait le ventre, on couchait dehors' (p. 725). When, after the division of land has taken place, Fouan claims he is still the master, Buteau retorts, 'Allons donc, vieux farceur, vous n'êtes rien du tout' (p. 633). As Zola puts it, 'Fouan était comme rayé du nombre des vivants' (p. 731).

The eviction of Fouan from his own identity is described in graphic terms in the novel. Fouan's identity is metaphorically expressed in descriptions of the Fouan ancestral home, a building described thus: 'Ah! la pauvre vieille maison patrimoniale des Fouan, bâtie il y avait trois siècles par un ancêtre, aujourd'hui branlante, lézardée, tassée, raccommodée de toutes parts, le nez tombé en avant sous le souffle des grands vents de la Beauce!' (p. 701). Zola's description of Fouan, his body curving progressively closer towards the land which will ultimately reclaim him, echoes that of his ancestral home:

> Dans sa face amincie, décharnée, il ne restait que son grand nez osseux, qui s'allongeait vers la terre. Un peu chaque année, il s'était courbé davantage, et maintenant il allait, les reins cassés, n'ayant bientôt qu'à faire la culbute finale, pour tomber dans la fosse. (p. 732)[18]

The structure of Fouan's identity is dismantled, a process he equates with his own home:

> Déjà il n'avait plus de terre, et bientôt il n'aurait plus de maison. Il lui semblait qu'on sciait les vieilles poutres, qu'on enlevait les ardoises, au-dessus de sa tête. Désormais, il n'avait pas même une pierre où s'abriter, il errait par les campagnes comme un pauvre, nuit et jour, continuellement; et, quand il pleuvrait, la pluie froide, la pluie sans fin, tomberait sur lui. (p. 563)

These words predict Fouan's fate in the novel as he subsequently wanders homeless in a storm, 'étranger et perdu' in the village which has long been his home (p. 727).

Fouan thus cannot retain possession either of the land or of the identity reinforced by it. Ownership passes to his offspring in general and Buteau in particular. Buteau usurps his father's documents, replacing him to collect their financial rewards: 'Buteau agissait en son lieu et place, touchait et signait, sous le prétexte que le bonhomme [Fouan] perdait la tête' (p. 731). Buteau possesses his father's land and to an extent, his signature and the identity it represents. However, as this chapter demonstrates, *La Terre* is a novel that, via its characterization, questions the very possibility of ownership at the level of property. Buteau's possession of the land and the reflective ratification it offers is no more secure than was that of his father. Buteau repeatedly picks up handfuls of earth in the course of the novel. As his father's land is being divided, Buteau reaches to grasp that which he is about to inherit: '[...] ils [the onlookers] le virent qui se baissait, qui prenait dans sa main une poignée de terre, puis qui la laissait couler lentement, comme pour la peser et la flairer' (p. 395). He repeats this action in the course of the novel and, as Robert points out, each repetition of this gesture represents a moment of possession:

> [...] une quadruple répétition accroît la valeur symbolique du geste; on le voit deux fois au moment de l'arpentage, puis lorsque, peu après son mariage avec Lise, Buteau est tout à la joie de la possession et enfin quand [...] il va constater que Jean l'a [the earth] laissée intacte.[19]

However, symbolically, whilst this gesture may represent Buteau's desire to possess the land, it also simultaneously negates his ability to do so permanently and totally. His gesture is identical to that of his father and a long line of forebears, all of whom have grasped the land but been unable to hold it forever. Fouan, talking of his life and that of those like him expresses 'sa passion de la terre, du plus de terre possible, de la motte grasse, qu'on touche, qu'on pèse au creux de la main' (p. 434). In repeating his father's gesture, far from asserting ownership of both his actions and the land, Buteau reveals that his fate will be that of his father and the endless line of forebears before him. As the textual property of Zola's novels as a whole passes from director to director in a series of often related adaptations, so the land in *La Terre* passes between, but is never permanently possessed by, the members of the Fouan family.

It might also be argued that Zola's novel questions its own ability to possess the reality of La Beauce. The landscape of the novel is repeatedly depicted in liquid terms. Zola describes it thus:

> Quand le soir tombait, des façades lointaines, vivement éclairées, étaient comme des voiles blanches, des clochers émergeant plantaient des mâts, derrière des plis de terrain. Il faisait froid, les ténèbres élargissaient cette sensation humide et murmurante de pleine mer, un bois lointain s'évanouissait, pareil à la tache perdue d'un continent. Buteau, par les mauvais temps, la regarda aussi, cette Beauce ouverte à ses pieds, de même que le pêcheur regarde de sa falaise la mer démontée, où la tempête lui vole son pain. (pp. 531–32)

However, not only does the phrase 'à perte de vue' recur in Zola's descriptions of the landscape, but so too do the words 'sans bornes' (p. 367, p. 566, p. 709). Onlookers watch the land: '[...] ils avaient la face rêveuse et figée, la songerie des matelots, qui vivent seuls, par les grands espaces' (p. 396). Repeatedly the author depicts the land in fluid terms which appear to seep beyond the boundaries of his pages, exceeding the senses.

As Buteau's repeated gesture of grasping the earth, discussed above, suggests, Zola parallels his exploration of literal inheritance (land) with the metaphorical variety represented by *race* or genetics. Zola writes in his highly contested work *Le Roman expérimental*: '[...] j'estime que la question d'hérédité a une grande influence dans les manifestations intellectuelles et passionnelles de l'homme'.[20] Buteau's genetic inheritance from his father's identity expresses itself via a parity of words and of gestures. Both, as previously mentioned, equate the loss of the land with the loss of limbs. As Fouan cries when Jésus-Christ allows land to pass out of the family, so Buteau weeps before his father when land he thinks of as his own passes to Jean and Françoise.[21] Zola makes clear that Buteau's mother does have some part in her son's genetic make up: 'Il tenait de son père le désir brutal, l'entêtement dans la possession, aggravés par l'avarice étroite de la mère' (p. 381). However, it is Buteau's father who makes his son, as Buteau recognizes when he twice retorts to Fouan, 'Fallait pas me faire comme ça!' (p. 381) He adds, on the second occasion, 'chacun son tour. Je suis de votre sang' (p. 632). Buteau not only inherits from his father, but, it is implied, he becomes him. His actions in literally and metaphorically dispossessing his father repeat those of Fouan himself. Fouan admits, 'Lui-même avait souhaité la fin de son père. Si, à leur tour, ses enfants désiraient la sienne, il n'en ressentait ni étonnement ni chagrin. Ça devait être' (p. 734). Fouan repeats the actions of his father: 'Et voilà qu'il avait vieilli, qu'il devait céder cette maîtresse à ses fils, comme son père la lui avait cédée à lui-même, enragé de son impuissance' (p. 383). Zola adds, 'De père en fils, on avait partagé ainsi', inserting their actions into a long line of anonymous ancestors (p. 396).[22] Jésus-Christ predicts that Buteau in turn will replicate their actions: 'La terre [...] Est-ce qu'elle n'était pas au vieux [Fouan]? et n'a-t-il pas dû la couper pour nous la donner? et toi, ne la couperas-tu pas, pour tes petits?' (p. 561). Buteau unwittingly adds weight to his brother's prediction by stating: 'Lorsqu'on a fait son temps et qu'on a passé la terre aux autres, on avale sa chique, sans les emmerder davantage' (p. 633). The anonymous 'on' not only sums up the inherited fate of a faceless series of his forebears, it also creates space for the insertion of Buteau himself into the personal pronoun.

Buteau is not the only character to inherit, in genetic terms, from his father. Lise, in some senses, becomes her father, Mouche. Following the division of land between his siblings, Lise's father is unhappy:

> Mouche, veuf depuis longtemps, vivait seul avec ses deux filles, Lise et Françoise, dans une aigreur de malchanceux, encore humilié de son mariage pauvre, accusant son frère et sa sœur, après quarante ans, de l'avoir volé, lors du tirage des lots; et il racontait sans fin l'histoire, le lot le plus mauvais qu'on lui avait laissé au fond du chapeau. (p. 394)

Mouche's words not only echo those of Buteau on the occasion of the division of Fouan's property, but are subsequently transferred into his daughter's mouth when Mouche's own property is finally divided between his offspring: 'Depuis le règlement définitif des comptes, chez M. Baillehache, elle [Lise] se prétendait volée, elle ne tarissait pas en accusations abominables, lancées d'une cour à l'autre' (p. 713). Such repetitions form part of a wider exploration of the theme of replacement and displacement, a theme which is, as Chapter 5 will demonstrate, so central to *La Bête humaine*. As Lise takes her father's place and Buteau that of Fouan, Jean, in a non-genetic context, almost replaces Buteau with Lise. He remarks of Buteau's belated proposal to Lise: 'Tu sais que tu fais bien de revenir, j'allais prendre ta place' (p. 516). *La Terre* resounds with echoes as events are often inhabited by the memories of their like in the past and suspicions that they will be repeated in the future. Fouan watches his land being divided: '[...] [il] rappelait que l'ancien partage entre lui, Mouche et la Grande, avait eu lieu dans le sens qu'il indiquait' (p. 397). Much has been made of the cyclical repetition of nature in the novel. As Ronnie Butler points out, the novel takes the reader through successive seasons:

> The novel opens with the description of the autumn sowing in October 1860 (I.I). Following the spring of 1861, the haymaking is described on two occasions in the summer of that year (II.IV), and subsequently in 1864 (III. IV). The account of the wine-harvest in October 1867 (IV.IV), is followed by that of manuring in September 1868 (V.I). Finally, the winter ploughing of 1868–69 (V.III) is the prelude to the closing scene of spring sowing in March 1869 (V.VI).[23]

Indeed, in an article entitled 'The Cycle Myth in *La Terre* of Zola', Lawrence E. Harvey points out that the circular patterns of nature are echoed in the structure of the book: 'Individual chapters often come full circle and end with the event by which they began.'[24] Jean opens Chapter 1 sowing:

> Jean, ce matin-là, un semoir de toile bleue noué sur le ventre, en tenait la poche ouverte de la main gauche, et de la droite, tous les trois pas, il y prenait une poignée de blé, que d'un geste, à la volée, il jetait. (p. 367)

Zola closes the same chapter with the same image, albeit later in the day: 'Il allait, il venait, à longs pas rythmés dans les labours; et le blé de son semoir s'épuisait, la semence derrière lui fécondait la terre' (p. 377). This reflected image appears a third time as Jean remembers it in the closing of the first part of the book, the section opened by this chapter:

> [...] dès que Jean se fut engagé dans le sentier de traverse, il se rappela le champ qu'il avait ensemencé à cette place, quelques jours plus tôt: il regarda vers la gauche, il le reconnut, sous le suaire qui le couvrait. (p. 438)

These cycles of nature are echoed by the cycles of human behaviour, cycles defined by the literal and genetic inheritance explored at the heart of *La Terre*.

Zola's text not only remembers earlier actions within the lives of characters and their ancestors; so too, it could be argued, it remembers the language and images of earlier texts in its pages. This chapter will now consider the way in which Zola's novel about cycles stages the return, in altered form, of aspects of Shakespeare's *King Lear*.

Zola's admiration for Shakespeare is well-documented. In a letter to Jean-Baptistin Baille in 1860, Zola writes: '[...] je vais tâcher de te dire le mieux possible la sensation que fait naître en moi ce grand écrivain.'[25] He makes clear what he admires in Shakespeare: '[...] je dirai que souvent dans Shakespeare la forme idéale recouvre une pensée réelle, un être humain'.[26] And he concludes: 'Un de ces jours je ne désespère pas de faire une étude consciencieuse sur Shakespeare.'[27] That *La Terre* is influenced directly by *King Lear* is clear. Plans for the work repeatedly reference the Shakespeare play in relation to Zola's protagonist Fouan: 'Pourtant il faut qu'à la fin Beaugrand [an earlier name for Fouan] soit pillé par ses enfants, le roi Lear. [...]. La fin, il faut la débâcle de tout.'[28] Zola notes in *Le second plan sommaire*: 'Calvaire du père. Ne parlant plus à personne. Le roi Lear repoussé par tous ses enfants. Sa vie végétative et ce qu'il pense'.[29] He writes: 'Retour chez Bonhomme [an earlier name for Buteau] longue agonie du père. Le roi Lear. Le gendre tous en file.'[30] He concludes in his character descriptions of Fouan: 'Et à la fin, le pain jeté comme à un chien, le roi Lear, avec la résignation, l'acceptation de la mort, tout seul.'[31]

The interaction, the textual commerce between *La Terre* and *King Lear*, has been signalled in varying degrees of complexity by a variety of critics past and present. Guy Robert picks up and comments on the way in which Zola's contemporary, Sarcey, commenting in *La France* on the depiction of 'le paysan' in *La Terre*, immediately hailed the scene in which Fouan wanders in the storm as being 'd'une grandeur Shakespearienne'.[32] Catulle Mendès, writing in *Le Journal* on 22 January 1902, claims that 'l'épopée de Zola [...] se souvient de la tragédie de Shakespeare'.[33] Emile Legouis, *maître de conférences* at Lyon in 1887, immediately discerned extensive links between Zola's latest novel and Shakespeare's play, links underlined by the following simple assertion: 'Le père Fouan, c'est Lear paysan.'[34] In a recent article, David Baguley moves persuasively to suggest that the ripeness of Zola's novel lies in its ability to combine the poetic and the grotesque in a manner comparable to that of Shakespeare's play.[35]

That the legacy of Shakespeare's textual property finds something of a place in Zola's work is clear. However, the nature of the Shakespearian legacy in Zola's novel is open to debate. If a Bloomian approach to textual relations is adopted, then the nature of that legacy would have to be seen in antagonistic, anxious terms. Certainly, aspects of Bloom's theory resonate with elements of the plot of Zola's novel. Bloom describes poetry as 'property' and evaluates the way in which interpoetic influence can be a 'filial relationship'.[36] In seeking to find the 'proper', the property of his own text and identity, the poet struggles with the textual forebears in whose wake he comes. Bloom writes: 'Do strong poets gain or lose more, *as poets*, in their wrestling with their ghostly fathers?'[37] In Zola's novel, Buteau literally wrestles with his father over property. Fouan opens *La Terre* as the dominating physical presence of the family: 'Il était seul debout et menaçant. La mère tremblait, comme si elle eût craint les torgnoles égarées. Les enfants ne bougaient plus, ne soufflaient plus, soumis, domptés' (p. 390). Yet Fouan is ultimately dominated by his son in very physical terms: 'Et, voyant la main vacillante du vieillard [Fouan] s'abaisser pour taper, il [Buteau] la saisit au vol, il la garda, l'écrasa dans sa poigne rude' (p. 633).

Such a reading of the textual relations between Zola and his textual predecessor, Shakespeare, might find support in the fact that Zola's novel, despite explicitly referencing *King Lear* in its preparatory stages, largely wipes direct reference to this work from its final form. Its Shakespearian legacy is largely implicit. Writing on textual relations in the novel *Pot-Bouille*, Robert Lethbridge enunciates Zola's relation to his own textual property precisely in terms of anguish: 'Zola, lui aussi, ressent cette angoisse de l'originalité face à la saturation du déjà écrit et du déjà lu'.[38] However, Lethbridge argues that Zola mobilizes the textual borrowing he undertakes in *Pot-Bouille* in order to forge something of a self-reflexive literary property and originality for himself:

> Et si Zola se 'refait une virginité', c'est, pourrait-on prétendre, par le moyen d'un réinvestissement transformateur de la composante textuelle; c'est-à-dire, non pas la reduplication d'un modèle générique constitué, mais plutôt un puisement dans ce que Genette nomme cette 'mémoire générique' qui incite, au delà d'un réseau immobile de ressemblances, à une différenciation forcément metatextuelle.[39]

Zola's relationship with *King Lear* is not one of anxiety. The nineteenth-century novelist does not wrestle with his ghostly forebear over textual property. Zola may efface Shakespeare's name from the body of his text, but he encourages his reader to recognize *en filigrane* the textual property of his English predecessor, to recognize sameness in difference in this novel in which textual repetition in slightly altered form is something of a narrative theme.

Zola's choice of forebear is far from insignificant. His novel about inheritance itself inherits aspects of the textual property of a Shakespearian text precisely about inheritance and property. The literal property at stake in both works is very different. In Shakespeare's play, Lear divides Britain between his daughters; in Zola's novel, characters squabble over nineteen *arpents* of farm land. Legouis claims of both works: 'La donnée est la même; les tribulations de Fouan sont celles de Lear, le milieu diffère. Les paysans ont remplacé le roi et les seigneurs.'[40] The social *milieux* in which the works are situated may differ, but the importance both accord to the space of the natural world is strikingly similar. G. Wilson Knight's words on *King Lear* might well be applied to *La Terre*:

> The world of *King Lear* [...] is a world of flowers, rough country, tempestuous wind and wild, or farmyard, beasts; and, as a background, there is continual mention of homely, countrified customs, legends, rhymes. This world is rooted in nature, firmly as a Hardy novel.[41]

Ultimately, the land appears to reclaim Lear's body as he dresses in weeds. As the play's dénouement approaches, Cordelia describes her father thus:

> Alack, 'tis he: why, he was met even now,
> As mad as the vexed sea, singing aloud,
> Crowned with rank fumitor and furrow-weeds,
> With burdocks, hemlock, nettles, cuckoo-flowers,
> Darnel, and all the idle weeds that grow
> In our sustaining corn.[42]

Lear ultimately merges with the nature of the land he gave away. In death, Fouan's body is also described in relation to the soil's products. The coffin metaphorically merges with the wheat the land produces. Jean sees it in the following terms:

> [...] il distingua le cercueil, diminué encore, avec son étroit couvercle de sapin, de la couleur blonde du blé; et des mottes grasses coulaient, le recouvraient à moitié, il ne voyait plus qu'une tache pâle, comme une poignée de ce blé que les camarades, là-bas, jetaient aux sillons. (p. 805)

The natural world, its land and its products lie at the heart of both works.

Moreover, the possession of land serves a similarly reflective function in relation to the metaphorical property of identity in both *King Lear* and *La Terre*. That property serves as a mirror for the individual identities owning it has already been suggested in relation to *La Terre*. The wealth that the land represents ratifies Fouan and subsequently Buteau in his place. Indeed, the reflective function of the land is extended to encompass money by Zola. Significantly, Fouan reputedly hides his 'magot', the secret funds which safeguard his identity, behind a mirror. According to Buteau, 'Certain soir, il avait cru voir son père prendre, derrière une glace, un petit rouleau de papiers' (p. 389). The money disappears as Fouan changes its hiding place, but the reflective function of wealth, be it financial or territorial, is established.[43] As property and the wealth it represents help to constitute Fouan's social body and the loss of this wealth triggers the disintegration of this form, so Lear enjoys a similar relationship with his retinue. When the number of his men is cut by his daughters, who haggle the same way as Jésus-Christ, Fanny and Buteau do to reduce the amount their father costs them, Lear expresses this process of loss in highly corporeal terms, deeming his daughter to be destroying his very flesh:

> But yet thou art my flesh, my blood, my daughter,
> Or rather a disease that's in my flesh,
> Which I must needs call mine. Thou art a boil,
> A plague-sore, or embossèd carbuncle
> In my corrupted blood. (II. 4. 214)

As Regan's fine clothes prove her social identity, so Lear's retinue shores up his social standing. The loss of his land and standing results in his gradual disintegration. In Zola's novel, as this chapter has already suggested, Fouan is referred to as being 'rayé du nombre des vivants' and the word 'rien' repeatedly applied to him. Zola's choice of words appears directly inspired by *King Lear* for there is an extended play on nothingness, on the empty space of identity when possessions literal (land and wealth) and metaphorical (identity and good name) are lost. The following speech between Lear and the Fool subsequent to the King's divesting himself of his property is revealing:

> LEAR: This is nothing, fool.
> FOOL: Then 'tis like the breath of an unfeed lawyer; you gave me nothing for't. Can you make no use of nothing, nuncle?
> LEAR: Why, no, boy; nothing can be made of nothing. (I. 4. 113–16)

The Fool adds, '[...] thou hast pared thy wit o'both sides and left nothing i'th'middle' (I. 4. 147–48). Once divested of both his literal land and the metaphorical property of his standing, Lear amounts to nothing.[44]

In Zola's novel the language of *King Lear* returns. Lear chastises Regan: 'I gave you all' (II. 4. 243). In a direct echo, Fouan laments of his offspring: 'Je leur ai tout donné' (p. 542). A prophecy uttered in *King Lear* is likewise fulfilled in *La Terre*. The Fool claims:

> Fathers that wear rags
> Do make their children blind,

> But fathers that bear bags
> Shall see their children kind. (II. 4. 44–48)

His prophecy explains Fouan's children's change in attitude when they discover that he has not quite given them all his land. Courtesy returns, where formerly contempt and disregard prevailed, thanks to the hope of further financial gain (p. 654). Similarly, Edmond's replacement of his father in *King Lear* prefigures Buteau's usurpation of Fouan's place, in *La Terre*. Having stolen his father's letter to betray him, Edmond claims:

> This seems a fair deserving, and must draw me
> That which my father loses: no less than all.
> The younger rises when the old doth fall. (III. 3. 20–23)

The images of Shakespeare's play return in Zola's novel. Surviving a storm homeless, in a manner comparable to Fouan, Lear hears the following words from Cordelia:

> Mine enemy's dog,
> Though he had bit me, should have stood that night
> Against my fire. And wast thou fain, poor father,
> To hovel thee with swine and rogues forlorn
> In short and misty straw? (IV. 6. 33–37)

Significantly, Fouan wandering in the storm is described in canine terms: 'Fouan s'écarta, avec la crainte qu'on ne l'aperçût à cette porte, comme un chien battu qui retourne à sa pâtée' (p. 725). As if to underline the metaphor, Zola depicts his protagonist as envying a dog: 'Le chien des Bécu, qu'il vit passer, lui fit envie, car cette bête-là, au moins, savait le trou de paille où elle dormirait' (p. 722). Zola's preparatory notes, moreover, underline that Fouan's presentation as a dog is far from unconsidered. He writes: 'Et à la fin, le pain jeté comme à un chien, le roi Lear, avec la résignation, l'acceptation de la mort, tout seul.'[45] Not only do the language and images of *King Lear* return in Zola's novel, but the very theme of things returning, the circular structures of the novel discussed earlier, could be argued to be drawn from Shakespeare's text. *La Terre* is structured around notions of a return. Seasons recur, fathers are metaphorically reincarnated as their sons, land is lost and regained, and even the movements of the local *abbé* are structured around notions of a seemingly eternal return. As Harvey points out, the abbé Godard must return each Sunday to Rognes from Basoches-le-Doyen. He leaves Rognes for good at one point, only to be forced to return to replace the abbé Madeline.[46] In *La Terre*, everything comes back. The cyclical structure of *La Terre* reflects and continues that of *King Lear*. The figure of the wheel is key to Shakespeare's play. Not only does Lear describe himself as a victim strapped to a burning wheel, but other characters make similar circular references. Kent appeals: 'Fortune, goodnight, / Smile once more, turn thy wheel' (II. 3. 155–56). Edmond, acknowledging his return to his former position echoes this metaphor: '[...] 'tis true. / The wheel is come full circle; I am here' (V. 3. 163–64). As Zola's novel comes full circle, opening and closing with scenes of sowing and implicit re-growth, so Shakespeare's play completes a full cycle and returns to something akin to its starting point. Lear opens the play asking Cordelia to speak her love for him: 'What can you say to draw / A third more opulent that your sisters? Speak' (I. 1. 80–81). A mad and bereaved Lear makes a comparable plea to Cordelia to speak at the play's close:

> Cordelia, Cordelia, stay a little. Ha?
> What is't thou sayst? — Her voice was ever soft,
> Gentle, and low, an excellent thing in a woman. (V. 3. 245–47)

To both pleas, Cordelia says not enough for her father's liking. In depicting the entire royal family on stage at the play's dénouement, a vision previously depicted only when the play commences, Shakespeare invites the viewer to consider the cyclical structure of his play, a cyclical structure echoed by the revolutions of Zola's text.

La Terre is neither an adaptation nor a replica of *King Lear.* Innumerable differences do exist. The means of death in relation to Lear and Fouan is a notable example. Yet even here Zola cultivates a sense of sameness in difference for the death he chooses for his protagonist is prefigured anecdotally in Shakespeare's work. Edgar, playing the part of Poor Tom, chants in his apparent ravings about St Swithin meeting the nightmare, a female monster who suffocates using her great weight:

> Swithold footed thrice the wold,
> He met the nightmare and her ninefold;
> Bid her alight
> And her troth plight,
> And aroint thee, witch, aroint thee! (III. 4. 106–10)

Whilst Zola had originally planned to have Fouan die in his fields, he subsequently altered his intentions for his novel's dénouement. Whilst St Swithin is able to tell the monster to get off in Shakespeare's play, Fouan is suffocated by his own monster, Lise. She not only instigates his murder, but, significantly, she also finishes him off by suffocating him with her girth: '[...] elle, montée sur le lit, s'asseyait, enfonçait sa croupe nue de jument hydropique' (p. 792). Zola's dénouement is prefigured, hidden in the fabric of Shakespeare's text. Moreover, the flames of the fire which subsequently burn Fouan in Zola's novel are already metaphorically alight in Shakespeare's play. Lear famously claims:

> I am bound
> Upon a wheel of fire, that mine own tears
> Do scald like molten lead. (IV. 6. 43–45)

The fire started in *King Lear* burns metaphorically throughout *La Terre* as the crops at harvest time are repeatedly depicted with flame-like imagery: '[...] l'air brûlait: on aurait dit qu'ils flambaient eux-mêmes d'une flamme invisible, dans la vibration du soleil' (p. 566). Again Fouan is metaphorically linked with the land as he will come to share its fate. Zola claims: 'La Beauce, à l'infini, s'étendait, écrasée sous un sommeil de plomb'. He continues to describe: '[...] la terre écorchée et cuite, à une odeur de roussi, à la chanson des grillons qui crépitaient comme des braises dans de la cendre' (p. 619). Fouan sleeps as soundly as the land with which he is linked after he has wandered homeless in the storm: 'Le sommeil l'y foudroya, il dormit à l'instant, sans un souffle, sous un écrasement de plomb' (p. 729). Zola repeats this vocabulary in a manner that appears far from incidental for, like the land whose burning was described in corporeal terms using the vocabulary of 'écorchement', Fouan will be burned at the novel's close: 'Dans l'abominable souffrance des brûlures, le père, mal étouffé, venait d'ouvrir les yeux, et ce masque atroce, noir, au grand nez cassé, à la barbe incendiée, les regardait' (p. 793). Furthermore, in another play on sameness in difference, Fouan's burning beard is predicted earlier in the novel when, in association with the Jacques Bonhomme interlude, the characters recount local legends. In one of these stories, bandits thieving money as rapaciously as Buteau and Lise pounce on their victim in order to obtain his wealth: 'Quand ils lui eurent allongé les pieds au-dessus des braises de la cheminée, ils allumèrent avec des brandes de la paille sa barbe et tout le poil de son corps' (p. 424). Yet, inverting this earlier image of conflagration, Zola transforms the man burned so that he would reveal the truth (the hiding place of his fortune) into Fouan, the protagonist who has already handed over his money and is then burned to prevent him from revealing the truth (of Françoise's death). Using the text of *King Lear* and the legends in his own novel, Zola uses repetition to engage in an exploration of sameness in difference.

Such an exploration can also be discerned in wider terms as something of a narrative theme in *La Terre*. Stories are told and retold, words uttered and re-uttered. Fouan tells his story of misfortune repeatedly: 'Fouan [...] se traînant de porte en porte, conta partout l'affaire. Dès qu'il pouvait arrêter un passant, il se lamentait sur son misérable sort' (p. 720). Stories are not only repeated, but they pass from mouth to mouth. Lengaigne's letter from his son Victor is a striking example. It revolves entirely around the price of wine in Lille: 'Et la lettre, dans ses quatre pages d'écriture appliquée, ne contenait guère autre chose. Le même détail revenait à l'infini, en phrases qui s'allongeaient' (p. 555). Not only do the listening crowd repeatedly echo the letter's contents in disbelief at the price of wine ('Tous, du reste, se récriaient chaque fois sur le prix du vin'), but the letter is re-read out loud, causing a series of altered echoes. Zola writes: 'On l'écoutait, des gens qui l'avaient déjà entendue cinq ou six fois, se rapprochaient. Il y avait bien seize sous le litre? oui, seize sous!' (p. 559). Stories are not only told and re-told in the novel, but words begin to circulate detached from any original author. Information on the fate of the war mobilization reaches the village from an unknown source: '[...] vers cinq heures, des renseignements déjà circulaient, venus de Cloyes on ne savait comment, par cette sorte de télégraphie aérienne qui vole de village en village' (p. 758). The circulation and re-circulation of words in Zola's text is reinforced by his consideration of the cycles of local gossip, cycles as repetitive as the structure of Victor's letter:

> [...] et, pendant les deux années, les mêmes commérages avaient évolué avec les saisons, revenant et se répétant, toujours des enfants faits trop tôt, des hommes soûls, des femmes battues, beaucoup de besogne pour beaucoup de misère. Il était arrivé tant de choses et rien du tout! (p. 487)

Words circulate in Zola's text, moving beyond their intradiegetic authors.

The presence of the texts within Zola's text is, moreover, signalled in other ways. The novelist inserts a work of fiction in his fictional pages when he has Jean read to the assembled company from 'un petit livre graisseux, un de ces livres de propagande bonapartiste, dont l'empire avait inondé les campagnes [...]: *Les Malheurs et le triomphe de Jacques Bonhomme*' (p. 428). Ronnie Butler suggests that the insertion of sections of this narrative serves only to hold up the novel's flow.[47] However, it could be argued that Zola uses this textual insert to allude to the textual insertions and borrowings at the heart of his work. The Jacques Bonhomme text covers approximately eight pages and Zola punctuates it with his own narrative, writing his text literally in the interstices of that of Jacques Bonhomme as the characters interrupt Jean's reading. Fouan not only interrupts the Bonhomme story, but he appropriates it, re-telling it unknowingly as he recounts his own life story:

> Alors, en quelques mots lents et pénibles, il résuma inconsciemment toute cette histoire: la terre si longtemps cultivée pour le seigneur, sous le bâton et dans la nudité de l'esclave, qui n'a rien à lui, pas même sa peau. (p. 433)

Zola thus underlines that the stories of Jacques Bonhomme and Fouan reflect each other and he inserts a variety of stories within the wider story of *La Terre*, exploring the question of shifting textual frames in his fiction.

As Zola's text interacts with its textual inheritance of earlier texts, so too it subsequently passes into the hands of André Antoine, a man who may be regarded as something of an heir to some of Zola's ideas in the sphere of theatrical production and performance. Antoine was responsible for the creation of the Théâtre Libre in 1887, a haven for innovative drama and more realistic performance techniques beyond the restrictive approaches of contemporary theatre. Antoine subsequently undertook a similar mission in his Théâtre Antoine, before becoming director of the more mainstream establishment, the Odéon, until 1914. Antoine then turned to work with the medium of film, working on eight films between 1914 and 1922. According to Jean Chothia, Antoine's importance to the theatre and indeed to the cinema should not be underestimated: 'Antoine's idea of an independent theatre altered the process of theatre in the twentieth century and proved a major enabling device for subsequent dramatic writing and innovation. [...] He articulated ideas and instituted practices which have been absorbed and developed in both theatre and cinema.'[48] Antoine's work at the Théâtre Libre, a theatre he founded to be the equivalent of the 'Salon des Refusés' in order to showcase alternative work, began with four one-act realist plays (one of which was an adaptation of Zola) and quickly gained a reputation for furthering the cause of realist/naturalist drama. Antoine produced a stage adaptation of *La Terre* written by Saint-Arroman and Hugot, a play in five acts and ten scenes which was never published, appearing at the Théâtre Antoine on 21 January 1902. Significantly for the purposes of this chapter, Antoine, would, just two years later in 1904, stage a version of Shakespeare's *King Lear*, a play which, as Jean Chothia points out, was far from an obvious choice for French theatres:

> His [Antoine's] was the first [...] *Lear* in France with Fool, Shakespearean scene order and tragic ending. Indeed, it was only the fourth French performance of *Lear*, the first having been in 1783. When last performed in Paris, in 1868, in a translation by Lacroix, barely half of Shakespeare's text had survived. The Gloucester sub-plot was removed and Cordelia, played by the young Bernhardt, lived to become queen in Nahum Tate style. There had been an attempt to

> play a fuller text in 1837, at the Théâtre Imperial du Cirque after Macready's restorations in England had shown the way, but it had failed dismally and reinforced the tendency to play Shakespeare as historical romance.[49]

Antoine subsequently began the adaptation of Zola's *La Terre* into cinematic form in 1919, creating a film released in 1921.[50]

Antoine's position as something of an heir to aspects of Zola's conceptualizations of drama is clear. He wrote in his *Mes Souvenirs sur le Théâtre Libre*: 'La bataille, déjà gagnée dans le roman par les naturalistes, dans la peinture par les impressionnistes, dans la musique par les wagnériens, allait se transporter au théâtre.'[51] Antoine provided the space for this battle to take place both through his choice of plays and via the realism of their staging. Antoine was keen to underline, justifiably, the eclecticism of the theatrical programme of the Théâtre Libre: 'Je pense qu'une formule trop étoite serait la mort, et que, au contraire, il faut nous tenir prêts à accueillir largement tout le monde.'[52] However, writing in 1888 Antoine did admit: 'Si les poètes ont eu leur part dans la saison, les naturalistes ont fourni le meilleur et le plus significatif de l'effort'.[53] Antoine objected to what he saw as unfaithful adaptations of Zola's novels, adaptations he saw as betraying the naturalist ideal. He recounts his reaction to one such adaptation in 1888:

> *Germinal*, adapté par Busnach sur le grand livre de Zola, a fait au Châtelet un four assez embêtant qui retombe sur notre dos à tous. Aussi quelle idée de laisser ce vieux vaudevilliste tripoter ce chef-d'œuvre? Ce qui m'irrite, c'est qu'au fond, Zola s'était intéressé à la pièce beaucoup plus qu'il ne voulait en convenir, et, comme un soir je l'entendais en parler avec un peu de passion, et que je lui reprochais de livrer son œuvre à de pareilles mains, il me dit que cela valait mieux que rien, que ces adaptations réalistes faisaient lentement, mais sûrement, l'éducation du gros public. Et, peut-être, au fond, a-t-il raison.[54]

His admiration for Zola was pronounced ('rien ne peut amoindrir mon admiration pour Zola') and reciprocated.[55] Antoine's memoirs reproduce Zola's praise for him:

> Ce Théâtre-Libre a d'ailleurs l'avantage d'avoir pour directeur un artiste de talent, convaincu, intelligent, M. Antoine [...]. En résumé, ce que je considère comme certain, c'est que, grâce au Théâtre-Libre, une évolution tend à se produire en faveur de notre nouvelle école dramatique, que l'influence de cette école se fait sentir de plus en plus dans le public, et que le temps n'est pas loin ou une légion de jeunes auteurs la vulgariseront sur les autres scènes parisiennes.[56]

Antoine's declared intention in the theatre was to remain as subservient to the piece produced as possible. According to Chothia:

> Antoine repeatedly reminded his actors that their function was to re-create the author's imagined world and to speak the dialogue exactly as written, with no concessions to individual whim or fashionable expectations. He called cuts *tripatouillages* (tamperings) and was vocal against the liberties taken with texts in the Théâtre Français.[57]

In keeping with such statements, Antoine's film version of *La Terre* can be read as a cinematic close reading of Zola's earlier novel. Alterations were necessary. Certain aspects of the novel simply could not be shown on screen and so Antoine cut the most contentious scenes which had caused such outrage in the novel. Jésus-Christ's flatulence and scatological humour is replaced by nose jokes (he blows his nose on the gamekeeper's report and pretends that coins drip from his nose), the attempted rape, animal mating and deliberate family murders disappear. Antoine moves away from the horror of Zola's original dénouement where Fouan burns at the hands of his daughter-in-law and son, replacing it with Fouan dying in the fields, falling, face down on the earth, in a posture of metaphorical crucifixion. However, even in this alteration Antoine reveals his status as a close reader of Zola, for his chosen alteration is the dénouement Zola originally intended for his novel, before the idea of patricide imposed itself. Zola writes, for example, in his plans for the novel: 'Si je pouvais le faire mourir dans la terre, je le ferais lever, étant tout seul, sortir dans le jardin pour avoir un rayon de soleil, tomber, s'asseoir par terre, mourir là.'[58] Antoine was also forced to make cuts for the sake of brevity, cuts necessary for filmic success. Certain characters disappear: the teacher, the politicians, the drunken donkey. However, in some situations, in a manner comparable to a number of the umbilical scenes which will be explored in the course of this monograph, Antoine's film is able to gesture towards what it has omitted and changed, disclosing its narrative approach. The closed relationship between the church and the village in the novel, the lack of support each has for the other, is, in the film, symbolized by the Church's general absence. Fouan, wandering homeless in the village, seeking shelter, tries the church door and finds it locked. The *abbé* is as absent from the village in Antoine's piece as he hoped to be in that of Zola. In closing off the church and barring Fouan's entrance into it, Antoine subtly indicates the religious plot line he has had to bar from his adaptation of Zola's novel.

Such cuts aside, Antoine appears to revel in the detail of Zola's text, to present the viewer with a series of minute motifs gleaned from Zola's text. Zola's novel repeatedly links farm workers with ants swarming over the land: '[...] ils se multipliaient, pullulaient comme de noires fourmis laborieuses' (p. 377). Antoine consequently inserts a close-up of the same animals swarming over the earth when the shepherd and Fouan discuss working the land. As Zola used animals as mirrors for the reflection of his characters (a dog fight occurs immediately after Fouan and his offspring have battled in the *notaire*'s office, geese battle immediately after Jean and Buteau have fought), certain of the animal shots Antoine inserts in his film comment on the actions of his protagonists (p. 391 and p. 606). As Cousins points out, 'Jean's self-congratulation at the attention he receives [from women] is suggested by an associative montage close-up shot of a content turkey'.[59] Zola describes Rose's relationship to her husband, depicting her as existing obediently, 'dans son ombre, ne la quittant pas d'une semelle' (p. 380). In his film, Antoine italicizes Zola's metaphor, playing with Rose's shadow on the wall as she echoes her husband's laments about the quality of the produce their children give them. To underline the metaphorical barrier between Françoise and Jean even in the ultimate union of marriage, Zola places a literal barrier between them as they agree their betrothal: '[...] ils se secouèrent la main, en bons amis, par-dessus la barrière' (p. 691). Antoine does likewise, depicting them conversing through a wire fence. As Fouan constantly sees echoes of the past in the images before his eyes in the present (the verb 'rappeler' is often applied to the character's thought processes), so, as is to be expected in an adaptation, strong memories of the detail of Zola's text inhabit the minutiae of Antoine's images.[60]

However, Antoine not only translates aspects of the detail of Zola's novel into the currency of images, he also does likewise with some of Zola's key concepts. The emphasis Zola placed on the environment as a force acting upon and defining characters is well known and has already been explored in this chapter. Antoine affords the environment a comparable importance in his dramatic productions as a whole:

> Dans les œuvres modernes, écrites dans un mouvement de vérité et de naturalisme où la théorie des milieux et de l'influence des choses a pris une si large place, le décor n'est il pas le complément indispensable de l'œuvre? Ne doit-il pas prendre, au théâtre, la même importance que la description tient dans un roman?[61]

Seeking authenticity, Antoine reminisces about the use of reality in certain of his theatrical productions:

> Dans mon désir d'une mise en scène caractéristique, j'avais accroché [...] de véritables quartiers de viande qui ont fait sensation, et il y avait [...] au milieu de la place du petit village sicilien où se déroule le drame, un véritable jet d'eau qui a mis la salle en joie.[62]

In his stage production of *La Terre*, Antoine brought aspects of the countryside on to the theatre stage, using real bales of hay, real grass and plants.[63] However, to depict the changing landscapes of La Beauce, he had to resort to reproducing them through a series of eight different backcloths as Fouan wanders to his death. Offering as realistic a depiction of an environment as possible appears to be as important to Antoine as it is to Zola.

Antoine's characteristic use of authentic detail in producing *La Terre* for the stage was developed and magnified in his production of the piece for film. He was one of the first feature filmmakers in France to move almost definitively beyond the studio and instead film with his actors on location. *La Terre* was filmed in the village of Cloyes in the Beauce region. This, for Chothia, ensured that 'the farm buildings and the open fields of La Beauce starred legitimately, because the location filming compelled audience belief that they had before them not the brilliant subterfuge of a stage set, but the real thing, an unmediated image of places of Zola's novel'.[64] The documentary desires of Zola's fiction moreover find expression in Antoine's film which uses real actors alongside locals in the market scene, depicting everyday scenes of farm chores, market-day commerce and local produce. Zola's novel repeatedly underlines the endlessness of the Beauce landscape, presenting it, as this chapter has already suggested, as something which cannot fully be contained by Zola's narrative. The phrase 'à perte de vue' recurs in relation to the landscape as Zola depicts 'la perspective fuyante des terrains plats' (p. 369). Antoine echoes Zola's depiction of *milieu* in this respect. He underlines the immensity of the land in question by filming the same object from a variety of angles in order to disorientate the reader (the multiple shots of the harvester from various vantage points in the harvest scene provide a striking example). He also, as part of an exploration of boundaries woven through his film, plays with the edge and limits of his camera. In certain of Antoine's stage plays, he hired, at great expense, large numbers of extras, a practice described by Chothia in relation to Antoine's staging of *La Patrie en danger* in 1889 in the following terms: '[...] some figures were only partly on stage and some had to remain in the wings in order to imply that the stage life was flowing in and out from the real world'.[65] Sheep serve a similar purpose in the film version of *La Terre*. As Françoise and Jean walk out of the opening sequence of the film, sheep stream from the shot, at an angle, beyond the lower right hand corner of the camera, herded by a faceless boy. His importance lies not in his identity, but in his ability to signal life outside the lens of this film.[66]

Thus, Antoine's cinematic adaptation of *La Terre* clearly reflects some of the key concepts and details of Zola's earlier novel. However, the signature of Antoine is simultaneously visible in the film as a result of the use in the film of the innovative and distinctive performance techniques for which he became renowned in the theatre. Whilst these techniques harmonize with Zola's dramatic theories, they are of Antoine's invention and their appearance in his adaptation of Zola's *La Terre* marks the piece with Antoine's identity even while it reflects that of Zola. Antoine's notion of the 'fourth wall' is a key example. Over the course of the nineteenth century a declamatory acting style had become enshrined in French theatrical traditions as had fixed delivery positions. Actors spoke not to each other, but often turned their back or sides to each other, addressing the audience in order to remain visible to them at all times. Antoine was vocal in his criticism of this artificial acting style:

> Mlle Reichenberg, l'autre jour, monologuait debout, en brodant, comme les bonnes femmes tricotent au pas de leur porte. Pas une fois Clotilde et Lafont ne se sont pas adressés franchement l'un à l'autre. Mais, à la ville, au bout de deux phrases, vous diriez à votre interlocuteur: 'Regardez-moi donc, sacrebleu! c'est à vous que je parle!' et vous auriez raison. La vérité est qu'à ce théâtre nouveau, il va falloir des interprètes nouveaux. C'est une vérité élémentaire que je rabâche partout.[67]

Cousins points out the way in which this acting style and positioning of the characters is transferred into early cinematic adaptations of Zola. He cites Capellani's version of *Germinal* filmed six years before Antoine's *La Terre*:

> In the sequence when Souvarine advocates extreme measures [...], he is placed in the foreground with the miners in rows behind him. They remain facing the camera throughout in an arrangement recalling a theatrical production in which actors are advised never to turn their backs to the audience.[68]

However, Antoine's work at the Théâtre Libre in particular had seen him push for a far more natural acting style, and he had the actors perform as if a fourth wall existed in the set, separating them from the audience. He taught his actors not to address the audience who had previously been the focus of the action. Antoine also dimmed the house lights allowing only the action on stage to exist in the spectacle: 'Défense aussi de regarder dans la salle, d'ailleurs obscure. Presque toutes les scènes principales se jouent au troisième plan; les comparses tournant le dos et fixant les acteurs occupés au fond de la scène.'[69]

Antoine's use of his signature fourth wall is visible in his adaptation of *La Terre* from the outset. The film opens with a shot of Jean's back as he walks away from the camera. The camera will subsequently film Lise's back as she bars Jean entry into the house, a space into which the viewer has been allowed admittance. Chothia offers the following description of the audience in Antoine's stage productions:

> No longer the acknowledged core of the action, the audience experiences the illusion of looking in on another real, self-centred world, of being the unseen witness of a moment of actual existence. Each audience becomes a voyeur, a chance eavesdropper in whose unacknowledged presence the most intimate concerns of the characters are revealed.[70]

This notion of the viewer as voyeur is dramatized in Antoine's film from the outset. The action of the first sequence unfolds before the gaze of a hidden viewer, Buteau, who appears hidden behind a corner surveying the whole scene. Jésus-Christ later spies upon his father in the bushes. The camera positions itself behind him, spying on the person spying as Antoine underlines successive layers of intrusive, hidden viewers, gesturing to the hidden presence of the cinematic audience. Witnesses at windows are frequent in Antoine's film and the director frequently offers us their reaction to the events they watch through the frame of that window. Clerks watch Jésus-Christ arrive at the *notaire*'s office, as they do in Zola's novel. Fanny watches her father leave her house through the window, Lise watches Buteau argue with the man evicting them from their house through the window of the same house, having already watched her husband fight with Jean through that of the barn. Silent, at times hidden, witnesses are comparatively common in Zola's fiction.[71] Fouan, for example, is the initially silent witness to Françoise's murder in Zola's novel. Interestingly, he plays no such role in the film where instead the viewer takes his role as silent witness. Replicating the darkness of Antoine's theatre auditorium, we are positioned in the darkness of the barn watching as Antoine's film opens the locked door onto the reality and light of the world beyond. The camera pulls forward into this reality, leaving the darkness behind as the audience gains admission into the world on film.

That Antoine's film reflects the textual property of Zola, that it trades in the currency of his novel's images, is not surprising in an adaptation. However, what is more unusual is the manner in which the currency of Antoine's authorial identity circulates alongside and via that of Zola. Coins and currency play a key role in Antoine's adaptation. Both Jésus-Christ and La Trouille appropriate coins, placing them in their eyes. Such images not only underline the propensity of both to see only money, they also teasingly invert the cultural associations traditionally associated with coins and eyes. Instead of son and granddaughter placing coins on the eyes of Fouan as a corpse in order to pay for his safe passage into the afterlife, Jésus-Christ and La Trouille steal the coins they place in their eyes from their living father, hastening his transformation into that corpse. La Trouille displays her coin in her eye to her admirers whilst her father, in one of the film's rare direct address shots, smiles for the camera and the viewer with that which he has plundered in his eye. Antoine uses the coin to depict the shared genetic inheritance Zola describes as linking father and daughter. Moreover, Antoine uses coins to underline the genetic links between other generations of this family. He constructs a series of mirror scenes around the same collection of coins. Buteau calls grudgingly to pay his father some of what he owes him. His father sits at a table and twice gestures with his hand forcing Buteau to increase the sum. Immediately after, Fouan visits Jésus-Christ seeking the money his son owes him. The positions from the previous scene are reversed as son is seated at the table in the position his father previously occupied in his own home. Furthermore, Jésus-Christ will immediately after this scene repeat his father's double hand gesture to his own offspring, forcing La Trouille to increase the sum of coins (coins purloined from Fouan) she hands over to him. As coins are exchanged in this film, passing from hand to hand in different scenes, so too are certain recurrent images circulated and applied to different characters.

The vocabulary of plundering and the usurpation of original property and textual riches often appears in critical writing on adaptation, particularly when notions of fidelity are considered. Notions of plundering and the usurpation of property and wealth lie at the heart of Zola's novel *La Terre*. Not only are they prevalent on a narrative level as offspring seek to appropriate their father's wealth and indirectly his identity, but Zola gently highlights the way in which his text appropriates aspects of the textual currency and images of Shakespeare's *King Lear*. In a text about inheritance, literal and genetic, Zola might be seen covertly to situate his own text as inheriting from a text and author past. Zola's novel subsequently passes to Antoine, a dramatist and filmmaker who is something of an heir to Zola's ideas on performance. That Antoine's adaptation has a reflective relationship with Zola's text as its source is unsurprising for it is an adaptation. However, Antoine's adaptation is valuable not only as one of the important early adaptations of Zola's work, but because in terms of authorial presence the reflective surface of his own work not only offers an image of Zola, but also bears witness to the outlines of Antoine's own artistic identity. Zola is not robbed, for tribute is paid as Antoine adapts, but Antoine succeeds simultaneously in finding his own artistic currency in the exchange and circulation of Zola's images.

Notes to Chapter 1

1. Christopher Ricks cites Broadbent and subsequently meets the need Broadbent identifies, giving the opening section of his work *Allusion to the Poets* the following title: 'The Poet as Heir'. See Christopher Ricks, *Allusion to the Poets* (Oxford: Oxford University Press, 2002), p. 9.
2. Bloom, *Anxiety of Influence*, p. 5, p. 8. Melancholia, in a psychoanalytic-inspired work of criticism, is a loaded term. Freud situates melancholia as a pathological form of mourning. Mourning is the finite and inevitable reaction to the loss of a loved one, a reaction which loses its force as the bereaved detaches him or herself from the deceased. In contrast, Freudian melancholia, as Colin Davis puts it, 'occurs when for some reason the normal process of mourning is blocked; affect remains attached to the lost object and time's healing properties do not function to the expected degree'. Colin Davis, *Haunted Subjects: Deconstruction, Psychoanalysis and the Return of the Dead* (Basingstoke: Palgrave Macmillan, 2007), p. 132. For Bloom the poet cannot easily detach himself from the influence of deceased predecessors, his melancholy is thus potentially endless.
3. Bloom, *Anxiety of Influence*, p. 148.
4. See Russell Cousins, 'Antoine's Version of *La Terre*: An Experiment in Naturalist Cinema', in Gural-Migdal and Singer, eds, *Zola and Film*, pp. 15–26.
5. According to Brian McFarlane: 'As soon as the cinema began to see itself as a narrative

entertainment, the idea of ransacking the novel — that already established repository of narrative fiction — for source material got underway, and the process has continued more or less unabated for ninety years.' McFarlane, *Novel to Film*, pp. 6–7. Geoffrey Wagner echoes this vocabulary of theft in the context of Zola's works, suggesting that in the early years of the twentieth century, 'over in France Zola's canon had already been plundered for film'. Geoffrey Wagner, *The Novel and the Cinema* (London: Tantivity Press, 1975), p. 27.

6. Ricks, *Allusion to the Poets*, p. 147.
7. Robert, *La Terre d'Emile Zola*, p. 280.
8. For further details of the measurements of land involved, see Ronnie Butler, *Zola: La Terre* (London: Grant & Cutler, 1984), pp. 13–14.
9. Zola, *Les Rougon-Macquart*, IV: *La Terre*, (1966), pp. 391–92. Unless otherwise stated, subsequent references are to this edition and will be made in the text.
10. For an evaluation of French inheritance laws, largely in relation to a specific historical case study, see Margaret H. Darrow, *Revolution in the House: Family, Class, and Inheritance in Southern France, 1775–1825* (Princeton, NJ: Princeton University Press, 1989).
11. See Carter, *Zola and the Theater*, p. 41.
12. Zola, *Les Rougon-Macquart*, III: *Pot–Bouille* (1964), p. 221.
13. Guy Robert, *Emile Zola: principes et caractères généraux de son œuvre* (Paris: Belles Lettres, 1952), p. 81. Robert cites, for example, 'La Paralytique', a short story by Charles Grandmougin (1886): an elderly countrywoman goes to live with her nephew, her relatives hoping ardently for her death in order that they might be delivered from the care of her and benefit from her money. Ultimately Grandmougin's heroine will meet a fate similar to that of Fouan: she is suffocated by her relatives. Robert, *La Terre d'Emile Zola*, p. 96.
14. Zola, *Les Rougon-Macquart*, I: *La Fortune des Rougon* (1960), p. 202. Unless otherwise stated, subsequent references are to this edition and will be made in the text.
15. Zola, *Les Rougon-Macquart*, I: *Le Ventre de Paris* (1960), (p. 691). Unless otherwise stated, subsequent references are to this edition and will be made in the text.
16. Cited in Robert, *La Terre d'Emile Zola*, p. 168.
17. As the land is personified in *La Terre*, certain characters at times become dehumanized as man appears to become something of a machine. When Françoise and Buteau work on the land, Zola depicts their actions as machine-like: 'Et elle ne s'arrêta plus, le [un fléau] relevant très haut, le repliant comme sur une charnière, le rabattant ensuite, dans un mouvement mécanique et rythmé de forgeron; tandis que Buteau, en face d'elle, allait de même, à contretemps' (p. 601). The noise surrounding them is comparably mechanical: 'Durant deux heures, on n'entendit [...] que le toc-toc régulier des fléaux, que dominait au loin le ronflement prolongé de la batteuse à vapeur' (p. 601). The noises of man and machine merge and become one. Zola repeatedly depicts fields filled with legions of faceless farm workers, underlining their synchronicity, the machine-like nature of their rhythms. He writes: 'Au loin, les faucheurs s'avançaient sans un arrêt, d'un même mouvement rythmique, le torse balancé sur les reins, la faux lancée et ramenée, continuellement' (p. 479). He continues this image later: 'A perte de vue, des équipes manœuvraient du même train oblique, du même balancement des bras, les unes si voisines, qu'on entendait le sifflement du fer' (p. 566). Zola animates the inanimate and yet dehumanizes the living.
18. Variations of this curving towards the earth appear elsewhere in the text: '[...] il s'affaiblissait, il se courbait davantage vers la terre, qui semblait le rappeler à elle; et, deux fois, on l'avait secouru, le nez tombé dans ses plants de salades' (p. 549).
19. Robert, *La Terre d'Emile Zola*, p. 311.
20. Zola, *Œuvres complètes*, X: *Œuvres critiques I* (1968), p. 1184.
21. 'Le vendredi, la veille du jour où l'on attendait l'explusion, une scène surtout émotionna. Buteau, ayant rencontré son père près de l'église, se mit à pleurer comme un veau' (p. 703).
22. It could be argued that Zola moves to trace Fouan's ancestry in historical terms. Robert suggests that Fouan is 'une sorte d'incarnation éphémère de Jacques Bonhomme', the fictional peasant figure whose suffering at the hands of various political regimes lies at the heart of the book Jean reads out loud in the text. Robert, *La Terre d'Emile Zola*, p. 385.
23. Butler, *Zola: La Terre*, p. 21.

24. Lawrence E. Harvey, 'The Cycle Myth in *La Terre* of Zola', *Philological Quarterly*, 38 (1959), 89–95 (p. 90).
25. *Emile Zola: Correspondance*, ed. by B. H. Bakker, 10 vols (Montréal: Les Presses de l'Université de Montréal; Paris: CNRS, 1978–95), I (1978), 207.
26. Ibid., p. 208.
27. Ibid., p. 209.
28. Cited in Robert, *La Terre d'Emile Zola*, p. 163.
29. Ibid., p. 210.
30. Ibid., p. 212.
31. Ibid., p. 226.
32. Ibid., p. 450.
33. Cited in the introduction to the reproduction of Emile Legouis, '*La Terre* de Zola et *Le Roi Lear*', *Révue de la littérature comparée*, 27 (1953), 417–27 (p. 419).
34. Ibid.
35. David Baguley, 'Le Réalisme grotesque et mythique de *La Terre*', *Cahiers naturalistes*, 61 (1987), 5–14.
36. Bloom, *Anxiety of Influence*, p. 78 and p. 26.
37. Ibid., p. 88.
38. Robert Lethbridge, 'La Pot-bouille des genres: adultération et originalité chez Zola', *Cahiers naturalistes*, 74 (2000), 17–32 (p. 17).
39. Ibid., pp. 17–18.
40. Legouis, '*La Terre* de Zola et *Le Roi Lear*', p. 426.
41. G. Wilson Knight, *The Wheel of Fire: Interpretations of Shakespearian Tragedy* (London: Methuen, 1949), p. 180.
42. William Shakespeare, *King Lear*, ed. by Elspeth Bain, Jonathan Morris and Rob Smith (Cambridge: Cambridge University Press, 1996), IV. 3. 1–6. Unless otherwise stated, subsequent references are to this edition and will be made in the text.
43. Familial love in both *King Lear* and *La Terre* is strikingly arithmetical, repeatedly couched in the terms of currency and amount. Lear approaches his relationship with Regan in terms of debt: 'Thou better know'st / The offices of nature, bond of childhood, / Effects of courtesy, dues of gratitude. / Thy half o'th'kingdom hast thou not forgot / Wherein I thee endowed.' (II. 4. 170–74). Love is comparably measured in *La Terre*. La Grande considers helping Françoise and Jean: 'elle calculait la perte, le gain, le plaisir qu'elle y aurait' (p. 691).
44. Shakespeare returns to this link between land, standing and identity repeatedly. In *Antony and Cleopatra*, Antony feels his body literally melting away when his reputation melts after the battle of Actium: 'That which is now a horse, even with a thought / The rack dislimns and makes it indistinct / As water is in water [...] / My good knave Eros, now thy captain is / Even such a body. Here I am Antony, / Yet cannot hold this visible shape.' *Antony and Cleopatra*, ed. by Richard Madelaine (Cambridge: Cambridge University Press, 1998), IV. 14. 9–14. Richard II, when dispossessed of his crown expresses himself in comparably liquid terms: 'Oh that I were a mockery king of snow / Standing before the sun of Bullingbrook, / To melt myself away in water drops', *King Richard II*, ed. by Andrew Gurr (Cambridge: Cambridge University Press, 2003), IV. I. 259–61.
45. Cited in Robert, *La Terre d'Emile Zola*, p. 226.
46. Harvey, 'The Cycle Myth in *La Terre* of Zola', p. 95.
47. Butler, *Zola: La Terre*, p. 16.
48. Chothia, *André Antoine*, p. 188.
49. Ibid., p. 134.
50. For details of the production of Antoine's film, see Cousins, 'Antoine's Version of *La Terre*', pp. 15–26.
51. André Antoine, *Mes Souvenirs sur le Théâtre Libre* (Paris: Arthème Fayard, 1921), p. 9.
52. Ibid., pp. 143–44.
53. Ibid., p. 105.
54. Ibid., p. 93.
55. Ibid., p. 89.

56. Ibid., p. 127.
57. Chothia, *André Antoine*, pp. 82–83.
58. Cited in Robert, *La Terre d'Emile Zola*, p. 216.
59. Cousins, 'Antoine's Version of *La Terre*', p. 22.
60. Suffering in Buteau's house, 'Il [Fouan] se rappelait le soir où il avait rompu avec les Delhomme; et c'était ce soir-là qui recommençait, la même honte de n'être plus le maître, la même colère qui le faisait s'entêter à ne pas manger' (p. 634). When Fouan goes to the *notaire* to access his money, the narrative states: 'Ça lui rappela le samedi où il était venu décider le partage' (p. 648). Fouan watches the division of his land, underlining that 'l'ancien partage entre lui, Mouche et la Grande, avait eu lieu dans le sens qu'il indiquait' (p. 397).
61. Antoine, *Mes Souvenirs*, p. 200.
62. Ibid., p. 117.
63. For further details see Chothia, *André Antoine*, p. 47.
64. Ibid., p. 131.
65. Ibid., pp. 69–70.
66. Sheep are comparably linked with ungraspable infinity in Zola's novel as the following description of Jean walking out into the night suggests: 'Et, comme il levait la tête, il aperçut, à gauche, des centaines d'yeux phosphorescents qui flambaient, pareils à des chandelles, et qui se tournaient vers lui, au bruit de ses pas. C'étaient les moutons dans leur parc' (p. 619).
67. Antoine, *Mes Souvenirs*, p. 200.
68. Cousins, 'Antoine's Version of *La Terre*', pp. 25–26.
69. Antoine, *Mes Souvenirs*, p. 112.
70. Chothia, *André Antoine*, p. 25.
71. Ronnie Butler suggests of *La Terre* that it provides 'fresh illustration of Zola's permanent fascination with a recurrent figure in his works, the silent witness of violent crime, suffering and death.' Butler, *Zola: La Terre*, p. 52.

CHAPTER 2

L'Œuvre and the Translation of Reality: Moving Between Text and Image

Zola not only, as Chapter 1 demonstrated, explores his inheritance of the textual property of previous works, he also, as Chapter 2 will suggest, evaluates the ability of his pages to translate the techniques of different media. His novel *L'Œuvre* is a key case study for this line of argument, for it simultaneously depicts the world of art and assesses the novel's ability to translate aspects of this world's methods. *L'Œuvre* reveals Zola to be an author interested by and involved in the act of artistic translation from one medium to another. Moreover, translation is doubly resonant in the context of Zola's work. It lies at the heart of his personal definition of the artistic act, be it in prose or the visual arts. He conceives of art, whatever its form, as, ideally, a translation of reality, a translation mediated only by the consciousness of the artist. Reality is thus the original behind Zola's textual translation, the origin from which it stems. However, in a manner highly significant for debates on Zola and adaptation, revolving as they often do around notions of original and subsequent transformation, in *L'Œuvre*, Zola subtly destabilizes notions of origin and the original in a variety of ways. Whilst the author encourages the novel to be seen as something of a *roman à clef*, he will not give the reader the key to the reality apparently lying behind its pages. Zola does not allow any 'original' identities to be definitively deciphered, or reveal the real models for his textual creations. That Zola's obfuscation of origins and his originals is deliberate will be underscored by a consideration of the highly problematic relationship between Christine as model and her painted reproduction. *L'Œuvre* not only probes the possibility of translating word into image, it also evaluates its own difficult relationship with the reality it simultaneously seeks to translate.

Zola's links with the world of art are well established. The author's childhood friendship with the painter Paul Cézanne continued in adult life in Paris, leading to a certain degree of artistic and literary exchange. Cézanne used Zola in paintings such as *Paul Alexis lisant à Emile Zola* (1869–70), whilst Zola reminisced in print in his piece of 20 May 1866, 'A mon ami Paul Cézanne', about their shared ambitions:

> Tu es toute ma jeunesse; je te retrouve mêlé à chacune de mes joies, à chacune de mes souffrances. Nos esprits, dans leur fraternité, se sont développés côte à côte. [...] Nous cherchions des hommes en toutes choses, nous voulions dans chaque œuvre, tableau ou poème, trouver un accent personnel.[1]

Whilst Zola's assessment of Cézanne's work was ultimately a chequered one (he referred to him as a 'grand peintre avorté' in 1896) and their friendship appeared to cool, Zola enjoyed a comparable literary and artistic exchange with Edouard Manet.[2] Hailing Manet as a painter sharing his beliefs about the role of art in relation to reality, Zola wrote in defence of the controversial artist, publishing a brochure in support of him in 1867: 'Jamais le public ne sera juste envers les véritables artistes créateurs, s'il ne se contente pas de chercher uniquement dans une œuvre une libre traduction de la nature en un langage particulier et nouveau.'[3] In response, Manet painted Zola's portrait, whilst the author offered the dedication of *Madeleine Férat* to the painter in September 1868.[4] Zola came to know the circle of artists around Manet at the Batignolles studio and in the Café Guerbois (1863–66) and repeatedly wrote in support of the controversial impressionist school. The amount of art criticism stemming from Zola's pen is considerable and covers some twenty years, starting in *L'Evénement* in the 1860s and continuing in *Le Sémaphore de Marseille* and *Le Messager de l'Europe*.[5]

The boundary between word and image is comparatively permeable in Zola's art criticism. Peter Collier and Robert Lethbridge cite *L'Œuvre* as an exemplary novel for the illustration of the concept of *ekphrasis*, 'the literary description of a real or imaginary work of art'.[6] *L'Œuvre* is indeed filled with descriptions of paintings, but Zola's art criticism also uses words to reconstruct the images to which Zola refers. Zola summons and directs the reader's gaze, leading him/her through a series of paintings, at times present, at times not. Of Manet's *La Musique aux Tuileries* (1862), Zola addresses his reader with an injunction to see:

> [...] imaginez, sous les arbres des Tuileries, toute une foule, une centaine de personnes peut-être, qui se remue au soleil; chaque personnage est une simple tache, à peine déterminée, et dans laquelle les détails deviennent des lignes ou des points noirs.[7]

A similar injunction to see is found in relation to Manet's *Olympia* (1863):

> Regardez la tête de la jeune fille: les lèvres sont deux minces lignes roses, les yeux se réduisent à quelques traits noirs. Voyez maintenant le bouquet, et de près, je vous prie: des plaques roses, des plaques bleues, des plaques vertes. Tout se simplifie, et si vous voulez reconstruire la réalité, il faut que vous reculiez de quelques pas.[8]

In his art criticism Zola leads his readers through the nuances and lines of painted works, positioning their gaze.

As Zola reproduces images in words in his art criticism, so too his art criticism finds itself reproduced, to a degree, in his novel *L'Œuvre*. The text not only translates into fiction certain of Zola's key ideas on contemporary art, but in so doing it transposes, at points, metaphors and aspects of the very voice of Zola's art criticism. Criticizing the jury and their opinion on art, Zola, in his art criticism, utilizes a nutritive metaphor in relation to painting: 'Je finirai par penser que vous parlez de règles, par ouï-dire, pour nous faire accroire qu'il y a un parfait cuisinier de l'art où l'on apprend la recette des sauces auxquelles vous accommodez l'idéal'.[9] He describes romantic painting as being steeped in and coloured by 'le jus de bitume'.[10] *L'Œuvre* takes up precisely these metaphors in its fiction. It attacks 'les éternelles tartines de l'Ecole, cette peinture au jus de chique, honteusement cuisinée d'après les recettes', celebrating instead the new movement of *plein air* painting which it depicts as 'une fenêtre brusquement ouverte dans la vieille cuisine au bitume, dans les jus recuits de la tradition' (p. 44 and p. 130). Whilst *L'Œuvre* is not an exact literary reproduction of Zola's art criticism, the interaction of the two does begin to foreground questions about the translation of image into text and the adaptation of journalism into fiction.

The content of Zola's art criticism in some respects appears to appeal for a distinction to be maintained between images and words. Making repeated use of the vocabulary of language, Zola is scathing of those painters he calls 'des littérateurs fourvoyés, des gens qui croient renouveler la peinture, parce qu'ils ne peignent plus du tout et qu'ils se servent d'un pinceau comme d'une plume', slamming what he calls 'les gentillesses écœurantes des peintres-poètes'.[11] Such comments perhaps go some way towards explaining Claude's response to Sandoz in relation to his criticism of Claude's choice of title for a painting: *Plein air*. Sandoz states: '[...] ça ne dit rien.' Claude bluntly replies: 'Ça n'a besoin de rien dire' (p. 47). However, whilst the content of Zola's art criticism separates writing and the visual arts, its form blurs them, for Zola's prose appropriates the metaphors and vocabulary of the painted medium to such an extent that it perhaps passes beyond the level of a journalistic conceit. Speaking of his brochure on Manet, Zola writes: 'Ce travail, pour plusieurs causes, je le répète, ne saurait donc être un portrait définitif'.[12] He adds: 'J'espère qu'on cessera de traiter de rapin débraillé l'homme dont je viens d'esquisser la physionomie en quelques traits'.[13] Using the vocabulary of the visual arts, Zola presents his written account of the artist who has painted him, precisely as a portrait, a word picture. He sees broader sections of his art criticism in comparable terms: '[...] ce n'est pas ici le compte rendu d'une exposition; mais, si l'on veut, une série de médaillons, une simple collection de croquis à la plume'.[14] His aim is not to catalogue the salon, but rather, in some senses, to paint it: 'Je n'ai cependant pas l'intention de vous envoyer un rapport détaillé qui pourrait tout au plus présenter l'intérêt d'un catalogue. J'aime mieux tenter de brosser un tableau de la situation actuelle de notre école française.'[15] Zola's art criticism seeks to paint pictures with its words.

If Zola's journalism paints, so too the author attributes to painting the power of language. His art criticism repeatedly imbues painting with the ability to speak. Surveying 'Le Moment artistique' on 4 May 1866, he writes: 'Jamais je n'ai vu un tel amas de médiocrités. [...] Sur ces deux mille toiles, douze ou quinze vous parlent un langage humain; les autres vous content des niaiseries de parfumeurs'.[16] Sculpture too can speak, albeit, at times a dead language:

> [...] la sculpture, telle que l'entendait la Grèce, est devenue une langue morte pour nous, une expression artistique que nous ne saurions employer naturellement. Nos artistes parlent l'art grec, comme des élèves de sixième parlent le latin, à coups de dictionnaire, sans l'accent véritable, et avec d'affreux barbarismes.[17]

Zola conceives of art in the salon as a clashing of screaming voices: 'Des tableaux, toujours des tableaux; un kilomètre de taches violentes, des bleus, des rouges, des jaunes, criant entre eux, hurlant la cachophonie la plus abominable du monde.'[18] Good art, by contrast, is presented in terms of harmonious song. The colours of the vegetables in Zola's virtuoso still-life description of the landscape in *Le Ventre de Paris* sing:

> [...] les paquets d'épinards, les paquets d'oseille, les bouquets d'artichauds, les entassements de haricots et de pois, les empilements de romaines, liées d'un brin de paille, chantaient toute la gamme du vert, de la laque verte des cosses au gros vert des feuilles; gamme soutenue qui allait en se mourant, jusqu'aux panachures des pieds de céleris et des bottes de poireaux. Mais les notes aiguës, ce qui chantait plus haut, c'étaient toujours les taches vives des carottes, les taches pures des navets, semées en quantité prodigieuse le long du marché. (p. 627)

Art for Zola not only sings its words, it also appears, in a metaphorical sense, to write them. The journalist conceives of paintings precisely in terms of literary pages: 'Je voudrais que les toiles de tous les peintres du monde fussent réunies dans une immense salle, où nous pourrions aller lire page par page l'épopée de la création humaine'.[19] However art, for Zola is not just an 'épopée', it is also a poem. He sets the following challenge for painters: 'Nos artistes doivent trouver la poésie des gares, comme leurs pères ont trouvé celle des forêts et des fleuves.'[20] Surveying certain canvases by Millet, he sees them as having succeeded in their essentially poetic mission: '[...] et voilà qu'on avait la campagne ouverte devant soi, dans sa poésie vraie, dans sa poésie qui n'est faite que de réalité.'[21] Zola blurs the boundaries between image and word, be it spoken, written or sung.

The author repeatedly assesses Manet's pictures in particular using metaphors of language and speech. The artist's battles against the art world and indeed in relation to his own creativity are presented precisely as attempts to speak:

> Il avait sur le bout de la langue, comme on dit, le mot nouveau qu'il apportait, et il ne pouvait le prononcer. Puis, sa vue s'éclaircit, il distingua nettement les choses, sa langue ne fut plus embarrassée, et il parla.[22]

Words and images (painted or sketched) prove comparably interwoven in *L'Œuvre*. Paintings speak in Zola's novel. Christine looks at Claude's work and what she sees is 'rugueuse, éclatante, d'une violence de tons qui la blessait comme un juron de charretier, entendu sur la porte d'une auberge' (p. 23). Moreover, Claude's abilities to speak and paint are intertwined. Language flows as painting does: 'Quand son travail marchait, il s'allumait peu à peu, il devenait bavard [...]. Ainsi, à peine son ami eut-il repris la pose, qu'il continua d'un flot intarissable, sans perdre un coup de pinceau' (p. 43). However, the breakdown of Claude's painting is echoed by a concurrent break up of speech. Claude cannot capture the Parisian scene before his eyes: '[...] le croquis s'embrouillait d'un tel écheveau de lignes, se chargeait d'une si grande confusion de détails sommaires, qu'elle [Christine] n'y distinguait rien' (p. 216). The speech with which Claude seeks to supplement and explicate his work proves as fragmented as the sketch it describes. Zola perforates Claude's phrases with ellipses and the staccato rhythm imposed by an excess of exclamation marks:

> Rien au monde n'est plus grand, c'est Paris lui-même, glorieux sous le soleil... Dis? étais-je bête de n'y pas songer! Que de fois j'ai regardé sans voir! Il m'a fallu tomber là, après cette course le long des quais... Et, tu te rappelles, il y a un coup

> d'ombre de ce côté, le soleil ici tape droit, les tours sont là-bas, la flèche de la Sainte-Chappelle s'amincit, d'une légèreté d'aiguille dans le ciel... Non, elle est plus à droite, attends je te montre... (pp. 216–17)

Zola, as a novelist and journalist, depicts painting, be it fluent or stuttering and fragmented, in linguistic terms.

Just as Zola explores the boundary between language and image in his art criticism, Manet, the artist to whom his art criticism most frequently refers, interacts with Zola's fiction in his painted images. Manet not only painted a version of the character Nana from *L'Assommoir* which anticipated her subsequent novelistic incarnation in the novel bearing her name, a version explored in Chapter 3, but he also fashioned a piece of art around the figure of the author himself. Manet paints Zola's person in his portrait, but also the tools and products of his trade. The novelist sits, contemplatively, with a book in hand, his person framed by a pen and a fan of publications, including the pamphlet he wrote in support of Manet. As Zola plays with images in his prose, Manet plays with words in the form of his own signature, which appears only in the printed title of the aforementioned pamphlet. He does not, in some senses, sign his painting as Zola apparently does it for him. Henri Mitterand, drawing on the work of Théodore Reff, describes 'la brochure consacrée par Zola à Edouard Manet, avec le nom du peintre qui fait signature'.[23] This portrait, the stimulus for so many words, interpretations and articles, has been read as Manet's thank you to Zola for his support, as a symbol of a shared belief in the fraternity of the arts. Numerous critics have pointed out the altered reproduction of *Olympia* who smiles down on Zola, the writer who rose to her defence and who holds Charles Blanc's *Histoire des peintres.* According to Mitterand, the joint signature of the painting can be read as a 'manière d'associer encore plus étroitement le peintre et son modèle, l'homme de l'image et l'homme de la lettre'.[24] Certainly the idea of the complementary nature of the arts is explored in *L'Œuvre.* Gagnière annuls the boundaries between literature, painting and music. He claims: 'Berlioz a mis de la littérature dans son affaire. C'est l'illustrateur musical de Shakespeare, de Virgile et de Goethe. Mais quel peintre! le Delacroix de la musique, qui a fait flamber les sons, dans des oppositions fulgurantes de couleurs' (p. 201). However, Robert Lethbridge innovatively recasts Manet's portrait of Zola as a painterly correction to Zola's reading of his work.[25] Manet's own works are cropped in his portrait of Zola, testimony perhaps to Manet's belief in Zola's incomplete reading of them. Zola's art criticism does not fully acknowledge Manet's debt to past masters. Consequently, Lethbridge suggests, Manet seeks to correct this by placing certain of their incarnations behind the writer's head as he holds, but significantly neither reads nor engages with, Blanc's *Histoire des peintres*, the book from which Manet worked precisely because it contained reproductions of the Old Masters. Lethbridge points out that symbolically Manet's signature is half obscured (his first name does not appear) by the flamboyance of Zola's pen.[26] Whether one reads Manet's portrait of Zola as a symbol of the fraternity of the arts or conversely as testimony to the tensions between painting and writing, what is clear is that the painting, in precisely its demand to be read, explores the translation of language and text into images, just as Zola's *L'Œuvre* evaluates the mediation of images through text.

Zola not only writes about the world of art in his journalism, he incorporates the spaces of its exhibition into his fiction. The wedding party in *L'Assommoir* tours the rooms of the Louvre and in so doing surveys the history of art: 'Des siècles d'art passaient devant leur ignorance ahurie, la sécheresse fine des primitifs, les splendeurs des Vénitiens, la vie grasse et belle de lumière des Hollandais'.[27] As the wedding guests pass before, amongst others, *Le Radeau de la méduse* by Géricault with its images of starvation and *Noces de Cana* by Veronese with the splendour of its celebrations, Mitterand reads the tour of the Louvre as a reflection of Gervaise's destiny, as a prediction of her rise and fall: 'Voilà que toutes ces pièces maîtresses du Louvre, ces références de la culture universelle, commentent et annoncent le destin d'une petite blanchisseuse. En ordre inversé: la faim et la mort, pour commencer, la fête pour finir.'[28] However, the reflective function of the art in the Louvre spills beyond *L'Assommoir* to infiltrate the *Rougon-Macquart* series as a whole. The art contemplated in the Louvre reappears throughout the series. The wedding party gaze at 'les dieux de marbre noir muets dans leur raideur hiératique, les bêtes monstrueuses, moitié chattes et moitié femmes, [...] le nez aminci, les lèvres gonflées' (p. 444). This image echoes that of Renée in *La Curée*. In the hothouse, she merges with the black sphinx statue visible in the background as she takes on 'sa pose de chatte accroupie, l'échine allongée, les poignets tendus, comme des jarrets souples et nerveux. Elle était toute gonflée de volupté, et les lignes claires de ses épaules et de ses reins se détachaient avec des sécheresses félines'.[29] The fascination of 'le ménage Gaudron' in *L'Assommoir* with the Murillo in the Louvre (they stand 'béants, attendris et stupides, en face de *La Vierge* de Murillo' p. 445), gestures towards the pictorial depiction of Claire in *Le Ventre de Paris*. She has a 'figure rêveuse de vierge', a 'petite face d'un dessin noyé', 'elle restait un Murillo [...] selon le mot de Claude Lantier, un Murillo décoiffé' (p. 715). As the wedding party wander through the Flemish and Dutch sections of the Louvre in *L'Assommoir*, so Marie-Thérèse Barrett sees Zola's descriptions in *Le Ventre de Paris* as indebted to Flemish and Dutch still life painting. Zola not only mentions Rubens in his *ébauche* and novel, but Huysmans, as Barrett points out, sees Zola's descriptions as 'peintes avec la fougue et la couleur forcenée d'un Rubens'.[30] Madame Lorilleux is fascinated by 'la maîtresse du Titien' in the Louvre in *L'Assommoir* (p. 445). This figure is reproduced or reincarnated in *L'Œuvre* in the form of Irma Bécot. Irma creates herself as a walking work of art, 'si bien qu'une courtisane du Titien semblait maintenant s'être levée du petit voyou de jadis' (p. 176). As the wedding party gets lost in the wings of the Louvre in *L'Assommoir* ('Que de tableaux, sacredié! Ça ne finissait pas', 'les dessins n'en finissaient pas, les salons se succédaient aux salons', 'Jamais plus elle [la noce] ne sortirait' pp. 444–47), Zola's *Rougon-Macquart* series in a sense never leaves the labyrinths of art. The pictorial references pictured in the Louvre seep beyond the confines of *L'Assommoir* to echo and prefigure some of the pictures in the metaphorical galleries that are Zola's other texts.

As characters get lost in the labyrinths of the Louvre in *L'Assommoir*, so onlookers get trapped in the maze of the salon in *L'Œuvre*: 'D'autres, un à un, perdus entre les cadres, suivaient les sentiers étroits, renonçant à en sortir, tournant sans espoir de trouver jamais le bout' (p. 280). The attempt to find the edge or the boundaries of the spaces of art in Zola's novel is a difficult one, for the author depicts the places in which art is produced and exhibited in porous, fluid terms. Claude's lodgings are presented as a place of dissolution:

> L'ombre avait envahi l'atelier, une ombre violâtre qui pleuvait de la baie vitrée en un mélancolique crépuscule, noyant les choses. Il ne voyait plus nettement le parquet, où les meubles, les toiles, tout ce qui traînait vaguement, semblait se fondre, comme dans l'eau dormante d'une mare. (p. 139)[31]

Similarly, the paintings of the salon are described in liquid terms and metaphorically dissolve the structures of the building which houses them:

> Ah! ces trois mille tableaux placés bout à bout, [...] étendus en mares stagnantes, entre lesquelles on ménageait de petits sentiers filant le long des cadres, une inondation, un débordement qui montait, envahissait le Palais de l'Industrie, le submergeait sous le flot trouble de tout ce que l'art peut rouler de médiocrité et de folie. (pp. 279–80)

In Zola's novel, painting cannot be contained by the spaces designed to house it, by the museums, salons and studios in which it is found.

In *L'Œuvre* paintings not only dissolve the spaces that would contain them, they also metaphorically burn and cut through the frames and places in which they are housed. When Christine first looks at Claude's work in his *atelier*, she conceives of it in infernal terms. The narrative describes 'les esquisses terrifiantes, dont les murs flambaient' (p. 27). Zola also refers to 'les flamboyantes esquisses du Midi' (p. 92). The novel associates specific paintings with notions of 'éclatement'. The viewer witnesses 'des portraits, des paysages, des intérieurs, tous éclatant en notes aigres, dans l'or trop neuf des cadres' (p. 283). Claude's painting of his dead son is depicted in similar terms: '[...] la petite toile trop rude, éclatait férocement, dans une grimace douloureuse de monstre' (p. 293). Zola imbues painting with the ability to pierce the structures containing it as is evidenced by his use of the verb 'sabrer'. Christine is unnerved by Claude's painting with its 'tons violents, des grands traits de pastel sabrant les ombres' (p. 27). Claude later uses Sandoz as a model, 'sabrant à grands coups le veston de velours' (p. 44). Painting, for Zola, cuts through the frames and walls surrounding it. Describing the salon in *L'Œuvre*, the narrative states: 'De loin, à chaque pas, on voyait un tableau trouer le mur, ouvrir une fenêtre sur le dehors. Bientôt, les murs tomberaient, la grande nature entrerait, car la brèche était large' (p. 297).[32]

Fictional statements such as these parallel those made in Zola's art criticism underlining his belief that art, like literature, should mirror reality, taking the contemporary world as its subject matter. Consequently, in *L'Œuvre*, art pierces the boundaries which would contain it and seeps out into the streets of contemporary Paris. Claude looks at the city around him and sees in it ready-made pictures: '[...] il découvrait des tableaux partout, la ville entière, avec ses rues, ses carrefours, ses ponts, ses horizons vivants, se déroulait en fresques' (p. 203). His experience of Paris in *Le Ventre de Paris* is couched in similarly pictorial terms:

> Là, à travers la rue, il [Claude] trouvait un superbe sujet de tableau: les marchandes aux petit tas sous leurs grands parasols déteints, les rouges, les bleus, les violets, attachés à des bâtons, bossuant le marché, mettant leurs rondeurs vigoureuses dans l'incendie du couchant, qui se mourait sur les carottes. (p. 782)

Zola repeatedly uses his artist figure to draw the reader's attention to the potential paintings in the Paris skyline. In *L'Œuvre* Claude points to a section of the landscape, appealing to Christine to look at the painting he envisions (p. 212). This appeal is echoed by that previously made in *Le Ventre de Paris*: 'Tenez, dit-il [Claude] en s'arrêtant, regardez, au coin du trottoir. N'est-ce pas un tableau tout fait, et qui serait plus humain que leurs sacrées peintures poitrinaires?' (p. 624) This painting does not exist in the narrative itself and the reader does not know if Claude undertakes it. However, Zola, as far as he is able, paints in words a tableau in place of this absent painting:

> Le jour se levait lentement, d'un gris très doux, lavant toutes choses d'une teinte claire d'aquarelle. Ces tas moutonnants comme des flots pressés, ce fleuve de verdure qui semblait couler dans l'encaissement de la chaussée, pareil à la débâcle des pluies d'automne prenaient des ombres délicates et perlées, des violets attendris, des roses teintés de lait, des verts noyés dans des jaunes, toutes les pâleurs qui font du ciel une soie changeante au lever du soleil. (pp. 626–27)

This passage, with its play on light and shadow, explicit invocation of the fluidity of the water colour and specific shades bears out much of the critical attention which has underlined the way in which Zola imitates the methods of the painter. According to Kelly Basilio, writing on what she calls Zola's 'écriture peignante',

> Il semble alors que sa [Zola] plume se mette à faire des rêves de pinceau, de pinceau impressionniste. Car ce qui semble surtout visé à de tels moments, ce n'est plus tout simplement cet effet de réel auquel tout le texte puissamment travaille, mais ce que nous pourrions appeler un 'effet de pictural'.[33]

Mitterand concludes in relation to Zola's fiction, 'En tout cas on y dénote aisément les procédés et les instruments de la picturalisation, qui inscrivent à tout moment dans le texte du roman des simulacres des tableaux, et étendent ainsi à l'infini le musée textuel'.[34]

The 'musée textuel' that Zola's fiction at times represents is filled with a variety of categories of art. Numerous metaphorical still life paintings appear embedded in the narrative of *Le Ventre de Paris*. Claude dreams of but does not appear to paint 'des natures mortes colossales, des tableaux extraordinaires' when looking at Les Halles (p. 623). The narrative provides the reader with such a painting in Claude's place. It frames the contents of the *charcuterie* as a still life:

> Puis, dans ce cadre aimable, l'étalage montait [...]. Des colliers de saucisses, de saucissons, de cervelas, pendaient, symétriques, semblables à des cordons et à des glands de tentures riches; tandis que, derrière des lambeaux de crépine mettaient leur dentelle, leur fond de guipure blanche et charnue. (p. 636)

Objets d'art also make an appearance as the reader witnesses 'les choux frisés, dont les grandes feuilles ressemblaient à des vasques en bronze' (p. 627). Zola's character sketches at times take on the feel of portraits and indeed individuals are presented as works of art. Madame Coupeau in *L'Assommoir* lies in her coffin: 'Elle touchait de tous les côtés, un vrai tableau dans un cadre' (p. 666). Certain characters within Zola's narratives are at times sculpted into the form of statuary. In *L'Œuvre* Christine poses for Claude to paint her, but metaphorically becomes a statue as she does so, 'elle [...] retombait dans son néant de beau marbre, avec le sourire mystérieux et figé de la pose' (p. 115). Her textual sculpture stands alongside those of numerous other Zolian heroines in the *Rougon-Macquart* series. Hélène in *Une page d'amour* turns her head and 'son profil prenait une pureté grave de statue'.[35] Renée stands in the *tableaux vivants* of *La Curée* 'n'ayant plus de vivant, dans son corps figé de statue, que ses yeux' (p. 553). Désirée in *La Faute de l'abbé Mouret* resembles a statue in Plassans, 'une Cybèle, allongée sur des gerbes, œuvre d'un élève de Puget, sculptée au fronton du marché'.[36]

However, in the pages of Zola's 'musée textuel', the *paysage* predominates. Zola's images repeatedly invoke the language, structures and material of the visual arts. At times his narrative uses charcoal. In *L'Œuvre* the narration presents 'la silhouette des tours pointues du Palais de Justice, charbonnées directement sur le vide' (pp. 102–03).[37] In other places ink is the preferred method for visual reproduction. In *L'Œuvre*'s closing scene, a train is described thus: '[...] on distingua nettement, comme sur un transparent d'ombres chinoises, les découpures des wagons, jusqu'aux gens assis dans les trous clairs des fenêtres. Et la ligne redevint nette, un simple trait à l'encre coupant l'horizon' (p. 361). Zola throws into relief for the reader the 'touches' and 'taches' of his brushstrokes in his descriptions. Claude watches Dubuche walk away from him in a description which focuses on 'la tache noire de sa redingote' (p. 158). Zola subsequently offers the following description of Paris:

> Paris allumé s'était endormi, il n'y avait plus là que la vie des becs de gaz, de taches rondes qui scintillaient, qui se rapetissaient, pour n'être, au loin, qu'une poussière d'étoiles fixes. [...] Les plus reculés, sous les ponts, n'étaient que des petites touches de feu immobiles. (p. 339)

Zola might even be seen to apply varnish to his word paintings: 'Sous le soleil, couleur de blé mûr, les rangées des marronniers avaient des feuilles neuves, d'un vert tendre, fraîchement verni' (p. 117). Ultimately, frames can be discerned around certain of his descriptions. In *L'Œuvre*, 'Le long du Pont-Neuf, de grands omnibus jaunes, des tapissières bariolées, défilaient avec une régularité mécanique des jouets d'enfant. Tout le fond s'encadrait là, dans les perspectives des deux rives' (p. 213). Zola's narratives sketch, paint and exhibit their word pictures.

Zola's work references a variety of artistic movements. Zola takes care to situate Claude's art in *L'Œuvre* in the narrative trajectory of art history, presenting it as having moved away from Romanticism (Claude seeks to wash Delacroix from his artistic eye) and as being a close descendant of the Realists, the school embodied by the fading star Bongrand (p. 47). Moreover, Jean-François Thibault sees Claude's paintings as inspired successively by the impressionist, neo-impressionist and post-impressionist/expressionist schools.[38] William Kloss makes clear the influence of the Old Masters on the novelist's fiction.[39] However, by Zola's own admission, it is the impressionist movement which most informs his writing. He famously stated: 'Je n'ai pas seulement soutenu les Impressionnistes, je les ai traduits en littérature, par les touches, notes, colorations, par la palette de beaucoup de mes descriptions'.[40] Zola claims not just to have been influenced by the impressionists, but to have translated them. His choice of terminology reveals Zola as a writer intellectually engaged with the translation of one art form into another.

Zola translates a number of key impressionist techniques into his fiction. He gives the following definition of impressionist painters in 1876:

> On les appelle aussi impressionnistes, parce que certains d'entre eux paraissent vouloir rendre surtout l'impression vraie des êtres et des choses, sans descendre dans une exécution minutieuse qui enlève toute sa verdeur et l'interprétation vive et personnelle.[41]

Gagnière reiterates aspects of this definition of impressionism in *L'Œuvre*:

> Oh! ce n'est rien, vois-tu, quatre mesures, une impression jetée. Mais ce qu'il y a là dedans!... Pour moi, d'abord, c'est un paysage qui fuit, un coin de route mélancolique, avec l'ombre d'un arbre qu'on ne voit pas; et puis, une femme passe, à peine un profil; et puis elle s'en va, et on ne la rencontrera jamais, jamais plus. (p. 84)

However, more importantly, Zola himself enacts the process of focalization, the personal interpretation of the landscape he defines as key to the impressionist movement. As Pierre Aubery points out, he focalizes sections of the landscape through the gaze and viewpoint of his characters, providing us not with an omniscient narratorial perspective, but rather with individual perceptions from the characters: 'Ecrivain, il prêtera ces dispositions aux personnages dans lesquels il se projette le plus et il nous communiquera leurs aperçus, leurs "impressions" selon des procédés très proches de ceux qu'employaient ses amis peintres.'[42] A paragraph describing Claude's obsessive contemplation of an aspect of the landscape in different lights and seasons offers a striking example of this focalization, a focalization underlined by the repetition of 'il la vit':

> Sous une tombée de neige tardive, il la vit fourrée d'hermine, au-dessus de l'eau couleur de boue, se détachant sur un ciel d'ardoise claire. Il la vit, aux premiers soleils, s'essuyer de l'hiver, retrouver une enfance, avec les pousses vertes des grands arbres du terre-plein. Il la vit, un jour de fin brouillard, se reculer, s'évaporer, légère et tremblante comme un palais des songes. Puis, ce furent des pluies battantes qui la submergeaient, la cachaient derrière l'immense rideau tiré du ciel à la terre. (p. 231)

According to John Rewald, the defining feature of the impressionists was their exploration of light and its effects on the perception of reality.[43] Dominique Van Hooff identifies 'une véritable pulvérisation de la matière sous l'effet de l'intensité de la lumière' in Monet's *La Gare Saint Lazare* and in one section of the landscape described in Zola's *L'Œuvre*.[44] The sun and its light are repeatedly depicted in liquid terms throughout *L'Œuvre*: 'Et, au travers de la vaste pièce, la nappe de brûlant soleil, tombée des vitres, voyageait, sans être tempérée par le moindre store, coulant ainsi qu'un or liquide' (p. 23). It enjoys the ability to seep into the landscape, dissolving the structures and lines of reality. Thus, in the pages of the novel, the framework of Paris repeatedly dissolves, to be replaced by the canvas of a seascape: 'En bas, la place, aux trottoirs immenses, aux chaussées larges comme des lacs, s'emplissait de ce flot continuel, traversée en tous sens du rayonnement des roues, peuplée de points noirs qui étaient des hommes' (pp. 74–75). In the sun's haze, a row of houses come to represent 'une falaise rocheuse, s'enfonçant au milieu d'une mer phosphorescente' (p. 103). The colours of objects are no longer fixed and, to Christine's disapproval, change depending on the light in which they find themselves bathed. Claude's painting of Paris shocks precisely because of its new conceptualization of light and colour:

> Mais ce qui, surtout, rendait ce tableau terrible, c'était l'étude nouvelle de la lumière, cette décomposition, d'une observation très exacte, et qui contrecarrait toutes les habitudes de l'œil, en accentuant des bleus, des jaunes, des rouges, où personne n'était accoutumé d'en voir. (p. 206)

Zola explores light and the changes it effects not only in the paintings of Claude, but also in the broader word paintings that his own narratives create. Thus, for example, in *Le Ventre de Paris*, the narrative describes the urban landscape in the following terms: 'A chaque heure, les jeux de lumière changeaient ainsi les profils des Halles, depuis les bleuissements du matin et les ombres noires du midi, jusqu'à l'incendie du soleil couchant, s'éteignant dans la cendre grise du crépuscule' (p. 730).

Zola's depiction of the varying profiles of *Les Halles*, is just one of the series of word tableaux he paints, echoing the impressionist exploration of the changing face of reality over time. As artists such as Monet painted the same scene in different lights, times of day, weather conditions and times of year, so Zola translates this effect into his fiction. His narrative paints a series of tableaux. In *L'Œuvre* Claude studies, but does not paint, the same spot in a variety of weather conditions, fascinated by how it might appear in different light conditions:

> Il voulut la voir sous le soleil levant, se dégageant des brumes matinales, lorsque le quai de l'Horloge rougeoie et que le quai des Orfèvres reste appesanti de ténèbres, toute vivante déjà dans le ciel rose par le réveil éclatant de ses tours et de ses flèches, tandis que, lentement, la nuit descend des édifices, ainsi qu'un manteau qui tombe. Il voulut la voir à midi, sous le soleil frappant d'aplomb, mangée de clarté crue, décolorée et muette comme une ville morte, n'ayant plus que la vie de la chaleur, le frisson dont remuaient les toitures lointaines. Il voulut la voir sous le soleil à son déclin. (pp. 231–32)

The stasis of the repeated 'il voulut la voir' contrasts with the constant reincarnation of the landscape. Claude may not paint these scenes, returning instead to attempt to capture his first vision of the landscape, but Zola's narratives and words sketch them in his place. Indeed, as Jean-Pierre Leduc-Adine has pointed out, Zola's narrative paints the same spaces, the banks of the Seine, in four scenes, depicting them in summer, in winter, in September and in November.[45] These recurring locations both frame the narrative and translate the effects of impressionist paintings into Zola's fiction.

Impressionist experimentation in relation to notions of *décentrage* might also be seen to be anticipated in Zola's fiction as the writer explores unusual pictorial viewpoints. In *Le Ventre de Paris*, Florent contemplates a scene from an off-centre point of view: '[...] il regardait Saint-Eustache, posé de biais, comme lavé à la sépia sur le bleu du ciel' (p. 628). In *L'Œuvre*, Christine does not recognize Notre Dame seen from behind: '[...] il [Claude] dut lui nommer Notre-Dame qu'elle ne reconnaissait pas, vue ainsi de chevet, colossale et accroupie entre ses arcs-boutants, pareils à des pattes au repos, dominée par la double tête de ses tours' (p. 101). Zola not only explores the impressionist concept of *décentrage*, but he finds a narrative equivalent for the pictorial technique of cropping. As painters such as Manet in *Un Bar aux Folies-Bergère* take their viewer to the edge of their canvas, severing and cropping images to position their work as a slice of a much wider reality, Zola's narrative takes us to the edge of his pages, gesturing to that which he cannot show, to the mass which he has cropped. Through the repeated use of 'à perte de vue', a phrase which has already been discussed in relation to *La Terre* in Chapter 1, Zola cuts off his pages in *L'Œuvre*, whilst still gesturing towards the 'infini' beyond them: 'Et, entre les deux bordures vertes des contre-allées, l'avenue des Champs-Elysées montait tout là-haut, à perte de vue, terminée par la porte colossale de l'Arc de Triomphe, béante sur l'infini' (p. 74).

Zola thus translates certain of the methods of impressionist painters into his work. He does so, principally, because he identifies with what he suggests is their artistic mission: the attempt to translate reality into art. Zola annexes them, to an extent, to his own naturalist endeavour: 'Pour moi, le groupe d'artistes en question est simplement un groupe d'artistes naturalistes, c'est-à-dire d'artistes consciencieux qui en sont revenus à l'étude immédiate de la nature.'[46] Art, he suggests, should be as close a copy of reality as possible. Using precisely the terminology of copying, Zola, writing on Laurens, states: 'Je préfère aux grandes machines qu'il construit sur des textes historiques, le moindre des paysagistes qui s'assied tranquillement devant un arbre et le copie, en rapportant fidèlement l'impression qu'il en reçoit.'[47] He offers the following conceptualization of what art should ideally do:

> Ainsi, il est bien convenu que l'artiste se place devant la nature, qu'il la copie en l'interprétant, qu'il est plus ou moins réel selon ses yeux; en un mot qu'il a pour mission de nous rendre les objets tels qu'il les voit, appuyant sur tel détail, créant à nouveau. J'exprimerai toute ma pensée en disant qu'une œuvre d'art est un coin de la création vu à travers un tempérament.[48]

As these quotations make clear, Zola does not see good art as a mere copy of reality, an absolute reproduction.[49] He sees it rather as a recreation, in a different form, mediated by the consciousness and identity of the individual artist. He sees the best art as, as he puts it, a translation of reality. The vocabulary of translation abounds in Zola's assessments of what artistry should be not only in relation to painting, but the creative act more broadly. He writes: 'Jamais le public ne sera juste envers les véritables artistes créateurs, s'il ne se contente pas de chercher uniquement dans une œuvre une libre traduction de la nature en un langage particulier et nouveau'.[50] The ability to offer such a translation is, for Zola, the precondition of artistic greatness: 'Chaque grand artiste est venu nous donner une traduction nouvelle et personnelle de la nature. La réalité est ici l'élément fixe, et les divers tempéraments sont les éléments créateurs qui ont donné aux œuvres des caractères différents'.[51] Zola's admiration for the impressionists stems, in large part, from their ability to translate reality: 'Chacun d'eux, d'ailleurs, a heureusement pour lui sa note originale, sa façon de voir et de traduire la réalité à travers son tempérament.'[52] Zola, moreover, repeatedly sings the praises of Manet using the vocabulary of translation:

> Désormais, Edouard Manet avait trouvé sa voix, ou, pour mieux dire, il s'était trouvé lui-même: il voyait de ses yeux, il devait nous donner dans chacune de

> ses toiles une traduction de la nature en cette langue originale qu'il venait de découvrir au fond de lui.[53]

If Zola's art is itself a translation, then reality is the original or model behind it. However, origins, be they personal or textual, are as problematic in *L'Œuvre* as they are in *La Terre*. Zola not only questions the reader's ability to access the original reality behind his novel, he also destabilizes the one-way traffic between the prior source and its artistic reproduction, between the model and the work of art made from it.

As certain literal paintings in Zola's text were associated with 'éclatement' and the verb 'sabrer', promising to break through their frames and the walls of the buildings housing them to offer unmediated access to the reality lying beyond, so Zola's metaphorical word paintings do likewise. The narrative descriptions of reality that Zola offers frequently contain symbolic metaphorical holes. In *Le Ventre de Paris*, a fountain rips the landscape already cut by baskets: 'La fontaine, au milieu de la pelouse coupée de corbeilles, coulait, avec la déchirure de ses nappes' (p. 817). Holes appear in the same novel in the scenery of Les Halles: '[...] de gros radis noirs, rangés en nappes de deuil, laissaient encore quelques trous de ténèbres' (p. 627). They proliferate in the landscape of *L'Œuvre*. Christine sees Paris by night as 'une trouée immense' (p. 13). The narrative depicts the city as similarly fractured in daylight: 'Par les jours de ciel clair, dès qu'ils [Claude et Christine] débouchaient du pont Louis-Philippe, toute la trouée des quais immense, à l'infini, se déroulait' (p. 102). Such holes appear before the reader's eyes: '[...] une trouée s'ouvrait à gauche, jusqu'à l'île Saint Louis' (p. 213). The landscape is perforated by breaches: 'Alors, suivant le caprice du vent, c'étaient des mers de souffre battant des rochers de corail [...] des architectures entassées, brûlant, s'écroulant, lâchant par leurs brèches des torrents de larve' (p. 105). As the literal paintings in Zola's narrative promised to break their frames and open a window to reality (Zola's art criticism at times conceives of certain impressionist paintings in the same terms),[54] Zola's descriptions in *L'Œuvre* appear to make a comparable promise, breaking and fissuring themselves, suggesting the possibility of unmediated access to the reality that lies behind their images.

Whilst these holes in Zola's texts proffer an opening to reality, they also make clear the shared inability of the author, artist and reader to access it fully. The edges of Zola's pages, with their emphasis on 'fuites' into the 'infini' that lies beyond, as well as the fissures at their centre, underline that reality exceeds the attempt to grasp it. Zola makes use of two images in particular to emphasize this notion: water and fire. As Kelly Basilio puts it, 'C'est que la vie elle-même, par définition, ne saurait être contenue dans des limites; d'où cette importance du débordement chez Zola, de même que dans la peinture impressionniste'.[55] The 'débordement' that Basilio identifies finds expression in Zola's pages in the seeping, uncontainable fluid images so frequently incorporated into the author's artistic narratives. The liquidity of the landscape in *Le Ventre de Paris* is pronounced. Florent sees *Les Halles* and its vegetables as a rising sea against which he struggles (p. 633). This sea overwhelms, as Christopher Prendergast points out, both Florent and Zola.[56] Florent is unable literally to ingest the food he sees before him and Zola cannot do so metaphorically.

Florent turns away from the landscape depicted in Zola's narrative, unable to bear it. And Zola calls upon the image of water in the same depiction, unable to contain it (p. 633–34). Prendergast writes, 'et si l'image de la "mer" surgit ici encore une fois, si elle rentre dans le "tableau", c'est effectivement pour le noyer'.[57] The landscape proves as fluid in *L'Œuvre* and even more destructive. The water of the landscape eats into the very possibility of representation and men become mere splashes: 'En bas, la place, aux trottoirs immenses, aux chaussées larges comme des lacs, s'emplissait de ce flot continuel, traversée en tous sens du rayonnement des roues, peuplée de points noirs qui étaient des hommes' (pp. 74–75). Interpreting such scenes through the lens of the work of Michel Serres, Prendergast suggests, using Serres's contention that there is something of a 'vaporisation du signe' in the texts of Zola, that there is:

> [...] une perte de netteté dans les desseins esquissés par l'écriture, une sorte de voile scriptural, comparable à cette 'brume' qui si souvent flotte au-dessus du Paris de Zola. Au lieu d'une plénitude déscriptive, d'une cohérence et d'une totalité, on a plutôt l'impression d'un vide, d'un trou au cœur de la ville et de l'écriture qui voudrait la représenter.[58]

As water dissolves Zola's descriptions in places, fire burns through them elsewhere. The fragmentation enacted in the descriptions on Zola's pages is frequently enunciated in incendiary terms. The fire of the sun burns a hole in the artistic vision of Les Halles in *Le Ventre de Paris*: 'Elles flambaient dans le soleil. Un grand rayon entrait par le bout de la rue couverte, au fond, trouant la masse des pavillons d'un portique de lumière' (p. 633). The sparks of the sun pierce the landscape in *L'Œuvre*: '[...] l'astre [...] perçait ce rempart d'une telle poussée de lumière, que des traits d'étincelles jaillissaient, partaient d'un bout de ciel à l'autre, visibles, ainsi qu'une volée de flèches d'or' (p. 105). The flames such arrows convey not only light fires in the landscape, 'trouant les façades', but destroy its artistic representation in the form of Claude's painting, negating the possibility of such representations by turning passers-by into little more than destroyed indications: 'Les Tuileries, au fond, s'évanouissaient en nuée d'or; les pavés saignaient, les passants n'étaient plus que des indications, des taches sombres mangées par la clarté trop vive' (p. 206). Representation is consumed by the fire of light. Whilst Serres makes famous use of fire as one of his key themes in relation to the very possibility of representation, Blanchot's use of fire as a representation of the unrepresentable is also *à propos*.[59] Zola uses fire to depict the limits of his project from *L'Œuvre*'s opening scene, burning the edges of his metaphorical canvas: 'C'était une trouée immense, les deux bouts de la rivière s'enfonçant à perte de vue, au milieu des braises rouges d'un incendie' (p. 13). In burning holes in his pages, Zola fragments his own narrative, considers the limits of his fiction, hinting at the boundaries of his quest to translate reality onto the written page.

The holes pierced in Zola's word paintings may fleetingly imply that the reality behind them may be accessed, but Zola's narrative proffers such a possibility whilst negating it at the same time. Prendergast, considering the work of Serres, suggests the presence of a 'voile scriptural' in Zola's fiction.[60] Notions of veiling are key to *L'Œuvre* for Zola uses this novel to italicize the veil of his text, the material of his artefact, the gauze of art which separates us from the reality he seeks to depict.[61] The text is a veil, however thin, between the reader and the reality depicted. In his correspondence Zola explicitly likens writing to embroidery: '[...] j'écris tout doucement, en moyenne trois pages par jour, sans recopier: imaginez-vous une femme qui brode de la laine, point par point.'[62] He subsequently reveals in his fiction the very fabric of his craft. *L'Œuvre* depicts 'un voile de vapeurs' (p. 105). It describes 'un gazon d'une douceur de velours' (p. 142). Claude assesses the landscape in *Le Ventre de Paris* in textile terms:

> Les mous étaient d'un rose tendre, s'accentuant peu à peu, bordé, en bas, de carmin vif; et il les disait en satin moiré, ne trouvant pas de mot pour peindre cette douceur soyeuse, ces longues allées fraîches, ces chairs légères qui retombaient à larges plis, comme des jupes accrochées de danseuses. (p. 776)

In the same novel cabbages in Les Halles appear to be made out of velvet, whilst the structures of the building itself are likened to lace as Florent admires 'les dentelles noires des charpentes de fonte' (p. 892 and p. 621). Lace proves to be one of Zola's repeated metaphors in his artistic descriptions of the landscape. In *Thérèse Raquin*, another novel with a would-be painter (Laurent), 'les arbres des quais se couvraient de feuilles, d'une légère dentelle d'un vert pâle'.[63] Writing persuasively on the relationship between 'texte' and 'tissu' in Zola's novels as a whole, Hannah Thompson situates both the dressmaker in *La Curée*, Worms, and Octave Mouret in *Pot-Bouille* and *Au Bonheur des dames*, as the 'embodiment of the Naturalist novelist'.[64] In *L'Œuvre*, Zola exposes the very fabric of his narrative, drawing the reader's attention to the veil of his text, the textual and textile barrier lying between us and the reality that Zola's novel seeks to depict.

This veil is never breached in Zola's fiction. The reality behind the fabric of the text may be hinted at, but never accessed by the reader. The novel can give no access to the reality before art and consequently the reality depicted in its artistic pages persistently bears the marks of workmanship. The reader does not witness nature in an unmediated state, it is always artistic. The fish in Les Halles in *Le Ventre de Paris* are a striking example. Far from being untouched natural objects, Zola describes them as bearing the marks of craftsmanship and artistry:

> C'était comme les écrins, vidés à terre, de quelque fille des eaux, des parures inouïes et bizarres, un ruissellement, un entassement de colliers, de bracelets monstrueux, de broches gigantesques, de bijoux barbares, dont l'usage échappait. Sur le dos des raies et des chiens de mer, de grosses pierres sombres, violâtres, verdâtres, s'enchâssaient dans un métal noirci; et les minces barres des équilles, les queues et les nageoires des éperlans, avaient des délicatesses de bijouterie fine. (p. 698)

The fish are not natural, they are man-made objects in a text that recognizes itself as a mediation of reality. Potential acknowledgements of the artistry of his own pages, of the fabrication of reality appear elsewhere in Zola's texts. In *Une page d'amour*, for example, 'les grands arbres du quai étaient des merveilles. On aurait dit des arbres de verre filé [...] dont les caprices d'artistes avaient tordu les bras piqués de fleurs' (p. 1090). Zola underlines the mediated nature of the reality depicted in his pages, subtly inscribing it with the marks of craftsmanship, presenting it as already artistic.

In *L'Œuvre*, art, in a sense, at times precedes reality. An evaluation of the character Christine explicates this point. Claude's initial artistic depiction of Christine does not stem from the reality of their first encounter, rather it precedes this meeting. The picture of Christine exists, albeit in an incomplete state, before either the reader or the artist is introduced to her in textual reality. Claude sees her sleeping and recognizes her as his painting: 'C'était ça, tout à fait ça, la figure qu'il avait inutilement cherchée pour son tableau, et presque dans le pose. [...] Déjà, il avait oublié la jeune fille, il était dans le ravissement de la neige des seins' (p. 19). Art exists before reality from the outset of *L'Œuvre*. As Zola revealed the fabric of his fiction, the textual veil of his work, so he arguably also gestures to the textual fabric of Christine's identity. Claude looks at her, painting her: 'Brusquement, un frisson courut, pareil à une moire sur le satin de sa peau' (p. 20). Her skin, even before its pictorial representation on canvas, is already man-made. Christine is fabricated even before she enters the medium of paint.

Art is depicted in part not as a reflection of reality, but as competing with, and in some senses, killing it. Again the example of Christine is revealing. Few characters prosper from art. Irma Bécot in *L'Œuvre* is a notable exception. She transforms herself into a living masterpiece and makes a healthy living from the image she has painted and fabricated for herself:

> En quatre ans, elle était devenue autre, la tête faite avec un art de cabotine, le front diminué par la frisure des cheveux, la face tirée en longueur, grâce à un effort de sa volonté sans doute, rousse ardente de pâle qu'elle était, si bien qu'une courtisane du Titien semblait maintenant s'être levée du petit voyou de jadis. (p. 176)

She collects art, lives parasitically from artists (she bleeds Fagerolles dry) and fashions an image Zola repeatedly introduces in artistic terms. He sees her as a figure 'descendue d'un vieux cadre de la Renaissance' (p. 304). If art allows Irma to live, however, it kills Christine's textual reality. Claude's paintings suck the life force from her. The first time he paints her, her flesh begins to turn to marble. The reader sees her 'dans son néant de beau marbre, avec le sourire mystérieux et figé de la pose' (p. 115). The process continues when Claude paints her subsequently: 'Et les yeux au loin, elle gardait la rigidité d'un marbre' (p. 242). The artistic life of the image on the canvas is parasitically drawn from Christine's reality: '[...] quelle souffrance de prêter sa chair, pour que l'autre naquît' (p. 244). Ultimately the artistic version of Christine kills her: 'Et elle renaissait, cette image, elle ressuscitait, plus vivante qu'elle [Christine], pour achever de la tuer' (p. 254). Christine becomes an object, a 'mannequin vivant, qu'il [Claude] plantait là et qu'il copiait, comme il aurait copié la cruche ou le chaudron d'une nature morte' (p. 240). Art not only precedes the reality of the model, it subsequently kills the reality of its model.

L'Œuvre plays with reality as a point of origin in other specific ways. The novel, since its publication, has been read by a variety of critics as a *roman à clef*, as a literary reflection of an actual reality, a reality which can be deciphered and accessed if the reader looks and researches hard enough. Zola's novel takes care to depict the broad evolution of art history in the nineteenth century. It traces developments in the sphere of the visual arts using both real and imaginary painters. Real painters are referenced and pages of Zola's novel, aspects of Claude's speech, read like sections of Zola's art criticism:

> Tiens! le père Ingres, tu sais s'il me tourne sur le cœur, celui-là, avec sa peinture glaireuse? Eh bien! c'est tout de même un sacré bonhomme, et je le trouve très crâne, et je lui tire mon chapeau, car il se fichait de tout, il avait un dessin du tonnerre de Dieu, qu'il a fait avaler aux idiots qui croient aujourd'hui le comprendre... Après ça, entends-tu! ils ne sont que deux, Delacroix et Courbet. Le reste, c'est de la fripouille... Hein? le vieux romantique, quelle fière allure! En voilà un décorateur qui faisait flamber les tons! Et quelle poigne! Il aurait couvert les murs de Paris, si on les lui avait donnés: sa palette bouillait et débordait. Je sais bien, ça n'était que de la fantasmagorie; mais, tant pis! ça me gratte, il fallait ça, pour incendier l'Ecole... Puis, l'autre est venu, un rude ouvrier, le plus vraiment peintre du siècle, et d'un métier absolument classique, ce que pas un de ces crétins n'a senti. Ils ont hurlé, parbleu! ils ont crié à la profanation, au réalisme, lorsque ce fameux réalisme n'était guère que dans les sujets; tandis que la vision restait celle des vieux maîtres et que la facture reprenait et continuait les beaux morceaux de nos musées... Tous les deux, Delacroix et Courbet, se sont produits à l'heure voulue. Ils ont fait chacun son pas en avant. Et, maintenant, oh! maintenant... (pp. 44–45)[65]

In depicting Claude and the group around him, fictional as they are, as the movement replacing these painters, Zola encourages the reader to place them in the context of nineteenth-century reality, to identify them, at least in some respects, with the impressionists.

Zola encourages the reader to look not only for the reality of artistic movements, but of individual artists behind the veil of his pages. He presents *L'Œuvre*, in a variety of ways, as the fictional depiction of an ontological artistic reality, a reality in which he was involved. The novel was announced in the *Bibliographie de la France* with a fragment which Mitterand, in his edition of the novel, suggests was written by Zola himself:

> *L'Œuvre*, le roman d'Emile Zola que la bibliothèque Charpentier publie aujourd'hui, est une histoire simple et poignante, le drame d'une intelligence aux prises avec la nature, le long combat de la passion d'une femme et de la passion de son art, chez un peintre original, qui apporte une formule nouvelle. L'auteur a mis ce drame dans le milieu de la jeunesse, il s'y est confessé lui-même, il y a raconté quinze ans de sa vie et de la vie de ses contemporains. Ce sont des sortes de Mémoires qui vont du Salon des Refusés de 1863 jusqu'aux expositions de ces dernières années, un tableau de l'art moderne, pris en plein Paris, avec tous les épisodes qu'il comporte.[66]

Zola's private statements to friends and colleagues reinforce this idea that he wished his reader to seek the truth, the original reality behind his fictive copy. He wrote the following in a letter to Céard in February 1886: '[...] je n'ai fini *L'Œuvre* que ce matin. Ce roman, où mes souvenirs et mon cœur ont débordé, a pris une longueur inattendue'.[67] In a letter to Van Santen Kolff of the 6 July 1885 he made a comparable claim: 'Je me suis mis à mon prochain roman [....]. J'ai repris mon Claude Lantier du *Ventre de Paris*. C'est toute ma jeunesse que je raconte, j'ai mis là tous mes amis, je m'y suis mis moi-même.'[68] Zola's preparatory work for the novel reinforces this suggestion. Making notes on the character who will become Claude, he writes:

'Un Manet, un Cézanne dramatisé; plus près de Cézanne'.[69] The part of Fagerolles is anticipated as borrowing from the contemporary painter Gervex. Zola envisions: 'Un autre peintre, le Gervex de la chose, le peintre à l'hôtel'.[70] The character who will develop into Jory is described as an adaptation of Zola's friend, the writer Paul Alexis: 'Alexis, dramatisé et rendu mauvais, grand baiseur. Toujours des femmes nouvelles'.[71] Zola's preliminary work on the novel links nearly all of the characters with a pre-existing and real model, a link emphasized both in publicity material and Zola's letters. In the words of Adolfo Fernandez-Zoïla:

> L'écrivain va se complaire à brouiller les pistes, à introduire les souvenirs 'vrais' et des situations fictives. Chacun y trouvera de quoi satisfaire des dons cachés de détective. De Cézanne à Manet, en passant par Pissarro, Guillemet, Monet, voire André Gill, Gustave Moreau ou même Odilon Redon, les ressemblances et les clefs susciteront intrigues et polémiques. Zola savait faire du 'marketing'.[72]

Zola asks his readers to play at being detective, to locate the keys to his characters' ontological identity behind the veil of his text.

A variety of critics have, understandably, taken Zola at his word and produced a number of insightful works seeking to unlock Zola's *roman à clef*. Robert J. Niess's work, *Zola, Cézanne and Manet: A Study of L'Œuvre*, states its intention to 'attempt to measure with some exactness the scope of the biographical elements of the book and to assay its "real life" content'.[73] Another attempt at decryption is made in Patrick Brady's appropriately titled *L'Œuvre de Emile Zola: roman sur les arts, manifeste, autobiographie, roman à clef*.[74] Henri Mitterand dissects the character of Bongrand: 'Ce personnage est un prudent et habile amalgame de Delacroix (par sa situation dans l'évolution de la peinture), de Millet (auquel font songer les paysans de la "Noce"), de Manet (pour le voyage en Espagne), même peut-être de Courbet (par les thèmes).'[75] Nor is the urge to solve the mystery of Zola's novel new. Vizetelly, an English translator of Zola's novels, again assessing Bongrand, claimed: 'Bongrand is a commingling of Courbet, Cabanel and Gustave Flaubert'.[76] Alexis read the novel and wrote: 'Et Flaubert, et Cézanne, et moi, et nous tous! *Notre* jeunesse à tous est dans ce livre'.[77] From the novel's publication, a whole host of names have been proposed as potential keys to unlock the reality behind the veil of fiction.

However, as a consideration of the narrative of *L'Œuvre* makes clear, keys in this novel are not always available and the doorways they seal often remain locked. Claude and Christine lock themselves in Claude's *atelier* to safeguard her identity and reputation from Claude's friends: 'Dès que Christine était là, Claude enlevait la clef de la porte. Elle-même l'exigeait: de cette façon, personne ne viendrait les déranger' (p. 99). When Claude's visitors hear voices within, they do not pass through the locked door. When, by mistake, Claude and Christine forget to lock the door and Claude is forced to admit his friends, Christine hides and still they do not discover her presence or identity (p. 106). Keys in Zola's novel often do not open doors to reveal the truth of the identity lying behind them, rather they safeguard its secret. Claude goes to see a previously renowned painter, Courajod, a painter whom he thought was dead. Rather than gaining access to his life and news, Claude has the door shut and locked in his face: 'Bref, il m'a flanqué dehors, je l'ai entendu qui tournait sa clef violemment, qui se barricadait avec ses bêtes, contre les tentatives d'admiration de la rue' (p. 261). The metaphorical keys required to unlock the mystery of Zola's novel prove as elusive, as difficult to find and turn. Jacques is shut away from his father painting his mother, from this original piece of art. His mother covers the key hole with her clothes, 'de façon à boucher le trou de la serrure' (p. 242). Zola's reader finds himself/herself in a similar position, shut away from the identity of the painters Zola claims to depict, peering through a blocked keyhole at the reality or origin behind his pages.

If Zola's *L'Œuvre* encourages the reader, as the previously quoted passage from Fernandez-Zoïla suggests ('Chacun y trouvera de quoi satisfaire ses dons cachés de détective'), to play the part of the detective and solve the mystery the novel poses, later work in the *Rougon-Macquart* series warns of the difficulties of such an undertaking. *La Bête humaine* dramatizes the attempt to solve a mystery, to detect the original identity behind a crime. Yet, Denizet, the would-be detective of the piece, detects nothing at all. The keys to the crime elude him and his reconstruction of events and identities is false. Whilst it is a 'chef-d'œuvre de fine analyse', it unmasks nothing of the truth.[78] Moreover, the efforts of Denizet's detective doubles prove similarly fruitless. Misard's quest for his wife's buried fortune sends him around in circles. Infectious as his attempts at detection are (his second wife comes to share his obsession), rigorous as is the undertaking, the object sought is never unearthed and the novel closes with the quest still in progress (p. 1325).

Would-be detectives seeking the origin of and originals in *L'Œuvre* will meet a comparable fate. Writing on Zola's correspondence, Niess suggests that the clues offered simply do not add up:

> [...] they [the letters] indicate clearly that the novel has autobiographical elements, but they do not, unfortunately, give any but the vaguest clues as to the identity of the persons, living or dead, who might have served as models for the figure of Claude Lantier or the other characters in the book.[79]

Put simply, *L'Œuvre* is a novel to which Zola will not give the reader the key. The fictional door protecting the identity of the original artists and works remains closed and locked. Zola provides not a direct translation of a living artist, but rather an overlapping series of possible suspects. Critics past and present identify a whole host of artists and creative figures as the models for Zola's characters and they do so for a reason. Zola deliberately blurs the boundaries of his characters' originals, hinting at but obfuscating the models from whom he borrows. His preparatory work for the novel may identify specific characters with existing artistic figures, but Zola shifts between originals, substitutes names, adapts a series of models to create one character. Fagerolles, the character he linked with Gervex, subsequently moves to borrow from Maupassant's personality: '[...] le Gervex devient le Maupassant, très malin, tournant contre la bande, se mettant à part, cajolant les critiques'.[80] Characters simultaneously borrow from a variety of sources. Zola envisions the character who would become Bongrand as 'Un Manet très chic, un Flaubert plutôt'.[81] The attempt to unlock the originals of *L'Œuvre* leaves reader and critic alike, not with a fixed origin, but rather a series of overlapping origins. According to Mitterand: 'Il convient [...] d'être prudent dans la recherche des modèles. Car toutes sortes de souvenirs, d'idées, d'inventions, se superposent et se mêlent ici'.[82] Niess concurs:

'When he [Zola] did borrow events or details or even personal characteristics from his friends and acquaintances, he so combined, transposed, and modified them that it is almost impossible to recognize any of them surely'.[83]

Zola's obfuscation of the space of origin may be interpreted in a variety of ways. It was perhaps an attempt to safeguard himself and his work from reprisals. Monet, to an extent, sees it in this light:

> Vous avez pris soin, avec intention, que pas un seul de vos personnages ne ressemble à l'un de nous, mais malgré cela, j'ai peur que dans la presse et le public, nos ennemis ne prononcent les noms de Manet ou tout au moins les nôtres pour en faire des râtés.[84]

It was perhaps simultaneously a marketing tactic to encourage people to buy and decode his work. However, Zola's play on the key to his text feeds into the broader exploration of notions of original and translation, origin and reproduction undertaken by his novel. *L'Œuvre* not only evaluates its ability to access the reality behind its pages, italicizing the literary veil covering that reality, but it uses its narrative to explore the complex relationship between model and reproduction, a relationship still under evaluation in contemporary debates on adaptation.

Christine serves as a model for the series of copies, the paintings that Claude makes from her. Yet the relationship between Christine (the original) and the reproductions made of her is neither straightforward nor linear and Zola explores its intricacies. As has already been suggested, Christine is not fully the original from which the painting is created, for the painting precedes her in Claude's consciousness. When Claude looks at her sleeping, he sees not a woman whom he would like to paint, but a woman who corresponds to a painting that already exists in part on canvas and fully in his mind. And Zola complicates Christine's relationship with the painted reproduction made of her still further for as the reproduction precedes her, so too, in the course of the novel, does it replace her as a space of origin, consigning her to the status of inferior reproduction. Claude compares Christine, the model behind the painted reproduction, to that reproduction and finds her wanting: 'Ainsi, regarde-toi dans la glace: il y a là, près des aisselles, des poches qui se gonflent, et ça n'a rien de beau. Va, tu peux chercher sur son corps, à elle, ces poches n'y sont pas' (p. 254). Christine, speaking to Claude, does try to crush the artistic reproductions made of her, highlighting them as inferior copies: 'Tu m'as prise pour modèle, tu as voulu des copies de mon corps. A quoi bon, dis? est-ce que ces copies me valent?' (p. 348). Yet Claude chooses the copy over its original: '[...] elle sentait bien qu'il préférait sa copie à elle-même, que cette copie était l'adorée' (p. 244). Christine, the apparent point of origin, loses herself to her reproduction as the painting ultimately destroys whatever ontology the original enjoyed. Christine feels pain as she metaphorically gives her flesh to her painted rival, the rival increasingly described in the most animate of terms as Christine herself becomes inanimate: 'L'excès de la souffrance avait retiré tout le sang de son cœur, elle demeura évanouie par terre, comme morte, pareille à une loque blanche, misérable et finie, écrasée sous la souveraineté farouche de l'art' (p. 353). The reproduction does not translate the original, rather it replaces it. As Zola's novel points back to a whole host of artists as potential originals from whom it copies fragments, Zola's plot itself reveals the problematic relationship between model and painted reproduction.

Zola is actively and thoughtfully engaged with the processes of textual translation. His novel *L'Œuvre* situates itself as a translation on two levels. Zola not only explicitly claims to translate the impressionists into prose, but he also conceives of naturalist art, in its widest sense, as a translation of reality, the original source or model for his work. However, origins in Zola's novels are rarely unproblematic, as *L'Œuvre* suggests on three levels. First, Zola subtly makes the reader aware of the veil of the text separating them from the reality his novel depicts. Secondly, whilst the author encourages the reader to seek the point of origin lying behind his *roman à clef* in the shape of real artists and their work, he ultimately offers no keys, pinpointing no true models, just a series of clues to a series of original identities who cannot be found. This refusal is echoed at the level of plot as Zola destabilizes origins at a third level in the novel. Christine is never fully given the status of original to the series of artistic reproductions Claude makes of her. Her reproduction both precedes and supersedes her. Zola, thus, is not just an author who has been reproduced by or translated into the medium of film, he is an author who explores the processes and problems of reproduction and translation in and through *L'Œuvre*.

Notes to Chapter 2

1. Emile Zola, *Ecrits sur l'art*, ed. by Jean-Pierre Leduc-Adine (Paris: Gallimard, 1991), p. 91. For further details of the Cézanne/Zola relationship, see Robert J. Niess, *Zola, Cézanne and Manet: A Study of L'Œuvre* (Ann Arbor: University of Michigan Press, 1968).
2. Zola, *Ecrits sur l'art*, p. 468.
3. Ibid., p. 167.
4. For contrasting approaches to the Manet/Zola relationship, a relationship about which much has been written, see Robert Lethbridge, 'Manet's Textual Frames', in *Artistic Relations: Literature and the Visual Arts in Nineteenth-Century France*, ed. by Peter Collier and Robert Lethbridge (New Haven, CT: Yale University Press, 1994), pp. 144–58 and Elizabeth Briggs-Lynch, 'Manet's *Nana*: The Connection with Zola's *L'Assommoir* and *Nana*', in *Emile Zola and the Arts*, ed. by Jean-Max Guieu and Alison Hilton (Washington, DC: Georgetown University Press, 1988) pp. 9–14.
5. For further details see Guieu and Hilton, eds, *Emile Zola and the Arts*, pp. xii–xiii.
6. Collier and Lethbridge, eds, *Artistic Relations*, p. 8.
7. Zola, *Ecrits sur l'art*, pp. 157–58.
8. Ibid., p. 160.
9. Ibid., p. 204.
10. Ibid., p. 358.
11. Ibid., pp. 202–03.
12. Ibid., p. 143.
13. Ibid., p. 145.
14. Ibid., p. 178.
15. Ibid., pp. 283–84.
16. Ibid., pp. 109–10.
17. Ibid., p. 225.
18. Ibid., p. 270.
19. Ibid., p. 149.
20. Ibid., p. 358.
21. Ibid., p. 129.
22. Ibid., p. 146.

23. Théodore Reff, 'Manet's Portrait of Zola', *Burlington Magazine*, 117 (1975), 35–44. Henri Mitterand, 'Le Musée dans le texte', *Cahiers naturalistes*, 66 (1992), 13–22 (p. 14).
24. Ibid., p. 14.
25. Lethbridge, 'Manet's Textual Frames', p. 156.
26. Ibid., p. 155.
27. Zola, *Les Rougon-Macquart*, II: *L'Assommoir* (1961), p. 445. Unless otherwise stated, subsequent references are to this edition and will be made in the text.
28. Mitterand, 'Le Musée dans le texte', p. 18.
29. Zola, *Les Rougon-Macquart*, I: *La Curée* (1960), pp. 488–89. Unless otherwise stated, subsequent references are to this edition and will be made in the text.
30. Marie-Thérèse Barrett, '*Le Ventre de Paris*, Claude Lantier and Realist Themes of Food and Markets in Seventeenth- and Nineteenth-Century Paintings', in Guieu and Hilton, eds, *Emile Zola and the Arts*, pp. 47–54 (p. 48).
31. 'La salle de l'architecture' is described in comparably liquid terms: 'Du plafond, tendu d'un écran de toile blanche, tombait une clarté égale, douce et morne, qui se reflétait, pareille à une eau de source immobile, dans le miroir du parquet fortement ciré' (pp. 130–31). In *L'Assommoir*, Mademoiselle Remanjou closes her eyes as she walks on the floor of the Louvre 'parce qu'elle croyait marcher sur de l'eau', so much does it shine (p. 444).
32. This quotation can be paralleled almost directly with the following retrospective statement on the impressionists in Zola's art criticism: 'Autrefois, lorsqu'on accrochait une toile de ceux-ci dans une salle, elle faisait un trou de lumière parmi les autres toiles. [...] C'était la fenêtre ouverte sur la nature, le fameux Plein air qui entrait' (Zola, *Ecrits sur l'art*, p. 469).
33. Kelly Basilio, 'Naturalisme zolien et impressionnisme: le rôle de la métonymie', *Cahiers naturalistes*, 66 (1992), 83–90 (p. 86).
34. Mitterand, 'Le Musée dans le texte', p. 21.
35. Zola, *Les Rougon-Macquart*, II: *Une page d'amour* (1961), p. 810. Unless otherwise stated, subsequent references are to this edition and will be made in the text.
36. Zola, *Les Rougon-Macquart*, I: *La Faute de l'abbé Mouret* (1960), p. 1261.
37. Charcoal also appears in Zola's description of the shadows of Florent and Claude in *Le Ventre de Paris:* 'Le soleil, au ras des coteaux de Suresnes, était si bas sur l'horizon, que leurs ombres colossales tachaient la blancheur du monument [...] de deux barres noires, pareilles à deux traits au fusain' (p. 806).
38. Jean-François Thibault, 'La Peinture en marche: académisme et modernité chez Claude Lantier', in Guieu and Hilton, eds, *Emile Zola and the Arts*, pp. 25–33 (pp. 31–32).
39. William Kloss, 'Zola and the Old Masters', in Guieu and Hilton, eds, *Emile Zola and the Arts*, pp. 35–45.
40. Cited by Henri Hertz, 'Emile Zola, témoin de la vérité', *Europe* , 30, (1952), 83–84.
41. Zola, *Ecrits sur l'art*, p. 313.
42. Pierre Aubery, 'Zola peintre et la littérature', in Guieu and Hilton, eds, *Emile Zola and the Arts*, pp. 1–8 (p. 3).
43. John Rewald, *The History of Impressionism* (New York: Moma, 1961), p. 338.
44. Dominique Van Hooff, 'Emile Zola et L'Impressionnisme ou la révolution positiviste en peinture', *Excavatio*, 1 (1992), 73–83 (p. 77).
45. Jean-Pierre Leduc-Adine, 'Paris et l'ordre spatial dans *L'Œuvre*', in Guieu and Hilton, eds, *Emile Zola and the Arts*, pp. 165–75 (p. 171).
46. Zola, *Ecrits sur l'art*, p. 313.
47. Ibid., p. 382.
48. Ibid., p. 81.
49. That Zola's conceptualization of art is more complex and nuanced than his use of the vocabulary of copying initially suggests is made clear by *L'Œuvre* itself. Chaîne fails as an artist because he copies his topic too minutely, replicating it in its entirety. 'Son triomphe', and it is his only triumph, 'était l'exactitude dans la gaucherie, il avait les minuties naïves d'un primitif, le souci du petit détail' (p. 68). Claude's reaction to his painting is one of pity.
50. Zola, *Ecrits sur l'art*, p. 167.
51. Cited in Anne Lecomte-Hilmy, 'L'Artiste de tempérament chez Zola et devant le public: essai

d'analyse lexicologique et sémiologique', in Guieu and Hilton, eds, *Emile Zola and the Arts*, pp. 85–99 (p. 87).

52. Zola, *Ecrits sur l'art*, p. 313.
53. Ibid., p. 147.
54. Ibid., p. 469: 'Tous des Manet alors, tous des Monet, tous des Pissarro! Autrefois, lorsqu'on accrochait une toile de ceux-ci dans une salle, elle faisait un trou de lumière parmi les autres toiles'.
55. Basilio, 'Naturalisme zolien et impressionnisme', p. 89.
56. Christopher Prendergast, 'Le Panorama, la peinture et la faim: le début du *Ventre de Paris*', *Cahiers naturalistes*, 67 (1993), 65–71 (p. 66).
57. Ibid., p. 66.
58. Ibid., p. 70.
59. For an analysis of Serres, fire and the question of representation, see Larry Duffy, *Le Grand Transit Moderne: Mobility, Modernity and French Naturalist Fiction* (Amsterdam/New York: Rodopi, 2005), pp. 67–72. See also Maurice Blanchot, *La Part du feu* (Paris: Gallimard, 1949).
60. Prendergast, 'Le Panorama, la peinture et la faim', p. 70.
61. The veil has been analysed in a different context in relation to other of Zola's novels. See Peter Brooks, *Body Work*. Significantly for the purposes of this chapter, Brooks, in a chapter entitled 'Nana at Last Unveil'd? Problems of the Modern Nude', maintains that although Nana performs a prolonged striptease both for the reader and her admirers in the course of the narrative, she is never truly divested of her final veil, a veil comparable with the gauze of text discussed here.
62. Bakker, ed., *Emile Zola: Correspondance*, II (1980), p. 438.
63. Zola, *Œuvres complètes*, I: *Premiers romans* (1966), p. 620.
64. Hannah Thompson, *Naturalism Redressed: Identity and Clothing in the Novels of Emile Zola* (Oxford: Legenda, 2004), pp. 39–40.
65. As Henri Mitterand points out in his note on this long quotation, this tirade echoes in part the preface Zola wrote in 1884 for the catalogue of the exhibition of Edouard Manet's works.
66. Cited in Zola, *L'Œuvre*, p. 1384.
67. Bakker, ed., *Emile Zola: Correspondance*, V (1985), p. 370.
68. Ibid., pp. 278–79.
69. Cited in Zola, *L'Œuvre*, p. 1354.
70. Ibid., p. 1355.
71. Ibid., p. 1355.
72. Adolfo Fernandez-Zoïla, 'Le Système écriture-peinture et le figural dans *L'Œuvre*', *Cahiers naturalistes*, 66 (1992), 91–103 (p. 92).
73. Niess, *Zola, Cézanne and Manet: A Study of L'Œuvre*, p. 26.
74. Patrick Brady, *L'Œuvre de Emile Zola: roman sur les arts, manifeste, autobiographie, roman à clef* (Geneva: Droz, 1967).
75. Cited in Zola, *L'Œuvre*, p. 1370.
76. Cited in Niess, *Zola, Cézanne and Manet*, p. 44.
77. Cited in Zola, *L'Œuvre*, pp. 1385–86.
78. Zola, *Les Rougon-Macquart*, IV: *La Bête humaine* (1966), p. 1307. Unless otherwise stated, subsequent references are to this edition and will be made in the text.
79. Niess, *Zola, Cézanne and Manet*, p. 5.
80. Cited in Zola, *L'Œuvre*, p. 1359.
81. Ibid., p. 1358.
82. Ibid., p. 1353.
83. Niess, *Zola, Cézanne and Manet*, p. 61.
84. Letter to Zola cited in Zola, *L'Œuvre*, p. 1387.

CHAPTER 3

❖

Nana: Copies and Originals

Origins and originals prove as central to Zola's 1880 novel *Nana* and certain of its adaptations as they are in *L'Œuvre*. The introduction to this volume analysed the way in which conventional approaches to adaptation privilege the notion that adaptations are an inferior copy of a superior textual original. However, this chapter underlines the way in which the complexity of the relationship between Zola's novel, Jean Renoir's 1926 silent film version, *Nana*, and Edouard Molinaro's 2001 television adaptation, *Nadia Coupeau, dite Nana*, pose a challenge to such approaches. Zola's novel destabilizes its status as literary original. The text will not allow the origins of its heroine to be fixed and simultaneously engages with the works and media it has itself adapted in order to exist. Renoir and Molinaro are not the only filmmakers to have adapted Zola's novel: Russell Cousins cites ten known film versions of *Nana*.[1] However, what sets apart and indeed links the versions made by Renoir and Molinaro, versions separated by nearly one hundred years, is their willingness to consider their own authorial act. Both dramatize their status as adaptations, highlighting their own interpretative strategies and self-reflexively performing their status as copies of an earlier text. Origins may be sought in relation to Zola, Renoir, Molinaro and their versions of *Nana*, but, in their place, a kaleidoscope of fertile reproductions is found.

Zola's novel destabilizes notions of origin on a number of levels. Its initial obfuscation of origin takes place at the level of characterization. Images of Nana's identity fill the pages of the text, but the basis of that identity is nowhere to be found. Zola provides the reader with a family tree to accompany the *Rougon-Macquart* series, a family tree in which Nana figures, and which should allow the reader to trace her genetic origins. However, far from fixing his heroine's origins, Zola disperses them. In keeping with Zola's theory that women's children often bear the imprint of their mother's first lover even though they have different biological fathers, Nana resembles not her true father Coupeau, but her mother's first lover Lantier, a man with whom she has no genetic bond. Nana points to an origin from which she does not come. Zola underlines the link between Nana and Lantier in *L'Assommoir* by means of repeated imagery. The novelist uses the same digestive vocabulary to describe both Nana and Lantier in relation to their lovers. Lantier metaphorically consumes Gervaise, Virginie and a whole host of other lovers: 'Il venait de manger une blanchisseuse; à présent, il croquait une épicière; et il s'établissait à la file des mercières, des papetières, des modistes, il était de mâchoires assez larges pour les avaler' (p. 730). Just as her symbolic father consumes his female lovers in *L'Assommoir*, Nana, in the novel bearing her name, is a 'mangeuse d'hommes' who eats a stream of lovers 'comme elle croquait [...] un sac de pralines'.[2] Nana ingests Steiner and his fortune: 'Il était gros, il était bête, et elle le bousculait, avalant les morceaux doubles, voulant en finir plus vite [...] elle finit Steiner, elle le rendit au pavé, sucé jusqu'aux moelles' (pp. 1454–55). However, Lantier is not Nana's only paternal point of origin; the novel obfuscates her origins still further by situating Bordenave, in a manner akin to the Pygmalion myth, as her maker. Bordenave launches Nana's stage identity and Fauchery describes her as the impressario's 'invention' (p. 1096). Bordenave quantifies his relationship with his protégé precisely in terms of paternity: 'Et il resta, grognant, heureux pourtant de la revoir; car, disait-il, cette sacrée Nana lui mettait du baume dans le cœur, rien qu'à vivre devant lui. C'était sa fille, son vrai sang' (p. 1389).[3]

The origin of Nana's identity is rendered still more problematic as a result of its essentially theatrical nature. In order to understand the performance at the core of the heroine's identity, it is necessary to explore the space of the theatre in the novel as a whole. As Roger Clark points out, Zola sets three chapters in the theatre (Chapters 1, 5 and 9) and, at first glance, both the theatre and the performances it houses are clearly delineated and contained by the novel. Zola undertakes something of a naturalist dissection of the theatre.[4] Chapter 1 introduces the reader to the surface of the theatre, to the exterior image of its spectacle. The action is viewed from a distance, focalized using the narrative '*on*' of the audience, and the reader, a little like the novices Hector de la Faloise and Georges Hugon, is initiated into the world of spectacle, albeit from a detached position.[5] The novel's second trip to the theatre, which takes place in Chapter 5, deconstructs the spectacular surface of the operetta staged. It takes the viewer, via the uninitiated gaze of Muffat, backstage:

> Déjà le comte Muffat se dirigeait vers le couloir des loges. La pente assez rapide de la scène l'avait surpris, et son inquiétude venait beaucoup de ce plancher qu'il sentait mobile sous ses pieds; par les costières ouvertes, on apercevait les gaz brûlant dans les dessous; c'était une vie souterraine, avec des profondeurs d'obscurité, des voix d'hommes, des souffles de cave. (p. 1206)

As Zola puts it in his notes, his aim was to show the reader the mechanics of the theatrical, the machinery which creates the performative surface witnessed in Chapter 1:

> Comme transition, amener le monde sur la scène et mettre là l'œil au rideau. Regard dans la salle. Le prince, Muffat, ils viennent. Chouard aussi. Alors, quand le prince traverse la scène, mettre les machinistes, le changement de décor, en un mot la scène, quand la toile est baissée. Un mot d'une petite qui regarde par l'œil du rideau. (p. 1717)

In the novel's final visit to the theatre, the text delves still further behind the illusion of performance, offering the reader a glimpse of the genesis of a play via its creation and rehearsal, a play the reader will never see. In the course of the novel Zola thus dissects the distanced view of spectacle he offers the reader in Chapter 1, successively taking us into the wings and backstage, before moving still further back to consider the birth of one such spectacle.

However, whilst Zola dissects the theatre in *Nana*, arguably it cannot ultimately be pinned down. The theatre proves to be as permeable and shifting a space as the museum and the salon are in *L'Assommoir* and *L'Œuvre* respectively. Moreover, just as the boundary between art criticism and fiction is permeable in relation to *L'Œuvre* as Zola transfers aspects of his art criticism into his novel, so too the boundary between Zola's dramatic criticism and *Nana* is at times a fluid one. Zola's writing on the theatre, *Le Naturalisme au théâtre* and *Nos auteurs dramatiques*, appeared in collected form in 1881, the year of *Nana*'s publication.[6] Zola's dislike of Offenbach and his productions is well known.[7] *Nana* enacts and comments upon this dislike. Clark persuasively teases out the way in which *Nana*'s opening performance in *La Blonde Vénus* clearly constitutes an allusion to Offenbach's famous *La Belle Hélène*, an operetta which had been staged at the Variétés in 1864.[8] The plot of *La Belle Hélène* (a light-hearted survey of Second-Empire society based on sex, Trojan heroes and Greek mythology) is clearly recalled in *Nana*'s *La Blonde Vénus*:

> Le premier acte de *La Blonde Vénus* se passait dans l'Olympe, un Olympe de carton, avec des nuées pour coulisses et le trône de Jupiter à droite. [...] Rose Mignon venait d'entrer, en Diane. [...] Son air d'entrée, des paroles bêtes à pleurer, où elle se plaignait de Mars, qui était en train de la lâcher pour Vénus, fut chanté avec une réserve pudique, si pleine de sous-entendus égrillards, que le public s'échauffa. (p. 1105)

Zola's novel, like his theatrical criticism on the topic, leaves us in no doubt as to the value of the piece. The play is deemed to be of minimal importance, badly performed and the audience reaction is the following: 'Un même mot courait: "C'est idiot"' (p. 1109). Zola's novel not only points back to another textual origin in the form of the opinions he expresses in his theatrical criticism in relation to Offenbach, it also destabilizes origin in another respect. Zola's characters perform parts on stage in a fictional play, a play which points back to Offenbach's operetta as a source. However, Offenbach's operetta itself points back to the Second Empire as its source, albeit a source disguised by the borrowed costumes of mythology. As Clark puts it, 'Zola [...] within a novel that elsewhere provides the bleakest of representations of Second-Empire personalities and structures, uses *La Blonde Vénus* to debunk Offenbach's operetta, itself already a parody of the parody that was Louis-Napoléon's cardboard empire'.[9] Zola perhaps alludes to the dizzying number of receding origins performed on stage in *Nana*'s *La Blonde Vénus* by means of the costumes the characters assume whilst already in the theatrical disguise of their roles on stage. The characters of the play disguise themselves as characters from Offenbach's *La Vie parisienne*, a piece appearing on 31 October 1866 which proved to be one of his greatest successes: 'Ils s'étaient déguisés pour garder l'incognito. Jupiter entra en roi Dagobert [...]. Phébus parut en Postillon de Longjumeau et Minerve en Nourrice normande. De grands éclats de gaieté accueillirent Mars, qui portait un costume extravagant d'Amiral suisse' (p. 1112). The layers of costumes within costumes and performances within performances make stable origins harder to find.

The theatre will ultimately prove to be an uncontainable space in *Nana*. Its performances are not sealed in by the walls of the building and gradually seep through to the world beyond. The action on the stage predicts and reflects that which will subsequently take place in reality. On stage, Vulcain, played by Fontan, expresses a desire to slap Vénus, played by Nana (p. 1108). Fontan reprises his role as Vulcain in reality in the flat he shares with Nana: 'Fontan mimait le désespoir, avec ses airs drôles de Vulcain pleurant Vénus' (p. 1291). And he repeatedly gives in to the urge to slap and hurt Nana as their relationship goes sour. Diane's anger at losing Mars to Vénus is echoed by that felt by the actress playing her, Rose Mignon, as she loses Steiner to Vénus/Nana (p. 1119). The conclusions of the 'chœur des cocus' on stage apply perfectly to those later drawn by the novel's most prominent 'cocu' in the society beyond the theatre, Muffat: '[...] ils aimaient mieux être trompés et contents, ce qui était la morale de la comédie' (p. 1120). The action on stage at the Variétés spills beyond the edges of the scenes, to infiltrate the whole of the novel and its society.

Just as *La Blonde Vénus* seeps beyond the confines of the stage, so too the very space of performance proves to be a shifting one. Acting and spectacle are not confined to the stage in the Variétés, rather, they move through various offstage areas. The attention of the actors on stage is distracted from their performance by the pantomime, described in highly theatrical terms, performed by Mignon in real life in the wings. He reacts with veiled violence to his wife's non-lucrative affair with Fauchery:

> Depuis quelque temps, tout le théâtre s'amusait d'une comédie qui se jouait dans les coulisses. Mignon, furieux du caprice de sa femme, vexé de voir ce Fauchery n'apporter au ménage qu'une publicité discutable, avait imaginé de se venger en le comblant de marques d'amitié. (p. 1199)

The space of performance shifts from the stage to the wings. And it moves further still, as Nana's performance to Muffat in the *loge* makes clear. She performs the part of the duchess to convince Muffat of her suitability, reprising it when defending herself to the cast: 'Elle se retint, elle exagéra le ton flûté de sa voix, avec un geste de marquise qui va marcher sur une pelure d'orange' (p. 1345). The role shifts still further as Muffat performs it, imitating Nana imitating the duchess, in the prop room. Fontan, one of Zola's many silent witnesses, listens to the repercussions of this performance in the theatre filled precisely with hidden audiences and gazes (p. 1344). Zola inscribes such gazes into the very structure of the building:

> Seule, l'avant-scène était éclairée. Une servante, une flamme de gaz prise à l'embranchement de la rampe, et dont un réflecteur jetait toute la clarté sur les premiers plans, semblait un grand œil jaune ouvert dans la demi-obscurité, où il flambait avec une tristesse louche. (p. 1323)

Performances, in this novel, shift and slip beyond the space of the stage.

Nana is the principal means by which performances pass beyond the confines of the theatre to the society lying beyond. As David Baguley puts it, 'Nana's life is series of performances. [...] She not only makes her way in the world of the theatre, but transforms the world into theatre'.[10] As Zola makes clear, Nana performs everywhere. In the novel she rushes her role on stage in order to get home and perform 'son rôle nouveau de maîtresse de maison' (p. 1167). Her houses are described in supremely theatrical terms. So too are her servants: 'Ils se précipitaient, se bousculaient, faisant disparaître la table comme un décor de féerie, au coup de sifflet du maître machiniste' (p. 1185). Her house is 'machiné comme un théâtre' thanks to Zoé who directs much of her mistress's performance (p. 1351). Nana performs offstage in the theatre. She play-acts for the admirers who visit her dressing room: 'Elle risqua encore des mines hésitantes d'ingénue, se remuant comme chatouillée' (p. 1209). However, most importantly, she reprises both of her roles from the Variétés, Vénus and the lead of *La Petite Duchesse* beyond its walls. These reprisals are significant in relation to notions of origin in two respects. Zola uses Nana's reprisal of her Vénus role in order to question the ontology of his heroine herself. He uses her re-enactment of her role as a duchess to question the fixity and origin of the society surrounding her.

The reader is introduced to Nana as she performs the part of Vénus on stage. This performance subsequently shifts backstage as she reprises the role for her admirers in her dressing room: 'Nana, oubliant qu'elle était en pantalon, avec son bout de chemise, jouait la grande dame, la reine Vénus, ouvrant ses petits appartements aux personnages de l'Etat' (p. 1210). Nana then breaches the boundary between the theatre and the world to play the same role at the races: '[...] pour faire crever les autres femmes qu'enrageait son triomphe, elle leva son verre plein, dans son ancienne pose de Vénus victorieuse' (p. 1390). The boundaries between performance and original identity ultimately dissolve as Zola subtly indicates that performance is all that makes up the core of Nana's identity. Nana, having performed the part of Vénus, becomes her: the narrative twice addresses her as such in her dressing room. The first such address can perhaps be attributed to the focalization of Muffat as he touches her hair: '[...] les cheveux dénoués de Vénus lui [Muffat] roulèrent sur les mains' (p. 1214). However, the second such address is less clear cut. Highlighting Nana's assumption of her role, the narrative simply states: 'Vénus était prête' (p. 1215). The scene in which, in her own home, Nana examines herself naked in the mirror, that most privileged of naturalist tropes, is still more revealing in this respect. What Nana sees when she looks in the reflective surface is not an ontological identity, but instead her mythical role: 'Ça la surprenait toujours de se voir; elle avait l'air étonné et séduit d'une jeune fille qui découvre sa puberté. Lentement, elle ouvrit les bras pour développer son torse de Vénus grasse' (p. 1270). Nana is not a person in the mirror, but a performance. And a performance of an endlessly reproduced part at that. The mythical allusion to Vénus, far from fixing Nana's identity, rather posits her as the latest reproduction of a myth endlessly reproduced and adapted over time. Nana is not a point of origin, she is a performance, the latest in a series of reinterpretations.

Nana's performance and subsequent reprisal of the lead role in *La Petite Duchesse* proves comparably significant. She plays the part of a duchess on stage, imitating society women of the Second Empire. Her performance is a bad one and reactions to it are resoundingly incredulous. Bordenave is in no doubt about Nana's inability to play the part: 'Allons donc! c'est fou!' (p. 1340). Fauchery is aghast: 'Ah! non, n'est-ce pas? c'est une plaisanterie... On rirait trop' (p. 1341). The audience is ultimately unconvinced: 'Elle s'y montra atrocement mauvaise, elle eut des prétentions à la haute comédie, qui mirent le public en gaiété. On ne siffla pas, tant on s'amusait'

(p. 1346). Nana is an inauthentic copy of a society lady. The novel deems her performance so bad that it passes over the play in its entirety, allowing its short theatre run little narrative space. Nana, however, reprises her role as a society lady beyond the confines of the theatre. The reader has no reason to suppose Nana's acting skills improved, but the impact of the heroine's reprised role is an unusual one. Luce Irigaray, writing in a feminist context, investigates the power of imitation to question the ontology of the original it copies.[11] Aspects of her argument are perhaps unwittingly anticipated by Nana. Far from being a point of origin, society women of the Second Empire turn to imitate Nana as she performs a part she has borrowed from them. Nana claims: 'Oui, je vais lui en donner de la grande dame, à ton Paris' (p. 1346). Shortly after Zola states: 'Elle [Nana] donnait le ton, de grandes dames l'imitaient' (p. 1347). They copy a copy of themselves and the cycles of imitation seem unending as Zola queries the origins not just of his heroine, but also of the society in which she lives.

As Sandy Petrey puts it, 'Des chambellans de l'impératrice aux prisonnières du monde du petit vice, tous jouent leur rôle, chacun porte son masque.'[12] Nana unwittingly reveals these masks. Muffat, undone by his desire for Nana, briefly tries to resuscitate his social persona as he watches his wife's infidelity from the street below, an act of infidelity he will subsequently tolerate and imitate. His attempted resuscitation is described in theatrical terms which make clear its performed nature:

> Puis, comme, malgré tout, il ne détournait pas les yeux de cette fenêtre, sa colère se fondit dans une imagination de moraliste: il se voyait député, il parlait à une assemblée, tonnait contre la débauche, annonçait des catastrophes; et il refaisait l'article de Fauchery sur la mouche empoisonnée, et il se mettait en scène, en déclarant qu'il n'y avait plus de société possible, avec ces mœurs de Bas-Empire. (pp. 1279–80)

Muffat's wife's virtuous persona proves likewise constructed as her fall into adultery underlines and Chouard's acceptable social veneer is as performed as the theatre in which he finds himself so at home. He wanders its corridors with 'l'air enchanté d'un homme qui se retrouve chez lui' (p. 1207). The masks of Chouard and Muffat fall. So too does that of the government they represent, the government Zola opposes. The head of the Second Empire is implicitly linked with notions of performance. Fontan adopts the stance of Napoleon as he performs the rhetoric of patriotism: 'Il parlait de s'engager. Quand l'ennemi était aux frontières, tous les citoyens devaient se lever pour défendre la patrie; et il prenait une pose de Bonaparte à Austerlitz' (p. 1474). Moreover, the theatrical nature of Nana's life implicates that of the regime with which she is so closely linked. As Brian Nelson points out, Nana and the Second Empire were both born in 1852, and both will die in 1870; each ascends to power rapidly, living by means of the same extravagance.[13] Nana, appearing with the son she has named after the emperor, wears the regime's colours in the supremely theatrical setting of the race course (there is an audience, the carriages function as theatrical boxes and Nana receives the same acclamation that she did at the Variétés). Zola makes clear the theatricality of Second Empire reality or the reality of Second Empire theatricality when royalty, albeit foreign, is taken backstage. In *Nana* an actor playing the part of a king and a real prince drink champagne together, and the distinctions between the copy and the original become blurred: 'On ne plaisantait plus, on était à la cour. Ce monde du théâtre prolongeait le monde réel, dans une farce grave' (p. 1210). The 'héritier d'un trône' finds himself completely at home 'dans cette mascarade de la royauté' (p. 1210).

Whilst Nana unveils something of the problematic nature of the Second Empire, her own identity and body are never fully revealed. The novel, like the majority of its characters, revolves around Nana and devotes itself, as Peter Brooks points out in his chapter 'Nana at Last Unveil'd? Problems of the Modern Nude', to undressing her.[14] David Baguley concurs, characterizing the novel as 'one long, frenzied, vertiginous peep show, a veritable orgy of voyeurism'.[15] However, as numerous critics have pointed out, whilst Nana may be looked at, she can never fully be seen.[16] Her identity constantly shifts. Having explored the problematic performative reflection of Nana delivered by literal mirrors in the novel, it is necessary also to consider the multiple reflections of Nana offered by the wide range of doubles the text positions around her. As has already been established, Muffat impersonates Nana for Fauchery, trying to ratify the image she has performed. Nana makes reflective use of Georges. Dressing him up in her clothes, she moulds him into a strange mirror image of herself, delighting in aspects of their resemblance and in his being as thin as she is (p. 1236). Nana's reflective doubles initially appear to have the effect of reinforcing and delineating her identity for the reader. Satin serves as a reflection in the lower end of society, whilst Sabine serves a similar function in society's upper echelons. Reine Pomaré, 'la chiffonnière', and Irma D'Anglars, the regal-looking landowner, predict two possible trajectories for the future of Nana's sexual career (p. 1374 and p. 1254). However, far from fixing Nana's identity, these doubles rather serve to disperse it as they offer very different reflections of the heroine. The viewer is never truly allowed to see Nana. Her image is constantly focalized through the gaze of others. The initial view of Nana in the theatre is, as has been suggested, refracted through the eyes and '*on*' of the audience. When Nana famously contemplates herself in the mirror, performing the role of Venus, the origin of her identity is not only obfuscated by her own performance, it is also mediated by the fact that the scene is recounted to the viewer by Muffat's gaze. The vision of her is refracted through the biblical texts and images of his life:

> Et, ne pouvant détourner les yeux, il la regardait fixement [...]. Il songeait à son ancienne horreur de la femme, au monstre de l'Ecriture, lubrique, sentant le fauve. Nana était toute velue, un duvet de rousse faisait de son corps un velours; tandis que, dans sa croupe et ses cuisses de cavale, dans les renflements charnus creusés de plis profonds, qui donnaient au sexe le voile troublant de leur ombre, il y avait de la bête. (p. 1271)

The reader's final glimpse of Nana in *L'Assommoir* is likewise mediated by the gaze of a character. Lantier recounts seeing her to Gervaise:

> Vous ne savez pas, la mère! J'ai vu Nana, l'autre jour. [...] Elle était en voiture; moi, je pataugeais sur le pavé... Vrai, je vous le jure! Il n'y aurait pas à se défendre, car les fils de famille qui la tutoient de près sont bigrement heureux! (p. 747)

Nana closes with an unmediated vision of its protagonist, what Clark deems 'the one and only time in the course of the novel, [the reader] is left in solitary tête-à-tête with its heroine'.[17] The viewer is at last offered an unmediated vision of Nana. However, whilst the narrative offers a very physical description of Nana, it is simultaneously a vision of decomposition and ultimately absence. Nana's body, elusive in life, breaks down in death. The clarity of the candle throws light on an image of dissolution. Zola writes: 'Les pustules avaient envahi la figure entière, un bouton touchant l'autre; et, flétries, affaissées, d'un aspect grisâtre de boue, elles semblaient déjà une moisissure de la terre, sur cette bouillie informe, où l'on ne retrouvait plus les traits' (p. 1485). Nana's body cannot be mastered by the viewer's eye. We look at Nana, but what we see is a body becoming an absence.

Zola's probing of the question of origin in *Nana* extends beyond the level of characterization to encompass the novel itself. The text gestures towards the way in which it has borrowed from and transformed elements of Edouard Manet's painting of the same name. Manet's painting was created during the winter of 1876. Zola's novel *Nana* did not start appearing in instalments until October 1879. Manet's painting thus, in all likelihood, is inspired by Nana's appearance as a *cocotte* in the final pages of *L'Assommoir*, a novel he read in serialized form.[18] Probing the boundary between prose and art, and, in so doing, questioning the fixity of his genre, Zola appears to inscribe elements of the Manet painting into his work. Manet's painting depicts Nana in a state of undress, making herself up before the mirror as a desiring onlooker is sliced by the edge of the canvas. Zola's novel places Muffat in the onlooker's position and ascribes to him a sense of fragmentation and disintegration comparable with that of his painterly counterpart:

> Ce sentiment de vertige qu'il avait éprouvé à sa première visite chez Nana, boulevard Haussmann, l'envahissait de nouveau. Sous ses pieds, il sentait mollir le tapis épais de la loge; les becs de gaz, qui brûlaient à la toilette et à la psyché, mettaient des sifflements de flamme autour de ses tempes. Un moment, craignant de défaillir dans cette odeur de femme qu'il retrouvait, chauffée, déculpée sous le plafond bas, il s'assit au bord du divan capitonné. (pp. 1207–08)

As Clark puts it, 'This episode corresponds closely to the image of Manet as though, by an unusual effect of artistico-literary *chassé croisé*, the novelist were borrowing from the painter who had previously borrowed from him'.[19] However, probing notions of difference in sameness, notions which will be important when this chapter comes to consider Molinaro's television adaptation, Zola's novel alters and adapts what he borrows from Manet's painting. He may place characters in the same stances and the same occupations as Manet's painting, but he alters the emotions driving the scene. The vacant gaze of Manet's apparently worldly onlooker is replaced by that of Muffat, a man who watches the same scene, entirely focused on and consumed by his desire for Nana. Adaptations of Zola's text into film might be seen to engage with the borrowed origins of the novel. Maurice Cazeneuve's 1981 television adaptation of *Nana* is a case in point. It became something of a cinematic commonplace for films to acknowledge their status as adaptations, as cinematic readings of an earlier book, by physically having a book, often a book being read, in close up in their opening image. Episodes of Cazeneuve's adaptation *Nana*, however, open not with Zola's novel, but with a close up of Manet's painting of Nana. Fauchery not only stands before this painting to narrate the words of Zola's story, but the images of the film itself flow from Manet's painting as the camera pans sideways, segueing into the action.

However, Zola's interaction with Manet's painting not only probes the boundaries between prose and painting, underlining their interaction, it also raises the questions of performance so key to this chapter. Contemporary viewers looked at the piece and beneath the persona of Nana were easily able to identify the model for the painting: the well-known *demi-mondaine* Henriette Hauser. Manet's painting is also a performance, or more precisely, an anticipation of the theatricality of Nana's character. In the painted medium, Henriette Hauser performs the role of Nana, in a painting which, whilst it does not bear her name, still allows her true identity to be recognized. The dual identity of Manet's painting (Hauser as Nana) points forward to the layers of performances which inhabit personal origins in Zola's text. Moreover, the notion of identities within identities, personas beneath personas, echoes the layers of disguises the characters assume on stage when already in the disguise of their role. Like Hauser, their star personas as the recognizable darlings of the stage are readily visible to their audience as Zola's narrative makes clear: 'Quelques mains battirent, toutes les jumelles étaient fixées sur Vénus. Peu à peu, Nana avait pris possession du public, et maintenant chaque homme la subissaient' (p. 1119). The men in the audience watch Vénus, but they desire Nana.

This notion of identities within the identity of Nana is not unusual in reproductions or recreations of Nana, be they emulative or parodic. Catherine Dousteyssier-Khoze in her insightful work on the plethora of parodies and pastiches stemming from *Nana*, underlines the way in which specific works parody not just Nana, but, simultaneously, the actress who played her in the theatrical adaptation Zola authorized (and helped) Busnach to create. According to Dousteyssier-Khoze, 'Le personnage est surcodé: on voit apparaître [...] des Nana-Léontine Massin du nom de l'actrice qui incarne Nana au théâtre de l'Ambigu'.[20] A comparable plethora of identities and incarnations, albeit mythical and artistic ones, simultaneously inhabits Gill's famous caricature of Nana in *La Lune Rousse* of 19 October 1879. The caricature entitled 'La Naissance de Nana-Vénus' is an example of the plethora of 'nanaturaliste' and 'nanatomique' parodies created in the immediate aftermath of *Nana*'s publication.[21] In Gill's caricature, Nana is depicted not as a real figure, but as a creation of Zola's pen. She is conjured into existence and therefore is not a copy of an existing type or reality. Gill's copy, though, identifies Nana as a deformed artistic copy. The title of his caricature, 'La Naissance de Nana-Vénus', clearly refers to Botticelli's masterpiece of the same name, as do the details of the text. Whilst Botticelli's Venus rose out of a shell, Gill's stands in a 'cuvette', Zola apparently looking up her skirt. Gill's inscription, 'Motif à tableau pour les Bouguereau futurs', furthermore, references the reinterpretation of the myth inspiring Boticelli's painting effected by Bouguereau in his 1879 painting of the same name, a myth Gill's caricature assumes will itself be reincarnated by the 'Bouguereau futurs' to whom the caricature addresses itself, albeit it mockingly. Gill dramatizes a series of layered artistic identities and incarnations in his caricature of Nana.

If Zola's prose interacts with the painted medium via its dialogue with Manet's *Nana*, it does something comparable in relation to the genre of drama. Zola's novel, suffused as it is by the world of the theatre, brushes up against the genre of the theatre itself. Auguste Dezalay, having considered the musical repetitions in the novel, repetitions which occur in relation to Nana, ('L'évocation de Nana est ainsi pour toujours liée à l'introduction musicale de son personnage'), moves to characterize the novel as a 'ballet de la séduction dansé par tous les hommes autour de l'image de leur désir'.[22] David Baguley makes a comparable point, reading the structure of the novel as being reminiscent of the theatrical piece it depicts:

> The tenor of the theatre scene, like that of the novel as a whole, is captured by the rhythm of the prose, fast, furious, frenzied, fragmented, showing flashes of flesh [...]. The whole novel is a seemingly endless sequence of disconnected acts, beginning in the appropriately named 'Théâtre des Variétés'.[23]

Zola's prose brushes up against the stylistic medium of the theatrical genre it depicts.

Zola's novel was, as the introduction to this volume underlined, adapted into theatre by Busnach, albeit with Zola's help. Whilst the adaptation was comparatively successful in commercial terms when it appeared at the Ambigu (there was an initial run which reached over one hundred performances), the artistic reputation of the play was far from being secure.[24] Writing in *Le Figaro* of 30 January 1881, Auguste Vitu hails it as 'un médiocre mélodrame', suggesting that its production and performance might ensure its status as 'un succès de curiosité'.[25] Sarcey is even more damning in *Le Temps* of 31 January:

> [Nana] ne soulève pas, comme on aurait pu le croire, de hautes questions d'esthétique. C'est un mélodrame vulgaire, découpé avec adresse dans le roman par un habile metteur en scène qui possède et manie avec une dextérité rare toutes les ficelles du métier. Ce n'est pas encore cette fois que M. Emile Zola a livré sa grande bataille; la fameuse question du naturalisme n'a rien à voir dans cette pièce, qui est de fabrication courante. Il ne s'agit que d'argent à gagner et non de principe littéraire à défendre.[26]

As these two viewers perhaps suggest, Zola, meeting with criticisms similar to those which would confront so many of those who would adapt his works into cinema, was charged with two crimes by critics: firstly, that the play was not an accurate depiction of his novel; secondly, that the play betrayed his own naturalist ambitions for the theatre.[27] Zola, though never fully admitting his authorship of the adaptation, responded to these criticisms, in a manner perhaps useful to those who would later adapt him. He recognized the difficulties of the process of adaptation, acknowledging that a change of media and context often forces certain changes of style and content:

> Ils osent se plaindre qu'on n'ait pas mis tout le roman au théâtre. Parbleu! le roman est libre, le théâtre ne l'est pas. Pour le dramaturge, le problème n'était pas de transporter sur les planches certains tableaux impossibles, mais d'y tenter la plus grande somme permise de vérités, dans le cadre mélodramatique de l'Ambigu.[28]

Filmmakers for the large and small screen have had something of a love affair with Zola's novel. In the text itself the Prince jokes with Nana: '[...] c'est convenu [...] vous venez l'année prochaine à Londres, et nous vous recevrons si bien, que jamais plus vous ne retournerez en France' (p. 1213). Whilst Nana never makes the trip in the novel, adaptations of the novel have taken the character to Britain. A BBC adaptation of *Nana* appeared in 1968. Moreover, as Nana disappears, apparently travelling the world shortly before her death ('on apprit un beau matin qu'elle devait être partie la veille pour Le Caire; [...] Quinze jours plus tard, [...] quelqu'un jurait l'avoir rencontrée en Russie'), so too adaptations will take her all over the world (p. 1471). American director Dorothy Arzner adapted *Nana* (1934), a Mexican version starring Lupe Velez and Miguel Angel Ferriz appeared (1944) and a Swedish–French co-production entitled *Take Me, Love Me* (1982) also takes its place among adaptations of Zola's novel. 'Perhaps unsurprisingly', as Russell Cousins points out, '*Nana* has provided a fertile bed for experimental approaches and indeed exploitation.'[29] Certain adaptations are arguably as unfaithful in textual terms as Nana is in sexual terms in the novel. Dorothy Arzner's *Nana* prompted Zola's descendants to express their outrage at the deformation of the author's text.[30] Arzner's version of Nana has the heroine repent, take her life and reunite two brothers who have fought for possession of her.[31] However, deformation is a notion in some senses enacted in the text as stories about Nana twist and change as they pass from mouth to mouth, circulating freely with no verifiable point of origin. They circulate in a manner reminiscent of the authorless gossip already explored in *La Terre*. Zola writes of Nana's disappearance:

> Des mois se passèrent [...]. Lorsque son nom revenait, parmi ces messieurs et ces dames, les plus étranges histoires circulaient, chacun donnait des renseignements opposés et prodigieux. Elle avait fait la conquête du vice-roi, elle régnait au fond d'un palais, sur deux cents esclaves dont elle coupait les têtes, pour rire un peu. Pas du tout, elle s'était ruinée avec un grand nègre, une sale passion qui la laissait sans une chemise, dans la débauche crapuleuse du Caire. [...] Une légende se formait, elle était la maîtresse d'un prince, on parlait de ses diamants. Toutes les femmes bientôt les connurent, sur les descriptions qui couraient, sans que personne pût citer une source exacte. (p. 1471)

Whilst the cinematic and television versions of *Nana* are numerous, for the purposes of this chapter on Zola and origin, Jean Renoir's 1926 silent adaptation and Edouard Molinaro's 2001 film for television are of key importance. What sets them apart is their consideration of their own authorial act, a self-reflexivity which not only links them to each other, but also harks back to Zola's own authorial stance.

Zola's authorial stance is self-reflexive in a number of ways. *Nana* both anticipates and inscribes in its pages the negative reaction it triggered. It was not unusual to see naturalist works criticized as false, revolting works which did not merit the title of art. The critic 'Ferragus' (Louis Ulbach), put forward such a view when writing about *Thérèse Raquin* in *Le Figaro* in January 1868.[32] Nana reads a novel which could presumably be her own and her reactions are enunciated in a manner at least comparable to such critics:

> Elle avait lu dans la journée un roman qui faisait grand bruit, l'histoire d'une

> fille; et elle se révoltait, elle disait que tout cela était faux, témoignant d'ailleurs une répugnance indignée contre cette littérature immonde, dont la prétention était de rendre la nature; comme si l'on pouvait tout montrer! comme si un roman ne devait pas être écrit pour passer une heure agréable! (p. 1369)

Nana acts as critic to her own novel. It may also be argued that a degree of metatextuality is inscribed elsewhere in the novel. The image of the naturalist novelist, at times qualified by critics as a ragpicker, making his living out of the detritus of human life, finds expression in the novel in Nana's reflective double, Reine Pomaré, a ragpicker. Clark assesses the ragpicker in the following terms:

> As he (or in this case she) sorts through the detritus of the well-off, thereby exposing their secret lives to the public gaze, the ragpicker came to be perceived as a threat to the stability of the social order; the subversive nature of his task was in addition frequently seen as emblematic of the demystifying and equally scandalous enterprises of the realist creator.[33]

Such images are part of a wider allusiveness which Zola adopts in relation to his authorial role in *Nana*. In a manner far less explicit than the novel summaries offered in the text of *Le Docteur Pascal*, Zola inserts pointers to other texts in his authorial corpus in *Nana*. The plot synopsis of *La Petite Duchesse* sets its heroine up as a double of Renée from Zola's earlier novel *La Curée*. The duchess in the play in *Nana* goes to a 'bal masqué' at the house of 'une étoile d'opérettes' in order to explore the hold such women have on society men (pp. 1325–26). Renée goes similarly disguised in *La Curée* to 'un bal que Blanche Muller, une actrice en vogue, donnait aux princesses de la rampe', driven by the same curiosity (p. 441). It could also be argued that *Nana* points to the space *La Bête humaine*, which would not appear until 1890, will occupy in Zola's œuvre. Characters in *Nana* discuss and refute the key concept of heredity which will drive Jacques to his tragic destiny: 'Ces messieurs concluaient contre les nouvelles théories criminalistes; avec cette belle invention de l'irresponsabilité dans certains cas pathologiques, il n'y avait plus de criminels, il n'y avait que des malades' (p. 1372). Zola also includes something of a double of himself in the form of the journalist Fauchery. Fauchery's 'La Mouche d'or' article is not transcribed in the novel, it is hidden from the reader, glimpsed only as it passes through the consciousness of Muffat as he reads it (p. 1269). The article was, however, used by Zola as the advertising for his novel. Zola thus aligns Fauchery's authorship with his own, using it outside of the text to promote that text. Yet within the novel Zola goes to great lengths to convince the reader of Fauchery's lack of originality as a writer. His portrait of Bismarck is, he frankly confesses, a second-hand copy.[34] His portrait of Nana is badly written: 'Cette chronique était écrite à la diable, avec des cabrioles de phrases, une outrance de mots imprévus et de rapprochements baroques' (p. 1270). Thus, by anticipating the reaction to his novel, gesturing to other works within his corpus and inserting two less than attractive doubles of himself, doubles who represent the criticism repeatedly levelled at him, Zola evaluates the borders of his own authorship.

Jean Renoir's film not only reflects Zola's novel, as is to be expected in an adaptation, but it also reflects upon the very act of adaptation. Renoir's film may also be seen, unwittingly, to reflect the filmmaker's own life. Shooting began in

1925 and, as a joint Franco–German production, was split between the Gaumont studios in Paris and the Grunewald studios in Berlin. Just as Muffat ruins himself to fund Nana's acting career in Zola's novel, so much of the million-franc budget for the film, a star-vehicle for Catherine Hessling (Renoir's then wife), came from Renoir's own personal fortune. The film was not a commercial success and left Renoir financially compromised, in a situation perhaps somewhat akin to that of Muffat at the end of the novel. Muffat is, Zola informs the reader, '[r]uiné, vivant étroitement avec les débris de sa grande fortune' (p. 1465).

The theatre is as important a space in Renoir's film as it was in Zola's novel. As will be seen, the theatre, as a metaphor, allows Renoir both to reflect the text of Zola and to consider his own cinematic act of adaptation. Renoir's *Nana* opens in the theatre with a performance of *La Blonde Vénus*. However, whilst Zola focalized his opening chapter through the gaze of the audience, allowing us to enjoy, albeit only for a chapter, the surface of the performance, Renoir's film deconstructs the performance from the outset. The viewer is tantalized by brief fragments of the show only at the end of the opening sequence. Renoir's camera instead focuses on revealing the machinery behind this theatrical performance. The opening shots refuse the viewer a space in the audience and instead force us to climb, with Nana, the ladder above the stage from which she will make her entrance. The viewer is offered disconcerting shots of Nana's head, seen from above, as she hovers over the stage. The film delivers intrusive, flirtatious shots of her legs as she climbs. It uses strange shots of the cast from above the stage as they perform, beckoning Vénus, played by Nana, to come down from the heavens to join them, heavens Renoir shows to be shaky scaffolding from which Nana will descend on a rope. The spectacle is clearly unfolding and yet the viewer is not given access to watch it. Renoir will not indulge us in the illusion of theatre: the rope sticks and Nana is caught in mid air, flailing, much to the audience's amusement. She breaks out of character in annoyance. Renoir, reflecting Zola's naturalist dissections, cuts through theatrical illusion.

Moreover, Renoir, like Zola, uses the theatre and notions of performance to question the truth and fixity of the identity of certain characters. Using Nana as a conduit, Renoir underlines the way in which performance seeps beyond the space of the theatre. The scene in which Nana confronts Vandeuvres, the man who has come to remonstrate with her for the corruption of Georges, is a striking example. Though it takes place outside the theatre, it has all the elements of theatre. The scene has an audience: Georges is the unobserved witness in the next room. The décor of Nana's hôtel is reminiscent of the theatre in which she has just starred, with its heavy curtains and wide-open spaces. As Bordenave looked out onto the theatre box assessing Fauchery's seduction of Muffat's wife, so Nana spies on Vandeuvres as he waits for her. She adjusts her performance accordingly, deciding not to play the unrepentant seducer of young men that she is, opting instead for the role of the penitent sinner, a role she will reprise at the film's close in a dénouement to which this chapter will return. That she is acting when she plays this role to Vandeuvres is made clear in a number of ways. She wields a fan, a symbol of artifice and veiling, in this scene as she did in the prop room of the theatre. Moreover, she makes the same awkward hand gesture whilst performing to Vandeuvres that she did when rehearsing the role of the duchess for *La Petite Duchesse*. Nana is constantly associated with notions of performance. Indeed, Renoir refashioned parts of the text, notably in relation to the Bal Mabille, to offer Nana/Hessling more possibilities to perform. In a scene with no source in Zola's text, Hessling cancans for an audience in the open air fête, kicking top hats from male hands as part of her dance routine. The attention paid to the man directing the music, an attention comparable to that given to the conductor in *La Blonde Vénus*, encourages the viewer to consider this scene as a continuation of that earlier performance. Heather Howard sees Renoir's Nana as a puppet in Bordenave's stage machinery (in keeping with Fauchery's claim in Zola's text that Nana is Bordenave's 'invention').[35] However, it is possible to characterize both as co-stars in a wider theatrical performance in Renoir's production. As Bordenave directs Nana on stage, so Renoir's Nana directs him offstage, stage-managing and arranging his financial meeting with Muffat, prompting him with the appropriate lines before this meeting. Indeed, Muffat becomes something of a shared lover as he supports Nana, Bordenave and Nana's retinue. Having failed in her role as the duchess, Muffat pleads with Nana to leave the theatre for good. Whilst she does leave in literal terms, she cannot do so metaphorically and her performances continue ceaselessly.

In keeping with the novel, Nana's performances are bad ones. Her attempt to perform the part of the duchess is in rehearsal rejected with derision by the cast members. Renoir's film deems her performance of this role before the audience within the film so inconsequential that it spares us from it entirely. The viewer sees only a poster advertising it and, immediately after, another cancelling it. When Nana reprises this role for Vandeuvres, playing the virtuous woman, he too does not deem it credible. The script has him smile, seduced by Nana's body, but unconvinced by her performance, uttering the words 'Cabotine, qui débauchez les enfants'.[36] Renoir underlines Nana's incapacity as an actress by placing significant objects in the background as she performs a horrific version of the duchess for Muffat in her dressing room, trying to persuade him to fund the role. She leans against a dressmaker's dummy, an object that hints at her lack of prowess as an actress. A wooden doll serves a similar function in the prop room, appearing as it does just behind her head as she watches Muffat buy her the part at which she will fail so miserably. Renoir's film mirrors its reality, for Catherine Hessling's performance was deemed so bad, so stylized that it contributed to the film's commercial failure. Critics past and present are scathing. Howard compares Hessling's Nana to Zola's original and finds her wanting: 'Hessling [...] fails to exude a similar sensuality on screen and instead appears as a whirling dervish of mere gesture and facial contortion.'[37] Katherine Golsan summarizes critical responses to Hessling's role: 'Her exaggerated stance and make-up are so excessive that she has been compared to an automaton, an animated doll, a Charlie Chaplin in skirts, with Kabuki theater-like gestures.'[38] It should be recalled, however, that Zola's heroine, is, as the narrative takes care to underline from the outset, a terrible actress. The collective judgement of the audience upon first seeing her on stage is damning: '[...] elle ne savait même pas se tenir en scène' (p. 1107). Nana herself shares her audience's judgement of her own talent: 'Elle attendait, pas gênée, familière, entrant tout de suite de plain-pied avec le public, ayant l'air de dire elle-même d'un clignement d'yeux qu'elle n'avait pas de talent pour deux liards' (p. 1108). The terms Zola uses to depict his heroine are those used to criticize Hessling's performance.

Nana's presence and performances in Renoir's film question the fixity of the identities around her. Her bad performance to Vandeuvres in an attempt to convince him she is virtuous, reveals the staged nature of his virtuous persona, a virtuous persona that has seemed largely credible to this point. He comes on a mission of virtue to save his nephew Georges, but leaves tolerating her liaison with Georges and having secured a space in her copious affections for himself. Paradoxically, this scene in which both parties lie, reveals the truth of Vandeuvres's character. Muffat's virtuous mask will also fall, or at least be shaken. Identities prove fluid within Renoir's film. La Faloise mimes the death of Vandeuvres for a group of women. This mime has a literal value for it disseminates news of Vandeuvres's death, but it also has a metaphorical value for La Faloise, as ardent an admirer of Nana as the dead man was, could quite easily have met Vandeuvres's fate in his place. Likewise, Renoir takes care to blur the personas and boundaries of the identities of Muffat and Vandeuvres. As Vandeuvres waits for Muffat outside Nana's dressing room, he stands facing a poster of Nana as 'La Blonde Vénus'. The camera immediately cuts to Muffat standing in Nana's dressing room, his back to exactly the same poster. Muffat and Vandeuvres are, as this transition shows, two halves of the same whole, united by their fascination with Nana.

As Renoir's film plays with the origin and integrity of characters and their identities, so he concurrently plays with the boundaries and illusion of his own cinematic text. Renoir repeatedly draws attention in the fabric of his film to the act of looking. Characters peer through eyeglasses and opera glasses. The camera adopts unusual angles, offering shots which disorientate the viewer, drawing attention to themselves, shots such as that looking down on Nana's head as she hovers above the stage and that depicting the severed image of Nana's legs in her home, an image to be discussed later. As Renoir's Bordenave, the theatre director, looks out through a hole in the theatre curtains to spy on the unsuspecting audience, so Renoir's film itself reverses the system of gazes to force the viewer to consider his/her hidden status as spectator in the film. At the races, the camera twice hides in the bushes to observe Vandeuvres plotting to cheat the system, both the screen and the act of hiding, in the second of these shots, italicized by the foliage hanging into the shot. At Nana's hôtel, the camera awkwardly conceals itself like a silent witness behind a column as the viewer spies on Muffat and Vandeuvres opening their hearts to each other about Nana and their degradation at her hands. Renoir's camera is personified and the viewer pulled into the fabric of the film. Our viewing experience is not glossed over, but rather we are pushed to confront our hidden status, our place as theatrical viewer to the performance of Renoir's text.[39] Renoir throws into relief the machinery of his cinematic text.

Renoir's *Nana*, in a manner comparable with that explored in Chapter 5 in relation to *La Bête humaine*, plays with its status as a literary adaptation by exploring the role of text in its images. Reliant as all films of this era are on text such as intertitles and posters in the scenery as a means to ensure comprehension, Renoir's film secretes messages in its action, messages which take great joy in underlining notions of infraction. Bordenave strikes a match on a no smoking sign. A poster for *La Blonde Vénus* appears pasted over and partially obscuring what appears to be a sign prohibiting posters. Characters happily walk down backstage areas marked no entry, whilst Renoir beautifully inscribes his film's inability to offer sound by having characters perform and speak before a large backstage sign marked 'silence'. Words are not only written on walls in this film, earlier texts also circulate in this adaptation of an earlier text, frequently coming back to harm their author. Muffat is financially compromised by his signature on the credit note and Vandeuvres's signature on the fraudulent agreement with the bookmaker returns to prove his guilt. Vandeuvres will commit suicide in a moment of textual destruction, burning both the nameplate of the horse Nana and the love letter he had begun to the horse's namesake on its back. Nana's death, hinted at by the double destruction of her name on this burning page and by the presumed destruction of the horse named after her, is predicted in the solemn funeral cortege of her lovers when the performance of *La Petite Duchesse* has buried her acting aspirations. This cortege, intended to be accompanied by the Funeral March, not only hints at the impending death of at least two of the three admirers, it also gestures towards that of the heroine herself. Renoir's *Nana* not only italicizes the machinery of its own existence, it also dramatizes the perils caused by earlier texts.

Renoir's film, moreover, points to the limits of its ability to adapt Zola's text. It shows us what it cannot show us, what it is not, in its social context, allowed to do. Nana's scenes of naked self-love in the mirror are a striking example. Explicit and controversial in the novel, the adaptation has to cut them and underlines this fact by cutting to a shot of Nana's calves, severed by the edge of the camera. Her nudity is presumed but cannot be shown. Renoir again shows the limits of his adaptation in the scene in which Georges dies. Whilst the viewer sees Georges stab himself, we are not permitted to see his dead body. It is blocked by a doorway and we witness only Nana's horrified reaction to it. Nana, in fear, backs herself up against the mirror, a privileged trope for the naturalist project and its aims to see and show everything in fiction. Significantly, echoing the obfuscation of the scene in question, the mirror here is empty as Renoir acknowledges what his film will not or perhaps cannot show.

Renoir's film not only crops aspects of Zola's text, it also, like so many of the films made from *Nana*, crops Zola's ending. Cutting the solitary horror of the putrid, decomposing and unrepentant Nana depicted in Zola's novel, Dorothy Arzner made Nana kill herself, atoning for her sins whilst Christian-Jacque had society punish Nana as Muffat, in a rage, strangles his faithless lover. Renoir too replaces Zola's ending. In his version, a majestic Muffat climbs the stairs to her sickroom, a room abandoned by all and sundry, to comfort her and lead her to repent before death. Nana closes Renoir's film begging for celestial forgiveness, haunted by the spectres of the men she has ruined. Renoir acknowledged his alteration of Zola's text, citing it as a transposition rather than outright infidelity:

> D'aucuns nous feront peut-être grief de cette fin qui n'est pas exactement

> conforme à la lettre du roman de Zola. Cependant, nous pensons respecter, en ce faisant, l'esprit même de l'œuvre. Puisqu'il ne nous était pas possible de montrer, comme l'a fait le grand romancier, Muffat éperdument mystique dans l'acte de l'amour, ne pouvions-nous, par transposition le montrer tel en face de la mort.[40]

Critics at the time, as Heather Howard points out, hailed the ending a success. Howard cites the following statement of Lucien Wahl in *Information* of 3 May 1926: 'Elle [Nana] revient à la pleine sincérité en face de la mort, quand la petite vérole s'est déclarée.'[41] The dénouement of *Nana* was hailed as a moment of truth at the end of Nana's incessant performances and deceit. Whilst it is tempting to read Renoir's dénouement in this light, notions of performance are inscribed at its heart as Renoir seems to push us to distrust the altered ending he offers. In a shot which needed to be written into the film as it had become a staple of Werner Krauss's performances, Muffat walks majestically, his back to the camera, up the stairs to Nana's sickroom. In technical terms, the shot echoes that of Nana descending the stairs, a 'plongeant', to play act and perform in the scene when Vandeuvres has come to play, albeit fleetingly, the role of the concerned uncle. Muffat, moreover, is surrounded by the cast who performed at the theatre in the film's opening scene. The final shots in this film consequently have the feel of a theatrical encore. Notions of performance are also built into the decor. The film's opening scene in the theatre depicts Muffat in a box with laurel wreath wallpaper behind him, the laurels, symbols of victory, providing an ironic comment on this man who will subsequently lose wife, lover, fortune and respectability. As Muffat enters Nana's sickroom, the same laurel wallpaper appears behind his head, indicating that, whilst the theatre has been left, we are still in the realm of performance. Nana does repent, placing her hands together in prayer. But the viewer has already seen this gesture of supplication, in the theatre as she pleaded with the altogether more earthly gods of the theatre (the director, financier and author) to afford her a specific role. She may plead with another god in the dénouement, but one wonders if it is just another role. In any case, attentive readers of late-nineteenth-century French novels, readers such as Jean Renoir, have long been taught to be suspicious of such miraculous conversions. Such readers have been put on their guard by the suspect deathbed repentance of generations of heroines like that of Flaubert's *Madame Bovary* (a novel Renoir himself adapted), and Honoré de Balzac's character Valérie in *La Cousine Bette*. Renoir's Nana certainly makes the gestures of repentance, but, having seen her perform throughout, one wonders if it is necessary to suspect her sincerity to the last, if Renoir is asking his viewer to suspect the truth of the critically and socially acceptable ending he perhaps has to perform.

Edouard Molinaro's film career spans some sixty years and, like Renoir, adaptation occupies a privileged space in his output. Molinaro's 2001 television version of *Nana* has much to offend the purist. It modernizes and alters Zola's novel considerably. Zola's Second-Empire prostitute becomes a nightclub hostess and subsequently a model for a range of jeans, sleeping not with leading figures in Napoleon III's regime, but with officials in the European Union. The Balkan conflict replaces the Franco–Prussian War and, rather than presenting us with Nana's rotting corpse alone in a hotel room as Zola's novel does, Molinaro's *Nadia Coupeau, dite Nana*, in a manner which tests plausibility, closes with an image of Nana as a would-be childcare assistant conducting a Christmas concert. Television adaptations of Zola's texts have garnered comparatively little critical attention, perhaps as a result of the dubious cultural legitimacy often accorded to the small screen. However, it is perhaps worth remembering that the cultural legitimacy of Zola's own novels was questioned by many, such as Ferragus, on their publication, a publication which took place, initially at least, in the serial form that television episodes are able to reproduce. Molinaro's adaptation has passed comparatively unnoticed.[42] However, what links this adaptation to Renoir's earlier film is its self-conscious approach to the act of adaptation. It both evaluates its own authorial act and considers its status as a copy of Zola's source novel.

Molinaro's *Nadia Coupeau, dite Nana* quite clearly situates itself as the latest in a chain of copies made of *Nana*. The film may wipe Nana's genetic heritage (she has no visible father and her son is the product of gang rape), but Molinaro italicizes the bloodlines which link his heroine to her previous artistic incarnations. Despite claiming in its opening images to be only 'librement inspiré du roman d'Emile Zola', Molinaro's television production does acknowledge aspects of the detail of Zola's text. The publicity Zola unleashed prior to the publication of his novel was such that Nana was a known quantity even before she had fully appeared. In a letter to Antoine Guillemet on 25 October 1879, Zola alludes, perhaps somewhat disingenuously, to the scandal which greeted *Nana*: 'Hein? font-ils un boucan! Qu'ont-ils donc, bon Dieu! à crier comme ça après moi! Je suis bien tranquillement au travail, ici.'[43] This sense of the *déjà connu* mirrors the experience of male characters in Zola's novel as they wait to see Nana on stage for the first time: large numbers of them are convinced they already know her from somewhere. Vandeuvres whispers to Fauchery in the theatre: 'Dites donc, mon cher, cette Nana, c'est pour sûr elle que nous avons vue un soir, au coin de la rue de Provence...' Fauchery responds: 'Tiens! vous avez raison [...]. Je disais bien que je la connaissais!' (p. 1114). However, it also reflects our own viewing experience as we prepare for the first time to watch Molinaro's adaptation of one of Zola's most famous heroines, a heroine recreated in at least ten cinematic adaptations since her publication. We desire the heroine about whom we have already read. However, Molinaro's adaptation not only references Zola's source text, it adapts subsequent adaptations of that text, playing with and harnessing this sense of the *déjà connu* in both its textual and cinematic aspects. The adaptation does so via its interaction with the Pygmalion myth and its modern descendants.

In Molinaro's film, Faugier (Molinaro's equivalent of Zola's Fauchery), the gutter press journalist, claims to be Professor Higgins and to have an ability to decipher the precise geographical provenance of Sabine from her accent. Molinaro's use of the Pygmalion story is significant on a number of levels. In the film, this tale of the king of Cyprus who created a statue he loved so much that Aphrodite answered his prayers and gave it life, functions as a metaphor for the way in which Faugier brings Sabine back to life in sexual terms after the celibacy at the heart of her marriage. Molinaro's allusion to Pygmalion also taps into Zola's novel's veiled use of the same myth. Not only is Bordenave, as was suggested earlier, depicted as the inventor of Nana, but Zola's novel opens with its heroine depicted in statue-like terms on stage: 'Et Nana, en face de ce public pâmé, de ces quinze cents personnes entassées, noyées dans l'affaissement et le détraquement nerveux d'une fin de spectacle, restait victorieuse avec sa chair de marbre' (p. 1120). Having been brought to a new life thanks to her exposure via Bordenave, the heroine arguably returns to a statue-like status at the novel's close. The last time she is seen alive is in her role in Bordenave's *Mélusine*: 'son rôle était une simple figuration, mais un vrai "clou", trois poses plastiques d'une fée puissante et muette' (p. 1471).[44] The use of myth in adaptation is potentially significant for, as Julie Sanders puts it, 'Mythical literature depends upon, incites even, perpetual acts of reinterpretation in new contexts, a process that embodies the very idea of appropriation.'[45] Symbolically, Molinaro's adaptation borrows not from Greek mythology, as Zola's novel does, but instead from its twentieth-century reincarnations/adaptations in the form of George Bernard Shaw's *Pygmalion* (1913). Such a move constitutes an allegory for the film's own modernized identity, for the film's interpretative and re-creative act, particularly since the Pygmalion myth revolves precisely around the act of creation itself. However, in citing *Pygmalion*, Molinaro not only taps into the mythical adaptation undertaken by Zola's novel, recasting his piece as the modern incarnation of that adaptation, he also adapts Dorothy Arzner's earlier version of *Nana* in which Nana is addressed by her would-be theatrical maker: 'Remember, I am the potter [...]. I'm going to model you.' Molinaro's television version adapts both Zola's text and subsequent adaptations made of it, inscribing itself in a chain of textual transformation.

Molinaro's adaptation, moreover, evaluates the fidelity of its reflection of Zola. Like Renoir's film, it shows what it does not show, acknowledging and giving space to what it has cut and altered from Zola's novel. It points to the absences in its own images. Zola's text is, as has been discussed, set in the world of the theatre as Nana performs as a musical star on stage. Molinaro's production cuts this context, transforming Nana instead into a fashion model. However, symbolically, his heroine still visits the theatre in the course of the adaptation to watch an opera. Molinaro has his protagonist visit the context he has amputated from his adaptation and, as if to underline this act of amputation, the shot by means of which this scene is portrayed is itself amputated. The viewer is offered a fifteen-second glimpse of Nana in the theatre stalls, the opera on stage heard but not shown, Zola's theatrical context acknowledged but foreclosed. Through this fleeting and unusual shot Molinaro acknowledges both his inheritance from and alteration of Zola's text. As Zola explored difference in sameness by replicating but subtly altering Manet's *Nana* in text, replacing the vacancy of Manet's onlooker with Muffat's all-consuming desire, Molinaro might be said to do something comparable. In a tongue in cheek scene with more than a passing allusion to another filmic narrative of prostitution, *Pretty Woman* (1990), what Molinaro's Nana watches in the theatre is not the bawdy, culturally dubious operetta in which her now canonical textual counterpart stars. On the contrary, Molinaro's heroine, a heroine existing in the apparently lowbrow medium of television, watches the highbrow culture which usually disdains televisual offerings such as the one in which she appears.

Moreover, it could be argued that Molinaro's adaptation refuses to naturalize itself as a textual artefact, instead unpicking, though not fully undoing, its own seams. This adaptation refracts Nana's image through a whole host of screens within the wider screen of Molinaro's adaptation. The fashion photographer, the gutter press and the blackmailing Vandeuvres all attempt to capture her in photos. Steiner seeks to capture her image in the advert for jeans in which she stars whilst Fontan tapes and replays her voice for the soundtrack. Whilst the variety of modern media woven into the film promises a host of possible Nanas, recreated, replayed and reprojected, interestingly, Molinaro does not fully deliver on this promise. He focuses on the processes whereby these media create an image of Nana in different forms, but he does not allow the audience to enjoy this final image. Nana's experience before the film camera for the jeans advert is a striking example. The viewer witnesses the financial, artistic and bodily preparations for the shoot. We see the process and machinery of filming. We even see how a technician lies on the floor behind the camera, propelling the balloons so central to the illusion being filmed. Yet the audience is never given uninterrupted access to the entirety of the advert. Whilst we are allowed a seat in the cinema when it is previewed, the camera's movements to detail reactions to it, subplots stemming from it and the continuing developments of Molinaro's film itself, disrupt the viewing process. Steiner subsequently pulls the advert before it is screened. Similarly, whilst Nana is repeatedly photographed for publicity billboards to accompany the campaign, our last glimpse of the end product in this campaign is the poster being rolled down and replaced on a bus shelter, withdrawn before it has fully been offered.

As part of its exploration of the process and production of images, Molinaro's adaptation makes us aware of the machinery behind its own existence. In a manner highly reminiscent of Renoir's film, Molinaro's piece italicizes the viewer's role in the cinematic pact. In this film in which there is always a hidden viewer, someone watching a scene unnoticed by the protagonist but not the audience, Molinaro makes us, as Renoir did, confront our own hidden viewing status. Desiring men repeatedly seek to take the same path through Nana's apartment to try to reach her body. However, as Nana lazes in the bath, the camera places the viewer in the position of desiring voyeur as it follows the discarded trail of Nana's clothes in a point of view shot which cannot be attributed to any one except the viewer. The remnants of this striptease lead us, and only us, for there is no one else in the apartment, towards the body desired by everyone in this film. Desiring men, like the chef in the restaurant, lust over Nana and the camera immediately follows the shots of their desire with point of view shots of fragments of Nana's body. Again the viewer shares the viewpoint of the desiring voyeur. However, like so many male protagonists in the novel, our desire as viewer is never fully satisfied as Molinaro unpicks the difficult relationship between copies and originals. In Zola's novel, Nana repeatedly adores herself in mirrors. In Molinaro's film, real mirrors are substituted for their metaphorical variety in the form of television screens. As Nana loves herself naked in the mirror watched by Muffat in Zola's novel, Molinaro's Nana watches herself on the screen of the advert as it is first shown in the studio. A variety of people watch her watching herself as the gaze of the camera, like that of the onlookers, moves back and forth between the real Nana and her copy on screen. However, this distinction between original and copy is a false one for this real Nana is always already a screen Nana, as much of a reproduction as her projected image within the film. The boundary between original and copy is repeatedly probed in Molinaro's film.

Whilst it is tempting to write off Edouard Molinaro's adaptation of *Nana* as just an unfaithful copy of a textual original, Zola's original novel undermines notions of origin in a variety of ways. The personal origins of its heroine cannot truly be fixed, being unstable both from the point of view of genetics and as a result of her endless performances, performances which in part replace her ontology. Questions of origin are also approached in relation to genre as Zola borrows from Manet's painting *Nana* in a novel whose self-reflexive approach to its own authorial act is pronounced. Molinaro's adaptation, like Renoir's silent film, enters into Zola's dialogue on origin. Both films play with the terms of their own existence, querying the authenticity and completeness of their own cinematic acts. Locating a point of origin in relation to Nana and these silent and television incarnations is something of an impossible task. Zola, Renoir and Molinaro delight in leading us through an array of productive, self-conscious, overlapping reproductions.

Notes to Chapter 3

1. 'There are ten known film versions of *Nana* as follows: 1912, dir. Knud Lumbye; 1914, dir. Camillo de Riso; 1918, dir. Nina Martoglio; 1926, dir. Jean Renoir; 1934, dir. Dorothy Arzner; 1944, dir. Celestino Gorsortiza; 1955, dir. Christian-Jacque; 1970, dir. Mac Ahlberg; 1982, dir. Dan Wolman; 1985, dir. Rafael Baledon.' Russell Cousins, 'Was Judas a Woman? Re-inventing Zola for the Cinema', in *New Approaches to Zola*, ed. by Hannah Thompson (London: Emile Zola Society, 2003), pp. 111–20 (p. 116).
2. Zola, *Les Rougon-Macquart*, II: *Nana* (1961), p. 1118 and pp. 1455–56.
3. Earlier ancestors to whom Nana has no genetic link might also be detected in the pages of the *Rougon-Macquart* as a whole. In a much commented-upon scene, Nana loves herself in the mirror watched by Muffat: 'Un des plaisirs de Nana était de se déshabiller en face de son armoire à glace, où elle se voyait en pied. Elle faisait tomber jusqu'à sa chemise; puis, toute nue, elle s'oubliait, elle se regardait longuement. C'était une passion de son corps, un ravissement du satin de sa peau et de la ligne souple de sa taille, qui la tenait sérieuse, attentive, absorbée dans un amour d'elle même' (p. 1269). Clorinde in *Son Excellence Eugène Rougon* appears to be one of Nana's textual predecessors, sharing her love for and in mirrors: 'Dans l'abandon où elle laissait sa personne, elle était ainsi prise parfois d'un accès d'idolâtrie pour son corps. Alors, elle inventait des raffinements, nue devant sa glace, se faisant frotter les membres d'onguents, de baumes, d'huiles aromatiques [...]. Elle aurait passé une journée à s'adorer.' Zola, *Les Rougon-Macquart*, II: *Son Excellence Eugène Rougon* (1961), pp. 301–02. Similarly, Renée's bathroom in *La Curée* is dominated by 'une glace de Vénise' before which 'la jeune femme aimait à rester [...] presque nue' (pp. 479–80).
4. See Roger Clark's assessment of the changing narrative stance adopted in relation to the theatre in each of these visits, Roger Clark, *Zola: Nana* (London: Grant & Cutler, 2004), pp. 43–49.
5. The identification between the contemporary reader of the novel and the audience of *La Blonde Vénus* is amplified by the fact that both were subjected to rigorous publicity campaigns exciting their anticipation ahead of Nana's appearance. In *Nana*, Fauchery claims '*La Blonde Vénus* sera l'événement de l'année. On en parle depuis six mois' (p. 1096). The narrator testifies to the efficacy of this campaign, claiming 'Une fièvre de curiosité poussait le monde, cette curiosité de Paris qui a la violence d'un accès de folie chaude. On voulait voir Nana' (p. 1100).
6. For further details see Clark, *Zola: Nana*, p. 49.

7. 'J'aboie, dès que j'entends la musique aigrelette de M. Offenbach', Zola, *Œuvres complètes*, x: *Œuvres critiques I*, p. 1058.
8. Clark, *Zola: Nana*, pp. 49–50. For further details on the plot, staging and reception of *La Belle Hélène* see David Baguley, *Napoleon III and His Regime: An Extravaganza* (Baton Rouge: Louisiana State University Press, 2000), pp. 324–26.
9. Clark, *Zola: Nana*, p. 50.
10. David Baguley, 'Zola, The Novelist(s)', in *Zola and the Craft of Fiction*, ed. by Robert Lethbridge and Terry Keefe (Leicester: Leicester University Press, 1990), pp. 15–27 (p. 22).
11. Luce Irigaray, *Speculum: de l'autre femme* (Paris: Minuit, 1974). Irigaray, exploring the status of women as inferior, excluded copies of a masculine original, posits mimicry as a means to question the truth and fixity of masculinity. She asks: 'Mais alors où sont les fantômes? Et les simulacres? Dehors? Ou dedans?' (p. 351).
12. Sandy Petrey, 'Anna-Nana-Nana: identité sexuelle, écriture naturaliste, lectures lesbiennes', *Cahiers naturalistes*, 69 (1995), 69–80 (p. 76).
13. Brian Nelson, '*Nana*: Uses of the Female Body', *Australian Journal of French Studies*, 38 (2001), 407–29 (p. 424).
14. Brooks, *Body Work*, p. 124.
15. Baguley, 'Zola, The Novelist(s)', p. 23.
16. Beizer 'Uncovering *Nana*: The Courtesan's New Clothes'; Brooks, *Body Work*, p. 155; Roy-Reverzy, 'Nana, ou l'inexistence: d'une écriture allégorique'; Auguste Dezalay, *L'Opéra des Rougon-Macquart: essai de rythmologie romanesque*.
17. Clark, *Zola: Nana*, p. 77.
18. For further details see Clark, *Zola: Nana*, p. 41.
19. Ibid., p. 41.
20. Catherine Dousteyssier-Khoze, *Zola et la littérature naturaliste en parodies* (Paris: Eurédit, 2004), p. 130.
21. For further details of these 'nanaturaliste' cartoons, see Dousteyssier-Khoze, pp. 113–30 and John Grand-Carteret, *Zola en images* (Paris: Juven, 1908).
22. Dezalay, *L'Opéra des Rougon-Macquart*, pp. 295–96.
23. Baguley, 'Zola, The Novelist (s)', pp. 22–23.
24. For further details of Busnach's adaptation, see Carter, *Zola and the Theater*, pp. 118–22.
25. *Le Figaro*, 30 July 1881. Also cited in Carter, pp. 121.
26. Sarcey, 'Chronique théâtrale', *Le Temps*, 31 January 1881. Also cited in Carter, pp. 121–22.
27. 'Un courant irrésistible emporte notre société à l'étude du vrai. Dans le roman, Balzac a été le hardi et puissant novateur qui a mis l'observation du savant à la place de l'imagination du poète. Mais, au théâtre, l'évolution semble plus lente. Aucun écrivain illustre n'a encore formulé l'idée nouvelle avec netteté.' Zola, *Œuvres complètes*, XI: *Œuvres critiques I*, p. 283.
28. Zola, *Œuvres complètes*, XV, *Théâtre et poèmes*, p. 805.
29. Cousins, 'Was Judas a Woman? Re-inventing Zola for the Cinema', p. 116.
30. For further details see David Baguley, '*Riduttore, Traditore*?', p. 208.
31. For further details of Arzner's film, see Yannick Lemarié, '*Nana*, un film de Dorothy Arzner', *Cahiers naturalistes*, 75 (2001), 243–54.
32. 'Il s'est établi depuis quelques années une école monstrueuse de romanciers, qui prétend substituer l'éloquence du charnier à l'éloquence de la chair, qui fait appel aux monstruosités les plus chirurgicales, qui groupe les pestiférés pour nous en faire admirer les marbrures, qui s'inspire directement du choléra, son maître, et qui fait jaillir le pus de la conscience', Ferragus, *Le Figaro*, 23 January 1868. Also cited in Zola, *Œuvres complètes*, I: *Premiers romans*, p. 515.
33. Clark, *Zola: Nana*, pp. 31–32.
34. 'Mon Dieu! madame, je vous avouerai que j'ai écrit ce portrait sur des biographies parues en Allemagne... Je n'ai jamais vu M. de Bismarck' (p. 1150).
35. Heather Howard, 'Staging the Courtesan: Taking Zola's Nana to the Movies', in Gural-Migdal and Singer, eds, *Zola and Film*, pp. 45–61 (p. 49).
36. Jean Renoir and Pierre Lestringuez, *Scénario: Nana* (Paris: Arte Editions, 2004), p. 49.
37. Howard, 'Staging the Courtesan', p. 46.
38. Katherine Golsan, 'From Theater to Cinema: Jean Renoir's Adaptation of *Nana*', in Gural-Migdal and Singer, eds, *Zola and Film*, pp. 62–68 (p. 63).

39. This performance or italicization of the audience's hidden gaze spreads beyond *Nana* in Renoir's œuvre. It appears, for example, as a key feature in another of his overtly theatrical works, *La Règle du jeu* (1939). The camera becomes an invisible guest at the party in the country house, getting trapped uncomfortably in the midst of the theatrical antics on and off stage.
40. Renoir and Lestringuez, *Scénario: Nana*, p. 7.
41. Howard, 'Staging the Courtesan', p. 56.
42. Gaël Bellalou discusses the adaptation in '*Nadia Coupeau, dite Nana*: A Modern Adaptation of Zola's Eponymous Work', *Bulletin of the Emile Zola Society*, 30 (2004), 16–22.
43. Bakker, ed., *Emile Zola: Correspondance*, III (1982), p. 394.
44. For an in-depth discussion of the popularity and incarnations of the Pygmalion myth in nineteenth-century French literature, see Nigel Harkness, *Men of their Words: The Poetics of Masculinity in George Sand's Fiction* (Oxford: Legenda, 2007).
45. Sanders, *Adaptation and Appropriation*, p. 63.

CHAPTER 4

❖

La Curée and the Hunt for Authorial Origin: The Pull of the Past[1]

Each of the chapters thus far has revolved around the notion of origin in and in relation to Zola's novels. Chapter 1 considered the role of literal and textual inheritance in the construction of individual identities in *La Terre*. Chapter 2 moved to explore the problematic status of reality as a point of origin in *L'Œuvre*, whilst Chapter 3 analysed Zola's depiction of identity as a performance rather than a point of origin in *Nana*. This current chapter continues this exploration of origin by turning to consider the 1965 adaptation of *La Curée* made by Roger Vadim. The critical reception of this film has, as the introduction to this book suggested, been largely hostile, as it is frequently cited as an unfaithful reproduction of Zola's original text. However, as Chapter 1 aimed to suggest in its analysis of Zola's covert use of *King Lear* in *La Terre*, notions of Zola's novels as a fixed point of origin are at times problematic as the author self-consciously explores his own textual antecedents. As *La Terre* borrows from Shakespeare covertly, *La Curée* borrows from Racine's *Phèdre* overtly as part of an extended exploration of authorship. Zola's novel analyses authorship on two levels: he explores the ability of the characters to author their own destinies as well as assessing his own creative act. In both cases, he depicts authorship, not as a point of origin, but as a palimpsest, constructed via the texts of earlier authors. The destinies of Zola's characters are authored by the blood of their ancestors. Zola's own authorship is itself no more stable an origin since he engages with the receding pages of the texts he himself has adapted. He italicizes the labyrinthine layers of these texts, encouraging the reader to hunt for an original author who can never truly be found. Vadim's adaptation, for all its infidelities, shares in this exploration and destabilization of origin, pointing to authorship, be it personal or artistic, as a place problematically constructed using the pages of past texts, genetic and literary. Vadim, like Zola, in a self-reflexive manner, considers his own authorial act in a film precisely about the possibilities and limitations of personal authorship.

Roger Vadim's place in the annals of cinema history is a disputed one. His *Et Dieu créa la femme* (1956) was hailed as reflecting a new spirit in French film, a spirit which would fuel the New Wave movement. Michel Mardore, writing in 1959, depicts the impact of this New Wave in the following terms: 'Ce bouillonnement, que des journalistes avisés baptisèrent "Nouvelle Vague", [...] continue encore à étendre ses ondes d'une manière assez spectaculaire pour qu'il se révèle superflu de lui accorder ici un surcroît de publicité'.[2] However, Mardore clearly situates Vadim as a New Wave precursor:

> Une certitude demeure: Vadim avait devancé tous ces jeunes loups, inscrivant à l'actif d'un cinéma fossilisé par l'ankylose des routines commerciales un ton neuf, un style signé d'une griffe inimitable, et tous les enchantements d'une vision moderne du monde.[3]

Writing in 1963, Maurice Frydland makes clear that despite the success of *Et Dieu créa la femme* (1956), Vadim soon fell into critical disregard:

> Le réalisateur qui battait les records de recettes de la saison ne rencontre plus que mépris chez les cinéphiles qui, en général, souhaitent pourtant le succès commercial à leurs cinéastes préférés. Vadim n'inspire plus le moindre 'succès d'estime', et chaque film voit la critique se faire plus dure.[4]

This critical disregard continues to this day. Critical readings of Vadim's work are rare and the majority of attention given to this filmmaker relates to his famous marriages and liaisons with Brigitte Bardot, Catherine Deneuve and Jane Fonda. Vadim certainly courted the publicity his personal life received, as the tag line for the English version of his life story makes clear:

> Roger Vadim is internationally famous — not only for the films he's directed, but for the women wedded and bedded. Now, the man who created *And God Created Woman*, and who has enjoyed romantic liaisons with the World's Most Beautiful Women, tells all.[5]

Such attention has undoubtedly detracted from Vadim's under-appreciated output, a corpus in which adaptation holds an important place. Vadim's *La Curée* is powerful precisely as a result of its willingness to engage with and probe questions of adaptation.

Vadim's film claims in its opening images to be 'inspiré du roman d'Emile Zola'. However, critics seeking fidelity to Zola's text have, by and large, pronounced themselves disappointed by Vadim's 'bad copy'. The film angers the section of filmgoers whom Mardore, writing on Vadim's earlier work, deems 'les comparateurs': those who seek the original text in the adaptation.[6] Vadim does make considerable changes to Zola's novel. Second-Empire decadence becomes 1960s hedonism, social and political commentary in large part disappears as the host of characters is condensed into a love triangle consisting of Maxime, Saccard and Renée (now a French Canadian played by Jane Fonda). The film also irritated the filmgoers whom Mardore deems 'Les Tartuffes', the audience who sees five minutes of nudity and cries obscenity. Jane Fonda's body is repeatedly placed in the foreground of the film as she exercises in her home gym, dances naked for Maxime and the viewer behind a series of veils, and strips in a sex game in the *serre*. According to Russell Cousins:

> Essentially, Zola's narrative has been reshaped to provide a star vehicle for Jane Fonda and the voyeuristic/exploitative contemplation of the star's body

> is established from the outset as Maxime tracks her down to her exercise gym through the lens of his movie camera. Thereafter, images of her body — dressed and undressed — dominate the screen.[7]

The sexual attention the camera pays to the female body is something of a constant in Vadim's work. The opening of *Et Dieu créa la femme* with Brigitte Bardot naked behind a sheet has become iconic and Frydland, writing in relation to Vadim's version of *Les Liaisons dangereuses* (1959), states: '[...] la caméra, après avoir caressé les pieds, découvre en mouvements langoureux la noble nudité de Mme de Tourvel, puis hésite sur le ventre pour venir enfin s'échouer comme une vague mourante sur la grève de ses seins.'[8] Critics have reproached Vadim for his intrusive sexual camera work. However, his adaptation's obsession with the heroine's body is in some senses a feature of Zola's novel. Whilst Zola's Renée does not intend to perform a striptease, the narrative depicts the progressive removal of the clothes from her body and dramatizes the attendant titillation of those around her. Renée's first appearance in society after the Bois de Boulogne is revealing and promises the imminent revelation of nudity:

> Quand Renée entra, il y eut un murmure d'admiration. Elle était vraiment divine [...]. Décolletée jusqu'à la pointe des seins, les bras découverts avec des touffes de violettes sur les épaules, la jeune femme semblait sortir toute nue de sa gaine de tulle et de satin, pareille à une de ces nymphes dont le buste se dégage des chênes sacrés; et sa gorge blanche, son corps souple était déjà si heureux de sa demi-liberté que le regard s'attendait toujours à voir peu à peu le corsage et les jupes glisser, comme le vêtement d'une baigneuse, folle de sa chair. (p. 336)

Renée's flesh is increasingly unveiled in the course of the novel and ultimately she contemplates her own nakedness at the novel's close: '[...] elle se contempla, les cils baissés, avec des rougeurs subites. Qui l'avait mise nue? que faisait-elle dans ce débraillé de fille qui se découvre jusqu'au ventre?' (p. 572). Zola's novel presents Renée's life from the moment she alters the dress given to her as a child to the novel's final images as a prolonged strip tease.

This chapter does not seek to enter into a debate about the fidelity of Vadim's version of Zola's original text, or to list the changes Vadim makes. Such a list would be long, given Vadim's statements on the nature of adaptation:

> [...] certains intellectuels adoptent vis-à-vis de l'adaptation une position qui m'irrite. Toucher à une œuvre littéraire implique nécessairement pour eux sacrilège et trahison. J'avoue ne pas les comprendre et me demander alors pourquoi ne pas interdire de photographier un tableau sous prétexte que la photographie déforme et modifie l'original. Je crois qu'il faut avoir une conception plus large, plus libre de l'adaptation. Comme un tableau, un roman existe tel qu'il est. Il y aurait trahison à récrire un livre mais non à l'adapter et il serait absurde de ne s'inspirer d'aucune source littéraire.[9]

Rather, this chapter seeks to underline the hunt for and problematization of authorial origin that takes place in these works by Vadim and Zola. Both Zola's novel and Vadim's film are bound together, as their shared title suggests, by images of the hunt. The prevalence of hunting is clear in Zola's novel. He inscribes the following lines from Auguste Barbier's 1830 poem of the same name on his manuscript: 'Du sang chaud, de la chair, allons, faisons ripaille, / Et gorgeons-nous tout notre soûl!'[10] Zola depicts Saccard, Maxime and Renée as hunters. Saccard is perhaps the most adept in this art:

> Les fumets légers qui lui arrivaient lui disaient qu'il était sur la bonne piste, que le gibier courait devant lui, que la grande chasse impériale, la chasse aux aventures, aux femmes, aux millions, commençait enfin. Ses narines battaient, son instinct de bête affamée saisissait merveilleusement au passage les moindres indices de la curée chaude dont la ville allait être le théâtre. (p. 362)

However, his son appears in the *tableaux vivants* dressed for the hunt: 'Narcisse, en demi-dieu rôdeur de fôrets portait un costume de chasseur idéal' (p. 544). Renée appears in 'cette fameuse robe de satin couleur buisson, sur laquelle était brodée toute une chasse au cerf, [...], des poires à poudre, des cors de chasse, des couteaux à larges lames' (p. 494). Renée will, as Hannah Thompson points out, ultimately become the beast hunted on her dress.[11] Yet her intention to hunt is nonetheless made clear by Zola's depiction of her 'griffes' as she looks down on Maxime as one would prey (p. 514). Zola's use of the metaphor of hunting was, in large part, a means to show his opposition to the Second Empire, as the following quotation from an article in *La Cloche* of 13 February 1870 makes clear:

> Ah! quelle curée que le second Empire! Dès le lendemain du coup d'Etat, l'orchestre a battu les premières mesures de la valse, et vite le thème langoureux est devenu un galop diabolique. Ils ont mis les mains aux plats, en plein dans la sauce, mangeant goulûment, s'arrachant les morceaux de la bouche. Ils se sont rués à la satisfaction de leurs appétits, avec un emportement de bête, et, lorsqu'ils ont été gorgés, ils ont mangé encore. Ils mangent toujours.[12]

Since Vadim sacrifices Zola's political critique and modernizes the era, he could dispense with the imagery of hunting. However, he is at pains to retain and even to augment it, inventing scenes to underline the chase. Renée pretends to hunt Maxime both in his room (she shoots his lights and talks of hunting monkeys like him on safari) and in a specific hunt scene created by Vadim in the country. Vadim works to underline the metaphor in terms of sound. Before a human voice has spoken, the film's opening introduces the viewer to the sound of dogs barking before the statue of a deer.[13] This sound perforates the film, reminding the audience, whether the dogs are visible or not, that a metaphorical hunt is in process. Dogs are heard when Saccard seeks to torture Renée's jealousy by telling her that Maxime is perhaps in love with someone else and when he manipulates Maxime into supporting him as he announces his divorce. Vadim retains Zola's hunt metaphor because both film and novel share in the hunt for a common quarry: original authorship. Both works explore notions of authorship within their texts. They dramatize the lack of authorship of their characters, but, importantly, they also explore their own problematic authorship.

Vadim's film pays homage to Zola's act of authorship by recreating the author's study of his characters' authorship of, or agency over their life. Having read the works of Hippolyte Taine, Zola famously adopted his view that individuals and their actions are determined and propelled by three factors: *race* (their heredity), *milieu* (their environment) and *moment* (the era in which they live). For Zola, man is not fully author of his own destiny, rather, the text of this destiny is written by the interaction of this triad of forces. Consequently, *Le Roman expérimental*, Zola's much-debated theoretical piece, claims that man is a 'machine': '[...] il y a un déterminisme absolu dans les conditions d'existence des phénomènes naturels, aussi bien que pour les corps vivants que pour les corps bruts'.[14] For all the changes Vadim makes, he nonetheless remains faithful to Zola's exploration of this triad of forces, integrating notions of *race*, *milieu* and *moment* into his cinematic adaptation and depiction of the personal authorship of his characters.

The importance of *race* to *La Curée* is clear. Maxime's actions are, to an extent, driven by his genetic inheritance:

> La race des Rougon s'affinait en lui, devenait délicate et vicieuse. Né d'une mère trop jeune, apportant un singulier mélange, heurté et comme disséminé, des appétits furieux de son père et des abandons, des mollesses de sa mère, il était un produit défectueux, où les défauts des parents se complétaient et s'empiraient. Cette famille vivait trop vite; elle se mourait déjà dans cette créature frêle. (p. 425)

Whilst much is made in the novel of Saccard's personal authorship, an authorship which will be discussed later in this chapter, *race* is still depicted as playing a role in his decision to marry Renée as Angèle lies dying in the next room: 'Tout le sang des Rougon, toutes ses ardentes convoitises lui remontèrent à la gorge' (p. 376). This Rougon blood circulates too in his sister: 'Elle était bien du sang des Rougon. Il reconnut cet appétit de l'argent, ce besoin de l'intrigue qui caractérisait la famille' (p. 373). Notions of heredity are already present in Renée in the novel as she battles to reconcile her outrageous debauched desires with the honest bourgeois blood of her father: 'Alors, devant les énormités de sa vie, le sang de son père, ce sang bourgeois, [...] se révolta' (p. 574). However, the importance of *race* to Zola's vision of personal authorship in this novel is further reinforced by a consideration of the theatrical adaptation he created from it, *Renée*.[15] The polluted maternal lineage of Renée is only hinted at in the novel via Béraud Du Châtel's marriage and the narrative's supposition: 'Quelque drame secret, dont la blessure saignait toujours, dut assombrir encore la figure grave du magistrat' (p. 379). However, Renée's corrupt maternal lineage is made explicit in the theatrical adaptation and situated as the predominant driving force behind Renée's actions. In the stage version Renée inherits her mother's infidelity. Béraud du Châtel states:

> Oh! j'ai vu cela cent fois, dans ma vie de magistrat. Ce sont les fatalités de la chair: la lésion est au fond, on a beau vouloir la guérir par des années d'éducation et de bons exemples, elle demeure, elle détraque les plus fortes, quand les circonstances le veulent... Toi, tu as recommencé la faute ancienne, tu m'as fait pleurer les mêmes larmes.[16]

Renée is, according to her father, the reincarnation of her mother:

> Vous ressembliez à votre mère, oh! d'une ressemblance troublante pour moi, avec ses cheveux, son regard, jusqu'à son rire. Un soir — vous aviez dix ans —, en vous entendant tout à coup rire derrière une porte, j'ai ouvert, bouleversé, et je suis demeuré tremblant, sous la gaieté de vos yeux, où luisait son regard.[17]

Yet her torment stems from the fact that she is also her father's daughter:

> Mais comprenez donc que, si je souffre, c'est que j'ai de votre sang! Ah! si j'étais une simple coquine, si un peu de votre honnêteté ne me gênait pas, par là, dans un coin, comme ce serait drôle, comme je m'amuserais.[18]

The actions and suffering of Renée, in her stage incarnation, are written in the blood of her ancestors and she is largely powerless in the face of her heredity.

Since Vadim's film does not trace the fate of a family over twenty novels as the *Rougon-Macquart* series does, but rather focuses on two members of that family (Maxime and Saccard), it cannot treat the influence of *race* with the same breadth as Zola's novel. However, the blood that links Maxime to his father is subtly underlined, as is its power to determine his actions. Father and son are ostensibly very different — the former a seemingly impassive machine, the latter a gregarious hedonist. Yet Vadim makes clear the bond of heredity, primarily by means of speech. Saccard twice echoes the speech of his son Maxime: 'Comme dirait Maxime, ça a été efficace', 'C'est chouette, comme dirait Maxime'. Similarly Maxime is not only able to predict his father's change in flight and the text of his telegram, but he unwittingly echoes his speech. When Renée asks Saccard for a divorce, Saccard details the financial difficulties he claims such a move will cause, in an attempt to dissuade her: 'Il nous restera la possibilité de chanter à la terrasse des cafés pendant que Maxime fait la quête.' When Saccard later announces his divorce to his son, mentioning its financial implications for Renée, Maxime protests his stepmother's wealth. Despite not having been privy to the earlier conversation, the bonds of blood are such that Maxime's terms are those of his father: 'Elle ne va tout de même pas chanter à la terrasse des cafés.' Saccard's words pass through the mouth of his son. Vadim demonstrates the kinship binding the two men, almost despite themselves, by means other than speech. Camera shots cut to parallel father and son lying in their beds when Renée has asked the father for a divorce to be with his son. Whilst this juxtaposition in part reflects the choice that Renée must make, it also predicts the ultimate unity of the men, epitomized by the emotional clasp of his father's hand that Maxime instigates in his final scene.[19] The two men toast 'la famille' in the scene before. Renée and Maxime try to ignore the bonds of family as demonstrated by the way in which they address Saccard in the abstract ('ton mari', 'ton père'), with Maxime calling him 'Saccard' or 'Alexandre' rather than 'Father'. However, the ties of kinship are such that they cannot be ignored for, as Maxime remarks in the opening scenes of the film, 'la famille, c'est la famille'.[20]

The influence of *milieu* in authoring an individual's actions is made clear in Zola's novel. When Renée and Maxime fall into an adulterous relationship, the act can in part be accounted for by the physical space in which it takes place: the room at the Café Riche in which society men entertain prostitutes and actresses. The *milieu* alters Maxime's behaviour, temporarily affecting the way he sees and treats his step mother. It sexualizes their relationship:

> Dans tout autre lieu, il lui aurait dit sans hésiter qu'il avait soupé le mercredi avec une dame, rencontrée sur le boulevard. Mais, depuis qu'il était entré dans le cabinet, il la traitait instinctivement en femme à laquelle il faut plaire et dont on doit ménager la jalousie. (p. 449)

He will later admit 'j'aurais dû me défier du cabinet' whilst Renée will realize that she would not have slept with him in a humble garret (p. 457 and p. 576). The nature of their love will vary according to the spaces in which it finds itself, as will Renée's personality:

> Chaque pièce, avec son odeur particulière, ses tentures, sa vie propre, leur donnait une tendresse différente, faisait de Renée une autre amoureuse: elle fut délicate et jolie dans sa couche capitonnée de grande dame, au milieu de cette chambre tiède et aristocratique, où l'amour prenait un effacement de bon goût; sous la tente couleur de chair, au milieu des parfums et de la langueur humide de la baignoire, elle se montra fille capricieuse et charnelle, se livrant au sortir du bain, et ce fut là que Maxime la préféra; puis, en bas, au clair lever de soleil du petit salon, au milieu de cette aurore jaunissante qui dorait ses cheveux, elle devint déesse, avec sa tête de Diane blonde, ses bras nus qui avaient des poses chastes, son corps pur, dont les attitudes, sur les causeuses, trouvaient des lignes nobles, d'une grâce antique. (p. 484)

The influence of the environment is so strong that, like the landscape of La Beauce in *La Terre* discussed in Chapter 1, rooms take on human characteristics, merging with the bodies they in turn shape. Renée's quarters are a striking example:

> Cette baignoire rose, ces tables et ces cuvettes roses, cette mousseline du plafond et des murs, sous laquelle on croyait voir couler un sang, rose, prenaient des rondeurs de chair, des rondeurs d'épaules et de seins; et, selon l'heure de la journée, on eût dit la peau neigeuse d'une enfant ou la peau chaude d'une femme. (p. 480)

The room moves between innocence and sexuality just as Renée does.

However, the influence of *milieu* on Renée's life is perhaps most clearly underlined by Zola's use of gold. Philippe Berthier underlines the way in which gold dominates the Hôtel Saccard both as a result of the legendary *coffre fort* of Saccard and the decoration for which it seemingly pays: '[...] comme la frange et les glands du lambrequin de la marquise abritant le perron — jusqu'à l'éclaboussement, le ruissellement du grand salon, il [l'or] manifeste sa présence, en touches discrètes ou en insolent étalage'.[21] According to Zola, the hôtel and its contents 'suaient l'or, égouttaient l'or' (p. 348). Gold is repeatedly depicted in liquid terms. Gold seems to seep from the landscape as Saccard looks at it from the restaurant in Montmartre:

> Il vint un moment où le rayon qui glissait entre deux nuages, fut si resplendissant, que les maisons semblèrent flamber et se fondre comme un lingot d'or dans un creuset. 'Oh! vois, dit Saccard, avec un rire d'enfant, il pleut des pièces de vingt francs dans Paris.' (p. 388)

Saccard is associated with this liquid gold. It flows over and into Renée's body: 'Elle assistait à son long effarement, à ce tapage de l'or et de la chair qui était monté en elle, dont elle avait eu jusqu'aux genoux, jusqu'au ventre, puis jusqu'aux lèvres, et dont elle sentait maintenant le flot passer sur sa tête' (p. 573). Renée's life, love and body in Zola's novel are in part propelled by the gold of her *milieu*.

Whilst the settings of the film are inevitably very different from those of the novel, the influence of these settings on the characters remains. Frydland points out the importance of setting to Vadim's work as a whole: 'Chez Vadim plus que chez tout autre cinéaste le décor se libère et se prend à vivre pour lui-même'.[22] It is largely by means of colour that Vadim expresses the influence of *milieu* on the life of his protagonists. Writing before *La Curée*, Mardore underlines the key question of colour in Vadim's films: '[...] Vadim ne sollicite pas les effets picturaux, mais s'attache aux couleurs franches, aux oppositions un peu vives, et une porte rouge dans le fond du décor a parfois une importance égale à celle de l'action qui se déroule au premier plan'.[23] Vadim's adaptation centres on the Saccard house, the citadel of Saccard's power. The house is dominated by the colour green, a colour associated with Saccard. The room in which Saccard invites Maxime to have a drink is awash with green, as is Saccard's bedroom at the hunting party. Moreover, Vadim transforms the fancy dress celebrations organized by Saccard around the *tableaux vivants* in the novel into a Bal vert, a green-themed ball, in the film. This choice of colour is not inadvertent given Saccard's pursuit of money and the French language's representation of the dollar as 'le billet vert'. As Zola's novel oozes with gold, Vadim's film is awash with the modern colour of money: green. Both Renée and Maxime live in environments associated with colours other than green. Renée's room, for example, is overwhelmingly white, as is her exercise room. The whiteness of these rooms is underlined by that of her clothes while she is in them. However, as the film progresses and Saccard's power over Renée and Maxime grows stronger, the colour green starts to infiltrate their spaces. The natural greens of the hothouse, greens the audience associates with the freshness and fertility of their love, are counterbalanced by a green shirt which Renée and Maxime wear one after the other, reminding the audience of the seemingly forgotten Saccard.[24] Even when they are away in the country touches of green appear in their clothing when they are at the rugby match, hinting that, free as they may seem, they are never out of the master's reach. On their return we notice the green carpet in Maxime's room, the green seats creeping into the entrance of Renée's room and the green dress Renée wears to finalize her divorce, unaware that she is being swindled by Saccard. Indeed, the close of the film represents a kaleidoscope of green as the guests, Maxime included, appear dressed in the colour in the Bal vert, symbols of Saccard's financial and amorous victory. The settings and colours chosen by Vadim are as integral to the action as those of Zola.

The influence of *moment* on the identities of Zola's characters is clear. He writes, in *Le Roman expérimental*, 'L'homme n'est pas seul, il vit dans une société, dans un milieu social, et dès lors pour nous, romanciers, ce milieu social modifie sans cesse les phénomènes'.[25] A host of Zola's characters in *La Curée* are clearly the products and creations of their age. Renée educates Maxime about the society of the Second Empire:

> Elle lui nommait le tout Paris impérial, gras, heureux, encore dans l'extase de ce coup de baguette qui changeait les meurt-de-faim et les goujats de la veille en grands seigneurs, en millionnaires soufflant et se pâmant sous le poids de leur caisse. (p. 410)

Zola depicts the corruption of the Second Empire as a contagion seeping into the life of his characters and pushing them to debauchery: 'Le vice, venu du haut, coulait dans les ruisseaux, s'étalait dans les bassins, remontait dans les jets d'eau des jardins, pour retomber sur les toits, en pluie fine et pénétrante' (p. 435). Having slept with her stepson, Renée breathes in the night air 'comme une assurance de honte partagée et acceptée par une ville complice' (p. 458).

Whilst Vadim modernizes *La Curée* in terms of epoch and excises Zola's political commentary, his work still explores the ability of *moment* or historic era to affect and author a character's life. The influence of era on Vadim's work as a whole is, as Frydland points out, pronounced:

> Des formes plus ou moins évidentes de contemporanéité se manifestent dans tous les films de Vadim. Certains lui reprocheront l'adoption d'un style Harper's Bazar ou une stylisation factice tout au plus digne d'*Elle*. Il faut reconnaître que Vadim est à la recherche du détail spécifique, celui dont on dit familièrement qu'il est dans le 'vent'.[26]

Mardore, comparing Vadim to Bresson agrees, 'Bresson calcule l'éternité, Vadim sollicite l'éclair fugace de l'instant irremplaçable'.[27] Vadim's desire to express the influence of his era on the personalities of his characters finds expression in both clothing and decor. However, it is in his use of music that the influence of *moment* is most tangible. The soundtrack to this film reflects and predicts the action. The music that accompanies the nightclub scene is a prime example. Metamorphosing Zola's use of the Café Riche, Vadim takes his plot to the Castel nightclub, a star-studded venue of the 1960s. Saccard's revenge in revealing to Maxime that he has resumed conjugal relations with his wife is accompanied by two songs sung by someone who would become one of the celebrated wild-children of the era, Arthur Brown. Before Saccard's confession to a silenced Maxime the audience hears the lyrics, 'Don't tell me, I'll tell you'. Whilst Saccard's actions are covert, the lyrics of the following song, which breaks through patches of his speech, make clear his intention: 'All right, listen to me. You hurt me, hurt me real bad. Now it's my turn. I'm going to tell you something.' Indeed, it might even be argued that the lyrics 'You're going to realize you loved me from the start' predict the film's dénouement with father and son reunited. A sexual love song reflects and anticipates the developments of paternal love in Vadim's film.[28]

Zola's novel makes a comparably considered use of music. The author conceives of *La Curée*'s relationship to the *Rougon-Macquart* series as a whole in musical terms:

> *La Curée* n'est pas une œuvre isolée, elle tient à un grand ensemble, elle n'est qu'une phrase musicale de la vaste symphonie que je rêve. [...] Cette note de l'or et de la chair, cette note du ruissellement des millions et du bruit grandissant des orgies, sonnait si haut et si continuellement, que je me décidai à la donner. J'écrivis *La Curée*.[29]

He embeds musical images into the action of his novel. Renée sees the noise of the street at the Café Riche as the orchestra accompanying her soirée with Maxime: 'Eh! c'est l'orchestre, dit-elle, comme il se plaignait du bruit. Tu ne trouves pas que c'est une drôle de musique? Cela va très bien accompagner nos huîtres et notre perdreau' (p. 451). The colours of the Hôtel Saccard are translated into musical notes by Zola's description: 'Les clartés du lustre, très délicatement fouillé, chantaient une symphonie en jaune mineur, au milieu de toutes ces étoffes couleur de soleil' (p. 350). Like Vadim, Zola uses music to predict the action of his plot. The piano in the sea resort anticipates the death throes of Renée's relationship with Maxime:

> Depuis qu'ils étaient seuls, le soir, en face de la mer, ils ne trouvaient plus rien à se dire. Elle essaya de chanter son répertoire du théâtre des Variétés sur un vieux piano qui agonisait dans un coin de sa chambre, à l'hôtel; mais l'instrument, tout humide des vents du large, avait les voix mélancoliques des grandes eaux. (p. 497)

Similarly, the piano accompanying the *tableaux vivants* echoes Renée's emotions and fate: '[...] le piano continuait sa plainte d'amour aiguë, coupée de profonds soupirs' (p. 545). The tears of the piano ('le piano préluda, d'une voix attristée, avec des tremblements de notes qui pleuraient', 'Le piano sanglotait mollement') anticipate the audience's final image of Renée (pp. 551–52). The heroine closes the novel thus: 'Les mains jointes, elle sanglota dans la nuit tombante' (p. 599). Both Vadim's film and Zola's novel use music to predict and comment on the actions of their characters.

Zola uses the interaction of *race*, *milieu* and *moment* to question the extent to which characters author their own life. He presents Renée as a mechanism moved by the world around her: 'Et, au milieu de son effarement grandissant, on commençait à entendre un râle, le détraquement de cette adorable et étonnante machine qui se cassait' (p. 514). Renée ultimately sees herself as a doll, the plaything of the world around her: 'Elle en était arrivée à cela, à être une grande poupée dont la poitrine déchirée ne laisse échapper qu'un filet de son' (p. 574). Not only are her limbs moved by this triad of influences, but she is also depicted as a 'fleur' grown in their climate. The Emperor deems her 'une fleur à cueillir, un mystérieux œillet panaché blanc et noir' (p. 440). Vadim translates this lack of agency, this powerlessness by underlining a sense of entrapment. There are trips outside in Vadim's film in the form of the hunting party and notably when Maxime and Renée experience the freedom of an escape from Saccard, a freedom translated by the wide open spaces of the countryside. However, the vast majority of the film takes place in internal spaces. When Maxime and Renée make love in one of those interiors (the hothouse), the two find themselves squashed into the screen as Renée sits naked behind Maxime, their faces at times cut by the edge of the shot. Whilst this may represent their closeness, it also demonstrates the lack of space that their relationship will find in the world. Characters are also trapped in the repetitions and mirror images of this film. The importance of the mirror to Zola's novel is clear. His stated intention was to mirror sections of the world and to provide a slice of reality in his work. His novel is structured around the idea of a reflective return. It closes, as it opened, with Renée returning to the Bois de Boulogne, trapped in an image of stasis: 'Au retour, dans l'encombrement des voitures qui rentraient par le bord du lac, la calèche dut marcher au pas. Un moment, l'embarras devint tel, qu'il lui fallut même s'arrêter' (p. 319). Mirrors and returns, literal and metaphorical, prove as important to Vadim. Characters are trapped in speech as we saw earlier with Maxime repeating Saccard's words. They are also trapped by recurring images. Symbolically, Renée is literally trapped by a mirror she takes for an open space at the end of a corridor when attempting to escape Saccard. The film opens with Renée driving with Maxime, yet it closes with Maxime driving with his father,

Saccard's ascendancy clear. Maxime wears his green Genghis Khan outfit when he begins his liaison with Renée who is dressed in white. He wears it again at the close of the film but this time for another woman dressed in white, Anne. Renée mocks her faceless lover Armand for using clichés to beg her to run away with him, yet she will later make the same clichéd plea to Maxime. The sounds and images of sameness permeate this film, be they dogs barking, vina music or the hypnotic reflection of water. Moreover, physical mirrors have a strong presence and serve to reflect the emotional reality of the characters. The two lovers look at a wall of mirrors shortly after their first sexual encounter, rather than looking at each other. Symbolically they are separated into different panes, the impossibility of their love emphasized once again. Vadim exploits a similar effect at the film's close. Zola's Renée stares into a mirror and recognizes the collapse of her existence: '[...] elle s'approcha de la glace, se regarda encore, s'examina de près. Elle était finie. Elle se vit morte' (p. 576). Renée's life has disintegrated and consequently when Vadim's heroine looks into the mirror, her face is segmented into the tiny panes of the looking glass.

Both Zola's novel and Vadim's film question the ability of characters to author their own life. Their querying of notions of authorship however, is not limited to the level of characterization. Rather, both novelist and filmmaker probe the boundaries of their own text and authorship, situating their art not as a place of fixed origin, but as a space constructed using the shifting pages of other texts. It has been argued that Zola's writing anticipates its future adaptation into the medium of cinema. Alice-Anne Busque suggests, for example, in relation to *Thérèse Raquin*, that Zola's descriptive gaze is pre-filmic.[30] Zola's lack of involvement in the nascent development of film perhaps renders such an argument problematic. Moreover, as this chapter hopes to suggest, the author's conceptualization of art is far from teleological. However, it might instead be argued that film nourishes itself from certain structures and techniques already in place in literature. Significantly, a number of literary critics use the vocabulary of cinema and its techniques when analysing Zola's fiction. For Colette Becker,

> Les premières pages du roman s'apparentent à un travelling: la description du Bois de Boulogne, qui progresse au rythme de la calèche de Renée, est une succession de tableaux, de points de vue, de gros plans sur le 'défilé' des voitures qui rentrent de la promenade.[31]

Philippe Berthier agrees in relation to the novel's description of the Saccard Hôtel itself. He refers to the 'parcours qui introduit progressivement son lecteur dans les diverses pièces de l'hôtel', as 'un travelling savamment calculé'.[32] According to Susan Harrow, 'The cinematic close-up on Saccard's boots as they stake out his new Paris territory, at the beginning of chapter II, creates the illusion of a Second-Empire colossus, towering over the city'.[33] The mobile nature of Zola's descriptions in *La Curée* is striking. They are not static, but often appear in a manner similar to the moving images of a film camera: 'A droite, filaient doucement des taillis, des futaies basses [...]; par instants, sur la voie réservée aux cavaliers, passaient des messieurs à la taille mince, dont les montures, dans leur galop, soulevaient de petites fumées de sable fin' (p. 322). The opening description does not focus on a section of the landscape, it pans from left to right, capturing colour and texture, before pulling back to give the reader a wider picture:

> Maintenant, à gauche, entre l'eau et la chaussée, se dressaient des petits bois d'arbres verts [...]. A droite, les taillis, les futaies basses avaient cessé; le Bois s'était ouvert en larges pelouses, en immenses tapis d'herbe [...]; les nappes vertes se suivaient, avec des ondulations légères, jusqu'à la Porte de la Muette, dont on apercevait très loin la grille basse, pareille à un bout de dentelle noire tendu au ras du sol; et, sur les pentes, aux endroits où les ondulations se creusaient, l'herbe était toute bleue. (pp. 323–24)

Moreover, the use of the fade to black technique toward the end of the paragraph, to change the focus of the narration, can also be detected:

> [...] il tombait de ces hauteurs pâlissantes une telle mélancolie d'automne, une nuit si douce et si navrée, que le Bois, peu à peu enveloppé dans un linceul d'ombre, perdait ses grâces mondaines [...]. Le trot des équipages, dont les ténèbres éteignaient les couleurs vives, s'élevait, semblable à des voix lointaines de feuilles et d'eaux courantes. Tout allait en se mourant. (p. 326)[34]

Other moments of fading are described in liquid terms which might be seen to mirror the technique of the dissolve: 'Puis, la nuit se fit, la ville devint confuse, on l'entendit respirer largement, comme une mer dont on ne voit plus que la crête pâle des vagues' (p. 390). Certain of the structural techniques of cinema, the medium which will adapt Zola as early as 1902, can already be found in the novelist's prose.

Whilst Zola was not involved in the adaptation of his works into film, he did, as this chapter has already established, adapt *La Curée* into a play entitled *Renée*. Zola's ambitions for the theatre were large. He writes in relation to *Thérèse Raquin*, *Les Héritiers Rabourdin* and *Le Bouton de rose*:

> [...] je publie mes pièces sifflées et j'attends. Elles sont trois, les trois premiers soldats d'une armée. Lorsqu'il y en aura une vingtaine, elles sauront se faire respecter. Ce que j'attends, c'est une évolution dans notre littérature dramatique, c'est un apaisement du public et de la critique à mon égard, c'est une appréciation plus nette et plus juste de ce que je suis et de ce que je veux. J'ai beaucoup d'entêtement et de patience. On a bien fini par lire mes romans, on finira par écouter mes pièces.[35]

Yet, *Renée* is one of the small number of performed plays which would appear only under Zola's name, as the majority of Zola's interaction with the theatre took the form of collaborative pieces, Zola's collaboration being at times explicit, at times covert. Zola's prefaces demonstrate a wariness towards the act of adaptation, a recognition of the challenges of such a process. He claimed in relation to the decision to adapt *La Curée*: 'Je résistais, d'abord parce que je suis convaincu qu'il est exécrable pour un auteur de mettre lui-même un de ses romans au théâtre'.[36] He made a similar claim in relation to *L'Assommoir*:

> Personnellement, je regardais la mise à la scène comme une tentative grave et dangereuse. Jamais je n'aurais risqué cette tentative moi-même. Fatalement, lorsqu'on transporte un roman au théâtre, on ne peut obtenir qu'une œuvre moins complète, inférieure en intensité; en un mot, on gâte le roman, et c'est toujours là une besogne mauvaise, quand elle est faite par le romancier.[37]

Interestingly, in adapting *La Curée* for the stage, a number of Zola's decisions anticipate those of Vadim. Zola, like Vadim, excises the political and social comment of his novel when adapting it to a new genre. In the words of Henri Mitterand: 'Il ne reste rien que l'intrigue passionnelle'.[38] Zola's approach to adaptation in relation to *Renée*, moreover, was not one which entailed the straightforward transposition of one source into another medium, for the play points back to more than one of Zola's works. As Sarah Capitanio puts it, 'Quant à *Renée*, il s'agit d'un drame dérivé directement du roman (on y retrouve le thème de l'inceste et la mort de l'héroïne), mais qui contient aussi de nombreux passages qui reproduisent presque mot pour mot ceux de la nouvelle, *Nantas*.'[39] Zola's adaptation received critical comments similar to those directed at Vadim's film. It was, as Zola points out, hailed as being unfaithful to the original novel:

> Ce qui m'a surtout frappé, dans le monceau de comptes rendus que j'ai lus d'une façon très attentive, c'est le désappointement des critiques, qui, connaissant *La Curée*, se sont fâchés de ne pas retrouver le livre dans la pièce. Cela achèverait de me faire condamner tout drame tiré d'un roman. Chacun, l'autre soir, au Vaudeville, était évidemment venu avec la pièce faite dans la tête.[40]

The seeds of *La Curée*'s adaptation for the stage are perhaps to be found in the novel itself. Not only is the theme of the theatrical prevalent in the novel, but performance and adaptation are key narrative themes. A number of critics have underlined the way in which Zola's novel borrows from the genre of drama. According to Anne-Marie Desfougères, 'Zola demeure plus largement tributaire qu'on ne croit de la dramaturgie classique'.[41] Desfougères underlines the language of the theatrical in Zola's preparatory notes as the novel divides into 'scènes' and 'drames'.[42] Becker goes still further, situating theatre as the structuring principle of the novel: 'Non seulement le développement de la métaphore du théâtre irradie la totalité du roman, mais il en est un élément de cohérence: on la trouve à tous les niveaux du sens; elle organise les constellations d'images.'[43] In the novel Maxime and Renée make a trip to the theatre. The influence of the theatrical extends beyond the confines of this stage to encompass the scenery of the Second Empire as a whole. The Bois de Boulogne is constructed around 'lignes théâtrales', has trees 'pareilles à des franges de rideaux savamment drapées' and is described as 'ce décor qui semblait fraîchement peint' (p. 322). Renée is likened to a famous actress: 'Renée montait, et, à chaque marche, elle grandissait dans la glace; elle se demandait, avec ce doute des actrices les plus applaudies, si elle était vraiment délicieuse, comme on le lui disait' (p. 333). Renée performs the songs she has she has heard and seen on stage whilst at the seaside (p. 497). Maxime imitates the actors he has seen on stage when asking Renée for a favour: 'Il prit son air drôle, la grimace et l'accent qu'il empruntait à Lassouche, chaque fois qu'il allait débiter une de ses plaisanteries habituelles: "Veux-tu, belle-maman chérie?"' (p. 330).

Vadim works to translate the theatrical nature of Zola's text by means of the themes of costume and make-up. Renée and Maxime fall into incest when they are in disguise in Vadim's film, play-acting the parts of Genghis Khan and one of his women. They will later play the part of a prostitute and her customer in a sexual role play. As Hannah Thompson points out, disguises, particularly in the form of a *bal travesti*, form a locus of crisis in Zola's work.[44] As Zola's Renée and Maxime fall into incest when Renée is disguised in a domino, Thompson explores the way in which the forbidden love of the married Henri for Hélène is uttered in *Une page d'amour* against the backdrop of *bal travesti* that his wife has arranged for their children. As Zola's Renée and Maxime star in *tableaux vivants* in the novel, Vadim's characters perform in a film made within this film, Maxime's home video. Moreover, they deceive Saccard, playing their former selves so as not to arouse his suspicion, unaware that he too is play-acting. Vadim's dénouement dramatizes the revelation of the truth by means of the metaphor of make-up being removed. Maxime wipes off his make-up, symbolically aided by his father, whilst the audience contemplates Renée, her face streaked with the remains of her make-up, dissolved by the water of the hothouse. She alone is not in disguise at Saccard's Bal vert and she is consequently regarded as strange and out of place despite being the only normally dressed individual in the whirl of bizarre costumes. The deception and disguise of Saccard's machinations, symbolized by the disguises of his guests, win the day as the truth of the lovers' bond is overwhelmed.

Janice Best has persuasively argued that the study of the theatrical adaptations made of Zola's texts helps the Zola scholar to understand better the author's work.[45] Such a claim bears fruit in relation to *La Curée*, for a consideration of adaptation, in the form of Vadim's film, underlines the extent to which adaptation itself is one of Zola's central themes in *La Curée*. Saccard's authorship of his own life is a case in point. Whilst Renée is the plaything of forces around her, Saccard appears to enjoy the ability to author his own life, shaping his destiny. The narrative characterizes his talents in terms of literary production. Saccard's schemes, as he attempts to persuade his wife to sell her property, are poetic: '[...] l'imagination du spéculateur travailla et finit par bâtir tout un poème. C'était une œuvre de scélératesse exquise' (p. 466). He is also a storyteller in his financial relations with his wife: '[...] l'histoire de ces billets le ravissait par le roman qu'ils mettaient dans l'affaire (p. 491). And Saccard's stage-management of his wife's appearances in public casts him as a dramatist: 'Il avait goûté le succès de sa femme en homme dont le coup de théâtre réussit' (p. 475). Robert Lethbridge makes the case for seeing Saccard as an incarnation of Zola as author figure in the text, a case strengthened by Zola's instinct to protect the character in *Renée*: 'Ce Saccard, j'avoue qu'il me tient au cœur, je suis furieusement tenté de le défendre'.[46] Saccard scripts a new identity for himself, obliterating his previous incarnation as he fabricates a persona more suited to the Second Empire: originally a Republican, he has changed his name to Saccard after the coup d'état, effacing the signature of that former identity.[47] Madame Sidonie symbolically scratches his address from the card given to Renée's aunt and borrows a bourgeois identity for him by renting a fully furnished flat (p. 376). However, the identity which Saccard scripts for himself usually has borrowing at its origin. The hôtel in which he lives, the hôtel which represents him (it is personified and described as 'une parvenue'), is, in terms of style, copied from elsewhere: 'C'était une réduction du nouveau Louvre, un des échantillons les plus caractéristiques du style Napoléon III, ce bâtard opulent de tous les styles' (p. 332). Not only is Saccard's style borrowed, so too is the finance supporting it. 'Cette mimique turbulente d'homme riche' is 'la façade dorée d'un capital absent' (p. 436 and p. 463). Saccard's identity is not a point of origin, it is rather adapted to suit the audience around him and borrowed financially from elsewhere.

Zola's narrative, moreover, explores and enacts notions of adaptation in relation to its own origins. To compare Vadim's film to Zola's novel as a fixed space of origin is, in some respects, a deceptive move. Zola's *La Curée* self-consciously points back to the authors upon whom it has written itself, to the works which it has adapted in order to exist. Zola's novel opens its pages, as Derrida puts it when writing on the archive, 'pour laisser entrevoir la possibilité abyssale d'une autre profondeur promise à l'excavation archéologique'.[48] Zola's novel may be considered to be an adaptation on a number of levels. In the first case, it is an adaptation of the reality that Zola seeks to represent. However, as Russell Cousins points out, 'the distant origins of the Phèdre story contained within Zola's fiction should not be ignored. For the nineteenth-century realist writer, French classical tragedy is the acknowledged source of inspiration'.[49] Zola famously claims: 'Décidément, c'est une nouvelle Phèdre que je vais faire'.[50] In a letter of 6 November 1871, he writes:

> *La Curée*, c'est la plante malsaine poussée sur le fumier impérial, c'est l'inceste grandi dans le terreau des millions. J'ai voulu, dans cette nouvelle *Phèdre*, montrer à quel effroyable écroulement on en arrive, lorsque les mœurs sont pourries et que les liens de famille n'existent plus.[51]

Indeed, Auguste Dezalay refers to 'le caractère presque obsessionnel des références à Phèdre dans la correspondance et l'œuvre de Zola'.[52] Maxime and Renée go to see *Phèdre* performed by La Ristori. Renée's experience watching the play is both uncomfortable and visceral for she identifies her life as an inferior copy of Phèdre. Casting herself as 'l'incestueuse des temps nouveaux', she wonders: 'Aurait-elle la force de s'empoisonner, un jour? Comme son drame était mesquin est honteux, à côté de l'épopée antique!' (pp. 508–09).

As the Vénus myth and its performance seep through the walls of the theatre to permeate the textual reality of *Nana*, echoes of Racine's *Phèdre* can be found throughout *La Curée*. Such is the reverence with which her society views Renée, that her status as something of a modern myth is clear. Maxime affords her a queenly social status, claiming 'tu règnes en souveraine' and 'On te salue comme une reine' (pp. 324–25). The death of Renée's mythical counterpart, poisoned by her own hand, is recalled as Renée, in frustration at Maxime's friendship with Louise, bites the poisonous leaves of the Tanghin plant (p. 358). Thésée, famous for his exploits in battle and love, finds something of a modern incarnation in Saccard. Battle vocabulary clusters around Saccard in his business affairs: 'En réalité, il voulait rester jusqu'à la fin sur le champ de bataille où il jouait son premier coup de cartes' (p. 386). He is depicted as having 'une armée d'ouvriers, d'huissiers, d'actionnaires, de dupes et de fripons' (p. 417). The skills of Hippolyte with his chariot and horses, skills hinted at by the presence of the Greek word for a horse, *hippos*, in his name, find something of a comic echo in Maxime's horse and tilbury. The narrative remarks: 'Et il fallait voir avec quelle légèreté, quelle science et quelle correction d'allures, il venait en dix minutes de la rue de Rivoli à la rue du Havre, arrêtait net son cheval devant la porte du lycée' (p. 409). Moreover, Racine reputedly invented a female love interest for Hippolyte in order to dispel any doubts about the sexual orientation of his hero. Despite situating Maxime in a heterosexual relationship, Zola takes care to inscribe a sexual ambiguity at the heart of the character. Similarly, Phèdre's father, Minos, the judge of the gates of Hades, is in some senses doubled by Renée's father, the man who resigns as 'président de chambre', retiring to his deathly home, 'après avoir refusé de faire partie d'une de ces commissions mixtes qui déshonorèrent la justice française' (p. 379). Hints of Greek mythology are to be found throughout the novel. The lodge of the concierge resembles a Greek temple (p. 330). The Bois de Boulogne is 'un bois sacré, une de ces clairières idéales au fond desquelles les anciens dieux cachaient leurs amours géantes, leurs adultères et leurs incestes divins' (p. 326).

Critics are largely divided in their assessment of the validity of Zola's association of *Phèdre* with Renée's life. Colette Becker and Philippe Berthier hail Zola's use of this model as parodic.[53] Albert S. Gérard underlines how Renée diverges from Racine's heroine.[54] Auguste Dezalay describes aspects of the novel as a 'burlesque' of Racine's tragedy.[55] In contrast, Janice Best maintains 'Zola fait de son incestueuse une "nouvelle Phèdre", une véritable figure tragique'.[56] Holly Woodson Waddell concurs, underlining 'the profound *similarity* in the lives of Renée and of the tragic queen [Phèdre]'.[57] Evidence to support both sides of the argument can be found in Zola's novel. Notions of Renée as a mythical parody are clear when the unfaithful, incestuous stepmother is likened in Zola's novel, whilst in her salon, to 'une Diane blonde s'éveillant dans la lumière du matin', a goddess associated with chastity (p. 351). However, elsewhere, Renée does appear fleetingly to don the costume and posture of a tragedienne: 'Une épouvante muette la courbait. Ses derniers vêtements, les dentelles de son linge, pendaient comme des lambeaux tragiques, sur sa peau frissonnante' (p. 515). However, whether Renée is a good or bad reproduction of Phèdre is not as important as the fact that she is a reproduction, not of a single text, but rather a series of layers of text. Zola uses Renée's interaction with *Phèdre* in the theatre to undercut the binary division between original and copy, showing instead a plurality of copies and identities mixing and merging outrageously in his heroine's consciousness:

> La Ristori n'était plus qu'un gros pantin qui retroussait son peplum et montrait sa langue au public comme Blanche Muller, au troisième acte de *la Belle Hélène*, Théramène dansait le cancan, et Hippolyte mangeait des tartines de confiture. (p. 510)

In *Phèdre* Renée finds not only the text of her own life, the identities of the actors involved, but also the text of Offenbach's *La Belle Hélène*, itself a depiction of the reality of the Second Empire, disguised in mythical costumes. Texts shift and mutate in *La Curée*.

Zola's choice of *Phèdre* as his novel's intertext is far from unconsidered. As Jean de Palacio points out, '*La Curée* s'inscrit dans une très grande vogue de la tragédie racinienne à la fin du XIXe siècle [...]. Les représentations de *Phèdre* abondent dans la fiction de l'époque: celle à laquelle Renée et Maxime assistent au Théâtre-Italien, avec la Ristori dans le rôle éponyme, n'est que la première d'une longue série où s'illustra notamment Sarah Bernhardt'.[58] The Phèdre myth experienced a variety of adaptations and recreations in the nineteenth century prior to that undertaken by Zola. As Auguste Dezalay points out, Zola's correspondence underlines that he had listened to a reading of M. Pagès du Tarn's *La Nouvelle Phèdre*.[59] His correspondence also thanks Paul Marguery, a fellow Aixois, for sending him his adapted version of the myth in 1864.[60] In choosing the Phèdre myth, Zola chooses a text which has a history of being reworked and adapted in the nineteenth century and before, a work which perhaps symbolizes authorship as a palimpsest.

Zola's novel points to its refraction of Racine's 1677 dramatic version of the myth, situating itself as an adaptation of this work. Yet Racine's text is not a point of origin, for it is based itself, with modifications, on the *Hippolytus* of Euripides and, to a degree, that of Seneca. Racine's play opens with Phèdre wanting to throw off her veils to reveal the substance of her identity:

> Que ces vains ornements, que ces voiles me pèsent!
> Quelle importune main, en formant tous ces nœuds,
> A pris soin sur mon front d'assembler mes cheveux?
> Tout m'afflige, et me nuit, et conspire à me nuire.[61]

However, revelation in the Racinian plot is a labyrinthine affair. Phèdre rewrites history in revealing her love to Hippolyte. Her speech places him in the labyrinth instead of his father, in order that he may marry her, merging past and present, chronological and genealogical order:

> Pourquoi, trop jeune encor, ne pûtes-vous alors
> Entrer dans le vaisseau qui le mit sur nos bords?
> Par vous aurait péri le monstre de la Crète,
> Malgré tous les détours de sa vaste retraite.
> Pour en développer l'embarras incertain,
> Ma sœur du fil fatal eût armé votre main. (II. 5. 647–52)

Phèdre's speech points then to another myth preceding the pages of Racine's text, the myth of the minotaur in the labyrinth.[62] Phèdre's act of rewriting perhaps echoes that of Racine as he borrows from Seneca and Euripides.[63] Racine adapts Seneca and Euripides: classicism reworks Roman tragedy, which itself reworks the Greek tradition. As William Levitan puts it, 'From its first beginnings with transplantations of Greek poetic texts, the Roman tradition formed itself as a self-conscious literature of aftermath.'[64] Zola's Renée watches a performance of Racine's play and adapts *Phèdre* in her head as the representation of her own life. Thus, the reader is offered an act of rewriting (Renée's) within a rewriting of Racine's text (Zola's), which itself exists by means to Seneca's rewriting of the version of Euripides, behind which, somewhere, hovers the myth itself. And, as Naomi Schor points out, one myth leads to another: 'Any attempt at airtight classifications violates the very Protean nature of myth'.[65] Schor's powerful argument that Zola, a writer obsessed with notions of origin, uses *La Fortune des Rougon* (a novel subtitled *Les Origines*) to posit, 'instead of an origin myth, a myth of transformation', resonates in relation to *La Curée*.[66] In Zola's novel the act of authorship is not a founding one, *La Curée* is not a place of origin, it is a palimpsest which has been written on the ever-receding pages of earlier authors.

As Zola's novel undermines notions of origin, pointing to the pages of texts gone by, so too does Vadim's film. Like Zola, Vadim presents authorship as a patchwork fashioned by a series of ever-earlier authors.[67] Vadim's film incorporates Zola's novel as well as a range of pre-texts. Biblical references are clear in the film. Renée is presented in distinctly Eve-like terms. In the hothouse that Vadim depicts as an Eden, with biblical overtones that are impossible to ignore, she and Maxime eat an apple, highlighting the sin and the fall associated with the incestuous act. This image is a refraction of Zola's original text refracting the Bible since Zola places the following words addressed to Renée in Maxime's mouth: 'Je dirais que tu as mordu à toutes les pommes' (p. 325). Playing with this biblical intertext, Zola describes the Saccard hôtel, decorated as it is with 'grandes femmes nues, jouant avec des pommes, prenant des poses, parmi les poignées de joncs' (p. 331).[68] Moreover, Saccard, discovering Maxime has borrowed Sylvia's bracelet for Renée exclaims: 'Ce polisson a toujours du fruit défendu dans les poches!' (p. 432). As Eve was cast out, so will Renée be in Vadim's film. Her exclusion from the world of Saccard is not only conveyed by means of costume as discussed earlier, but also in terms of windows. Zola claimed that he wanted his novels to be a window on the world, and, whilst Maxime and Saccard largely look out onto the world through windows, Renée will be left at the film's close looking in from outside, her hands almost covering her eyes from behind a closed door. In a further biblical intertext, when Renée leaves to arrange her divorce she commands Maxime not to watch her leave. He cannot resist the temptation to look. The punishment for this act of looking is that the two will never again meet on screen. Via this image, Vadim adapts the substance of the biblical tale of Lot into his work, imagery particularly appropriate to *La Curée* since, in a gender-inverted context, it invokes not only the wickedness of the world in question, but also hints at the theme of incest by means of Lot and his relationship with his daughters. Lot's wife was asked not to turn back and watch the destruction of Sodom, whereas for Vadim it is Maxime who is asked not to look. This inversion gestures towards the gender confusion that is such a key part of Zola's novel as Maxime is presented as effeminate and Renée in highly masculine terms:

> Renée était l'homme, la volonté passionnée et agissante. Maxime subissait. Cet être neutre, blond et joli, frappé dès l'enfance dans sa virilité, devenait, aux bras curieux de la jeune femme, une grande fille, avec ses membres épilés, ses maigreurs gracieuses d'éphèbe romain. (p. 485)

Interestingly, George Bluestone, writing on adaptation in a context not involving Vadim, parallels Lot's wife's fate with that of the filmmaker adapting a literary text:

> At times, the differences tempt one to argue that film-makers ought to abandon adaptations entirely in favour of writing directly for the screen. More often than not, the very prestige and literary charm of the classics has an inhibiting effect, shriveling up the plastic imagination. Like Lot's wife, the film-maker is frequently immobilized in the very act of looking over his shoulder.[69]

However, the request for Maxime not to watch Renée leave, the request which he cannot obey and for which he is subsequently punished, functions as a polyvalent image in Vadim's film. Whilst it evokes the Lot story cited above, it simultaneously interacts with the myth of Orpheus and Eurydice. The metamorphoses of myth, the workings and reworkings of mythical narratives over the ages, resonate with the adaptive process. As Roland Barthes writes in *Mythologies*, 'le caractère fondamental du concept mythique, c'est d'être *approprié*'.[70] Vadim chooses not only to insert mythical references in the fabric of his film, references which allegorize his adaptive act, he specifically selects the figure who has come to be considered, as Julie Sanders puts it, 'a prototype of the artist, be it musician, storyteller, painter or poet'.[71] Orpheus's lyric capacities are powerful enough to secure Eurydice's release from the underworld. Ovid, moreover, depicts Orpheus subsequently living in Thrace, the trees settling behind him to listen to his song, song powerful enough to ward off the objects thrown at him by the women he shuns. Indeed, killed by a group of females, in certain versions, Orpheus's decapitated head continues to sing until he is reunited with his lost love. Orpheus's story is most famously retold by Ovid, but it had already appeared in Virgil's *Georgics*. It has subsequently been worked and reworked across time and media as numerous authors, artists and filmmakers have used Orpheus as a symbol via which to reflect on their artistic act.[72] Vadim's deliberate insertion of an Orphic image parallels Zola's adaptation of the palimpsest that is *Phèdre*. Vadim, like Zola, explores the process of adaptation, inserting images borrowed from elsewhere, images whose provenance is multiple and cannot fully be forgotten.

Vadim's film adapts Zola's novel which itself adapts Racine's text, a text indebted to a variety of previous versions. As if to underline the series of texts lying beneath the surface of his own adaptation and Zola's source text, Vadim's film interacts with one of the versions of the Phaedra myth informing Racine's seventeenth-century tragedy: that of Euripides. Racine's heroine, presumably as a means to allow her to die on stage within the grounds of *bienséance*, poisons herself in an act of suicide. However, Euripides' character hangs herself early in the action and an accusation of rape is pinned as a note to her body. Vadim's film, adapting the text of Euripides in a scene which has no equivalent in Zola's novel, has Maxime stage the mock hanging of Renée's current lover Armand, a lover with whom she has just ended her liaison. Maxime hangs an empty suit for Renée to find, pinning a suicide note he has penned and signed in Armand's name to it. Vadim thus plays with the layers of texts informing his film, the multiple sources from which his work is adapted.

Vadim's film acknowledges, in a variety of ways, its status as an adaptation. Zola's theoretical texts underline his desire for his novels to be a mirror of the world. Consequently, his novels are filled with looking glasses, real and metaphorical, as well as instances of reflection. Chapter 1 commented upon the water in *La Fortune des Rougon*, for example, water 'dont la lune faisait un clair mirroir' (p. 202). Whilst the process of reflection in Zola's work is not always straightforward, the water of this novel's well seemingly produces a perfect reproduction of a slice of reality:

> Par les matinées de soleil, lorsque l'égouttement des cordes ne troublait pas la surface de l'eau, ces glaces, ces reflets du ciel se découpaient, blancs sur l'eau verte, en reproduisant avec une étrange exactitude les feuilles d'un pied de lierre qui avait poussé le long de la muraille. (p. 179)

Mirrors prove similarly important in Vadim's adaptation. The sex scene is shown to the reader by means of a mirror. Whilst Vadim at times hints at the purity of the love between Renée and Maxime, the corrupt nature of their love is shown by the kaleidoscopic contortions and blurred images that twist and turn in the sex scene mirror. However, this twisted mirror not only comments on the deformed nature of the couple's love, it is also Vadim's wink to the deforming nature of the act of adaptation. Vadim symbolizes his twisting of Zola's text in the twisted mirror he offers the viewer. Comparable acknowledgements of the act of adaptation can be found elsewhere in Vadim's corpus. Mardore offers a persuasive analysis of a scene in Vadim's adaptation *Les Liaisons dangereuses*. As he would later do with *La Curée*, Vadim modernizes the action, transporting Laclos's eighteenth-century narrative to twentieth-century France. Valmont walks in on a sleeping and chaste Cécile at a ski resort. He hesitates, unsure how to proceed. His eyes fall on an engraving on the wall, an engraving reminiscent of Fragonard, *La Dormeuse découverte*. Cécile and Valmont find themselves 'dans la position des personnages de la gravure' and Valmont appears to take inspiration from it, subsequently seducing Cécile.[73] In the words of Mardore, this scene constitutes an 'hommage discret au romancier [...] qui excuse l'impertinence de la transposition'.[74] Vadim points both to the borrowed origins and the inevitable deformation caused by the adaptive act by means of this scene. Vadim underlines his cinematic act in other ways, offering the viewer a self-reflexive cinema in a manner which is consonant with the visible filmmaking tendencies of the New Wave. Maxime's film camera frequently appears in the film and the viewer passes through the frames of Maxime's camera and that of Vadim, through a screen which Vadim, far from disguising, at one point floods red. Vadim makes his viewer comparably aware of his camera in *La Bride sur le cou* (1961) which closes with its heroine throwing a snowball at the camera. She exclaims 'encore des photographes' in the final line of a film made by a director who had previously made a living precisely by means of such photographs, working for *Paris Match*.

The original author may be hunted in Vadim's film and Zola's novel, but he will never truly be found for both artists point to the fabric of their texts, to the other sources from which they have woven their works. The original text may be looked for, but it will never be seen. Zola's novel and Vadim's film dramatize precisely this difficulty in seeing. Zola's text is in some ways a tragedy of myopia. The weakness of Renée's vision, is underscored from the text's opening pages: 'Renée [...] cligna les yeux, avec cette moue exquise que lui faisait faire la faiblesse de sa vue' (p. 319).[75] Moreover, the heroine's failure to see is underlined elsewhere in the text. She has recourse to the implements of vision: an eyeglass at the Bois de Boulogne and a magnifying glass when looking at portraits (p. 320 and p. 428). These tools do not, however, improve her blindness in relation to Saccard. She signs the promissory notes he brings her, unaware of the subtext of his deception. Vadim's film takes up this theme. Whilst the point-of-view shot in the car as Saccard watches his chauffeur's shoulders demonstrates the power and clarity of Saccard's vision (particularly since Maxime and his Chinese tutor bow to it), the camera more frequently associates itself with Renée's gaze. When a jealous Renée walks to see Maxime and Anne in the room at the hunting party, a point-of-view shot is established as the camera literally shakes with Renée's emotion. The focus of the camera also works to underline the haze of Renée's vision since only in scenes in which she appears are images unclear. In her bedroom the steam softens the lines of the shot whilst the focus of the love scene in the hothouse is soft. The camera even goes as far as to halo her with rainbow light on the screen. The euphoria of this muggy vision will fade, and ultimately the gentle obfuscation of soft focus will become dizzying visual distortion as the camera lens presents the guests at the Bal vert as contorted figures warped on the surface of her gaze. Making a dolly and the focus of the camera simultaneously move in different directions, Vadim reinforces the concept of visual distortion as Renée gazes at herself in the mirror in the final image of the film. She is pulled away from the space in which she finds herself, implicitly into the abyss of madness as a refuge from what she simply cannot bear to see.

The visual hunt for the author takes place on a number of levels within and between the work of Vadim and Zola. Notions of authorship and agency are rendered problematic in both film and novel as sources outside of the characters are shown to author their lives. Authorship proves equally diffuse in relation to the creative acts of Vadim and Zola. Vadim has been criticized for his adaptation of Zola's text, but his film plays with the idea of authorship on a number of levels, demonstrating the process of adaptation that lies at its heart. In so doing he provides a faithful reflection of Zola's exploration in *La Curée* of authorship as a palimpsest. The author may put his name to a text, but that name is written over the ever-receding signatures of earlier authors. One may hunt for the author as a place of origin, but this quarry will never truly be seen, much less caught, for it slips into the dizzying spirals of the pages of works gone by.

Notes to Chapter 4

1. This chapter is a continuation of the following article: Kate Griffiths, 'Hunt the Author: Zola, Vadim and *La Curée*', *Studies in European Cinema* 2: 1 (2005), 7–17. I am grateful to Owen Evans and Graeme Harper for permission to reproduce aspects of the argument pursued in the article.
2. Michel Mardore, *Roger Vadim* (Paris: Premier Plan, 1959), p. 23.
3. Ibid., p. 23.
4. Maurice Frydland, *Roger Vadim* (Paris: Seghers, 1963), p. 9.
5. Roger Vadim, *Memoirs of the Devil*, trans. by Peter Beglan (New York/London: Harcourt Brace Jovanovich, 1976).
6. Mardore, *Roger Vadim*, p. 26.
7. Russell Cousins, 'Refracting Zola; The Cinematic Prisms of René Clément and Roger Vadim', *Bulletin of the Emile Zola Society*, 7 (1994), 14–22 (p. 19).
8. Frydland, *Roger Vadim*, p. 68.
9. Vadim quoted in Frydland, *Roger Vadim*, p. 92.
10. Cited in Zola, *La Curée*, p. 1584.
11. 'Her dress, with its knowing reference to the *curée* evoked in the novel's title, represents an embroidered *mise-en-abyme* of her own story, which offers the careful reader (although ironically not its wearer) an insight into her eventual demise.' Hannah Thompson, *Naturalism Redressed: Identity and Clothing in the Novels of Emile Zola*, p. 39.
12. Zola, *Œuvres complètes*, XIII: *Chroniques et polémiques* (1969), p. 260. The metaphor of hunting features frequently in Zola's corpus. Macquart, the forefather of half the dynasty, is a poacher and the metaphor of the hunt is, as David Baguley points out, central to *Son Excellence Eugène Rougon*. David Baguley, 'Histoire et mythe dans *Son Excellence Eugène Rougon*', *Cahiers naturalistes*, 56 (1982), 46–60. Naomi Schor underlines the use of this metaphor in *La Conquête de Plassans*, *Germinal* and *Travail*. Naomi Schor, *Zola's Crowds*, p. 63. In each of these novels a character is

pursued by people throwing stones and, in each case, the chasing pack is described using the vocabulary of hunting. Etienne is described thus in *Germinal*: '[...] il se contenta de hâter le pas, comme sourd aux injures. Bientôt, ce fut une fuite, chaque maison le huait au passage, on s'acharnait sur ses talons, tout un peuple le maudissait d'une voix peu à peu tonnante, dans le débordement de la haine. [...] Il sortit du coron, blême, affolé, galopant, avec cette bande hurlante derrière son dos', Zola, *Les Rougon-Macquart*, III: *Germinal* (1964), p. 1519.

13. Vadim's opening is reminiscent of the novel's claim that in the era when Saccard is at his most successful, 'C'était l'heure où la curée ardente emplit un coin de forêt de l'aboiement des chiens' (p. 435).
14. Zola, *Œuvres complètes*, I: *Œuvres critiques I*, p. 1182 and p. 1176.
15. The play was written between 1880 and 1881 and, having been rejected by the Théâtre-Français, the Gymnase and the Odéon, was eventually staged at the Vaudeville. It ran for thirty eight performances. For details of the play, and its reception, see Carter, *Zola and the Theater*, pp. 48–55 and Zola's preface to the play in Zola, *Œuvres complètes*, XV: *Théâtre et poèmes*, pp. 417–35.
16. Zola, *Théâtre et poèmes*, pp. 439–50.
17. Ibid., p. 439.
18. Ibid., p. 470.
19. This clasp has its source in the novel, albeit driven by different emotions. In the novel's dénouement Renée sees father and son walking arm in arm in the Bois de Boulogne, a sight which upsets her: 'Saccard et Maxime marchaient à petits pas, au bras l'un de l'autre' (p. 595).
20. Vadim does not explore the role of heredity in relation to the character of Renée and her past. With the exception of one dialogue in the *serre*, the background of the film's heroine is largely excised. However, Vadim's heroine might be said to have her own heritage in relation to Vadim's cinematic corpus as a whole. Writing before Vadim's adaptation of *La Curée*, Michel Mardore describes the quintessential Vadim heroine, a genus to which Vadim's Renée can be considered something of a descendant: 'Ainsi s'explique l'ambiguïté relative de la position adoptée à l'égard des héroïnes: amorales, libres, traversant les tabous comme des ectoplasmes se meuvent au mépris des murailles, et jouissant en conséquence de toute notre sympathie, elles sont considérées par leur auteur comme irresponsables et un peu désaxées. Ce sont des êtres qui sèment la souffrance et jettent la discorde sans méchanceté consciente' (Mardore, *Roger Vadim*, p. 9).
21. Philippe Berthier, 'Hôtel Saccard: état des lieux', in *La Curée de Zola ou 'La Vie à outrance'*, ed. by David Baguley (Paris: Sedes, 1987), pp. 107–18 (p. 107).
22. Frydland, *Roger Vadim*, p. 72.
23. Mardore, *Roger Vadim*, p. 5.
24. Vadim, in contrast to Zola, underlines the purity of the love between Maxime and Renée by means of the Eden-like hothouse and the music that accompanies their first amorous encounter. However, the corrupt nature of their love is also thrown into relief, a corruption upon which Zola's novel focuses: 'Alors, l'incestueuse s'habituait à sa faute' (p. 510). Vadim's couple, like Zola's, love in a hothouse, an artificial space where things are grown in an unnatural climate. Their love, like the hothouse flowers which surround it, does not survive in the reality beyond. Moreover, by means of colour, Vadim underlines Renée's status as a scarlet woman. She dresses in red immediately after having slept with Maxime.
25. Zola, *Œuvres complètes*, X: *Œuvres critiques I*, p. 1184.
26. Frydland, *Roger Vadim*, p. 46.
27. Mardore, *Roger Vadim*, p. 12.
28. Moreover, Vadim also deploys contemporary music in an ironic sense in the closing scenes, as Russell Cousins points out: 'The celebratory masked ball with its ironical Rolling Stones track proclaiming enduring love is too much for the traumatised Renée'. Cousins, 'Was Judas a Woman?', p. 114. Love has been flouted on all levels: paternal, marital and sexual. However, the soundtrack accompanying the realization of these contraventions is that of perfect love: 'There will never be a girl like you. [...] I need you, can't live without you. Ain't no one else but you.'
29. Bakker, ed., *Zola: Correspondance*, II (1980), 304.
30. Alice-Anne Busque, 'Le Regard-caméra d'Emile Zola dans *Thérèse Raquin*', in *Zola et le cinéma*, ed. by Paul Warren (Sainte-Foy: Les Presses de l'Université Laval; Paris: Presses de la Sorbonne Nouvelle, 1995), pp. 177–94 (p. 179).

31. Colette Becker, 'Illusion et réalité: la métaphore du théâtre dans *La Curée*', in Baguley, ed., *La Curée de Zola*, pp. 119–28 (p. 121).
32. Berthier, 'Hôtel Saccard', p. 111.
33. Susan Harrow, *La Curée* (Glasgow: University of Glasgow French and German Publications, 1998), p. 52.
34. A similar fadeout can be found in the Café Riche scene: 'Les lueurs et les bruits allaient toujours en se mourant, la ville s'endormait, des souffles de tendresse passaient sur les toits' (p. 454). This narrative fadeout is immediately followed by a change of paragraph and focus: 'Lorsque la jeune femme se retourna, la lumière du petit lustre lui fit cligner les paupières' (p. 454).
35. Zola, *Œuvres complètes*, xv: *Théâtre et poèmes*, p. 413.
36. Ibid., p. 418.
37. Ibid., p. 783.
38. Ibid., p. 513.
39. Sarah Capitanio, 'L'Hypertextualité chez Zola: le cas de *La Curée*', *Cahiers naturalistes*, 68 (1994), 49–62 (p. 51).
40. Zola, *Œuvres complètes*, xv: *Théâtre et poèmes*, pp. 424–25.
41. Anne-Marie Desfougères, '*La Curée*: roman et dramaturgie classique', in Baguley, ed., *La Curée de Zola*, pp. 5–14 (p. 5).
42. Ibid., p. 7.
43. Becker, 'Illusion et réalité', p. 119.
44. Thompson, *Naturalism Redressed*, p. 121.
45. Janice Best, *Expérimentation et adaptation: essai sur la méthode naturaliste d'Emile Zola* (Paris: José Corti, 1986).
46. Robert Lethbridge, 'Zola et Haussmann: une expropriation littéraire', in Baguley, ed., *La Curée de Zola*, pp. 85–96 (p. 92). Zola, *Œuvres complètes*, xv: *Théâtre et poèmes*, p. 428.
47. The replacement and displacement of names, the signatures of the text of identity, is central to the novel. Bonnet, 'ancien raffineur du Havre', transforms himself by taking his wife's name to become M. de Mareuil (p. 433). Toutin-Laroche sells his name to a company in support of their venture ('il vendit le premier son nom à une compagnie véreuse', p. 395), as Saccard sells his to Renée to preserve her respectability. Names and identities are as unstable in this novel as texts. Written texts such as the business register Saccard creates with Larsonneau are faked, stolen and ultimately destroyed. Texts may also be dual as the story-telling abilities of Hupel de la Noue make clear: 'C'était sa spécialité; il avait toujours deux versions d'une anecdote, l'une pour les dames, l'autre pour les hommes' (p. 350).
48. Jacques Derrida, *Mal d'archive* (Paris: Galilée, 1995), p. 39.
49. Cousins, 'Refracting Zola', p. 20.
50. Cited in Zola, *La Curée*, pp. 1607–08.
51. Bakker, ed., *Zola: Correspondance*, II (1980), 304.
52. Auguste Dezalay, 'Déstruction et sacrilège chez Zola', in Baguley, ed., *La Curée de Zola*, pp. 195–201 (p. 196).
53. Berthier writes of 'une laborieuse parodie de *Phèdre*', Berthier, 'Hôtel Saccard', p. 117. Colette Becker concurs: 'La nouvelle *Phèdre* que souhaite écrire Zola, ne peut être, dans une telle société, qu'une parodie de la tragédie antique: l'inceste est consommé, l'histoire de la grande passion de Renée — mais s'agit-il réellement d'une grande passion? [...] tourne à la pièce de boulevard, son dénouement se déroule au son des flons-flons d'une valse, dans la débandade d'un cabinet de toilette, dont les eaux usées et les linges souillés rendent dérisoire la confrontation entre les amants et le mari, et lui enlèvent toute grandeur tragique', Becker, 'Illusion et réalité', pp. 126–27.
54. Albert S. Gérard, 'Zola's *La Curée* and Racine's *Phèdre*', in *Narrative Ironies*, ed. by Raymond A. Prier and Gerald Gillespie (Amsterdam/Atlanta: Rodopi, 1997), pp. 207–22 (p. 217).
55. Auguste Dezalay, '"La Nouvelle Phèdre" de Zola ou les mésaventures d'un personnage tragique', *Travaux de linguistique et de littérature*, 9: 2 (1971), 121–34 (p. 126).
56. Janice Best, 'Espace de la perversion et perversion de l'espace: la génération du récit dans *La Curée*', *Cahiers naturalistes*, 63 (1989), 109–15 (p. 115).
57. Holly Woodson Waddell, 'The Naked Truth: Renée and the Myth of Phaedra in *La Curée*', *Excavatio*, 18 (2003), 143–56 (p. 145).

58. Jean de Palacio, '*La Curée*: Histoire naturelle et sociale, ou agglomérat de mythes', in Baguley, ed., *La Curée de Zola*, pp. 171–77 (p. 172).
59. Pagès Du Tarn, *La Nouvelle Phèdre* (Paris: Gustave Havard, 1858). Dezalay writes: 'Dans une lettre du 5 mai 1860, Zola nous présente l'œuvre inédite d'un certain Pagès du Tarn: "Il y a eu une soirée hier chez moi [...] Nous étions douze, ma mère, Pagès (du Tarn), Chaillan, Pajot, moi: le reste ne vaut pas l'honneur d'être nommé [...] On a servi, comme consommations, trois douzaines de biscuits, deux bouteilles, une de champagne, une de malaga, puis le premier acte de la *Nouvelle Phèdre*, et le proverbe intitulé *Perrette*. On a fortement applaudi."' Dezalay, 'La "Nouvelle Phèdre" de Zola', pp. 121–22.
60. Cited in Dezalay, 'La "Nouvelle Phèdre" de Zola', p. 122.
61. Racine, *Phèdre* (Paris: Larousse, 1990), I. 3. 158–61. Unless otherwise stated, subsequent references are to this edition and will be made in the text.
62. As Dominique Jullien puts it, 'Mythological *contaminatio* is intimately related to the mental disorder created by incestuous desire. Mythological disorder is the sign and the language of incest, which disrupts the order of desire.' Dominique Jullien, 'Intertextuality as Labyrinth: The Presence of Racine in Michel Butor's *L'Emploi du temps*', in *Autour de Racine: Studies in Intertextuality*, ed. by Richard E. Goodkin (New Haven, CT: Yale University Press, 1989), pp. 108–24 (p. 117).
63. Racine's borrowings extend beyond Seneca and Euripides. They are, according to Richard E. Goodkin, multiple and, ultimately, untraceable in their entirety: 'To find all of the places where texts of Racine might be said to "point" to other texts [...] would already take several lifetimes.' Goodkin, *Autour de Racine*, p. iv. Furthermore, Joan de Jean testifies to the labyrinthine origins of Racine's *Phèdre*, identifying Sappho's presence refracted through the prism of Ovid's *Heroides* 15 in Racine's lines 'Je le vis, je rougis, je pâlis à sa vue; / Un trouble s'éleva dans mon âme éperdue; / Mes yeux ne voyaient plus, je ne pouvais parler; / Je sentis tout mon corps et transir et brûler' (I. 3. 273–76), Joan de Jean, 'Sappho, c'est moi, selon Racine: Coming of Age in Neo-Classical Theater' in Goodkin, ed., *Autour de Racine*, pp. 3–20 (pp. 5–6).
64. William Levitan, 'Seneca in Racine' in Goodkin, ed., *Autour de Racine*, pp. 185–210 (p. 198).
65. Schor, *Zola's Crowds*, p. 4.
66. Ibid., p. 8. Schor claims 'Zola's obsession with origins is inscribed at all levels of his text: it can easily be apprehended in his lifelong interest in theories of heredity, in the dynastic design of his three novelistic cycles, in the title of his "masterpiece" *Germinal*' (Ibid., p. xi).
67. Corinne Kubler in her article 'Intertextualités zoliennes' conceives of Zola's text precisely as a 'texte-patchwork', Corinne Kubler, 'Intertextualités zoliennes', *Cahiers naturalistes*, 63 (1989), 169–81 (p. 176).
68. See also Berthier, 'Hôtel Saccard', pp. 110–11 for further details on the mixture of mythological sources gracing the structures of the Saccard hôtel: 'Sur les frontons des pavillons, certaines de ces beautés jouent avec des pommes, d'autres prennent des attitudes dans des poignées de joncs: Eves curieuses ou naïdes en attente du satyre, les mythes païens et chrétiens se réconcilient dans l'exaltation de l'unique besoin de jouir.'
69. Bluestone, *Novels into Film*, p. 218.
70. Roland Barthes, *Mythologies* (Paris: Seuil, 1957), p. 226.
71. Sanders, *Adaptation and Appropriation*, p. 70.
72. Peter Collier demonstrates the way in which Auguste Rodin uses his sculptures of Orpheus to explore his own artistic mission. Peter Collier, 'Valéry and Rodin: Orpheus Returning', in Collier and Lethbridge, eds, *Artistic Relations*, pp. 278–90. Sanders herself points to the way in which Orpheus has been integrated into strands of modern film, notably Marcel Camus's *Orfeu Negro* (*Black Orpheus*) of 1959, a film which explores its own adaptive act of an age-old story: 'There is a self-consciousness throughout *Black Orpheus* that theirs is a pre-existent narrative, an old story. A marriage registrar jokingly tells Orpheus, persuaded by his fiancée Mira to obtain a marriage licence, that his bride-to-be's name should be Eurydice, and when Orpheus first meets Eurydice at her cousin's place, he laughs "Wonderful, I have loved you for a thousand years... It's a very old story"' (Sanders, *Adaptation and Appropriation*, p. 72).
73. Mardore, *Roger Vadim*, p. 28.
74. Ibid., p. 27.
75. For an analysis of the act of seeing in the novel, see Harrow, *La Curée*, pp. 35–44.

CHAPTER 5

❖

The Ghost of the Author: *La Bête humaine* and the Pull of the Future[1]

Chapter 4 focused on the pull of the past on Zola's works, underlining the way in which *La Curée* destabilizes its status as literary original, pointing to the texts it has adapted in order to exist. In contrast, this chapter moves in the opposite direction, turning to consider the pull of the future in relation to Zola's *La Bête humaine*. Focusing on the adaptations of this novel made by Jean Renoir (*La Bête humaine*, 1938) and Fritz Lang (*Human Desire*, 1954), this chapter explores the way in which Zola's text has been adapted and its adaptation re-adapted in the course of the twentieth century.[2] Julie Sanders underlines how frequently adaptations adapt other adaptations. She writes:

> Adaptation and appropriation also provide their own intertexts, so that adaptations perform in dialogue with other adaptations as well as their informing source. Perhaps it serves us better to think in terms of complex processes of filtration, and in terms of intertextual webs or signifying fields, rather than simplistic one-way lines of influence from source to adaptation.[3]

Renoir's *La Bête humaine* and Lang's *Human Desire* bear witness to such comments. Lang's film adapts that of Renoir whilst adapting Zola's source text. Despite the very real differences between the adaptations made by each filmmaker, the two films are tied together (and indeed to Zola's text) by an extended consideration of authorship. In French one can be *auteur* of a crime, one's destiny, a novel and a film. Renoir and Lang adapt Zola's novel, sharing in his dialogue about the extent to which his protagonist Jacques can be considered author of his crime. However, they also turn to evaluate their own authorial status, couching this evaluation in ghost-like terms. Just as Zola's Jacques is haunted by the ghosts of his heredity, Renoir confronts the spectre of his textual heredity, the phantom of Zola, in his images and Lang works with the traces of both earlier authors in his film. Moreover, all three, to an extent, dramatize the spectre of textual transformation, exploring the theme of replacement and displacement, perhaps gesturing towards their ghostly status in future adaptations as texts pass into different hands and media. As Zola queries his status as literary original in relation to *La Curée*, so Renoir and Lang, in adapting his novel, play with their status as textual copies accreted onto the surface of Zola's text, dramatizing the pull of the future and the transformations it entails.

In the first instance, concepts of authorship are explored in criminal terms at the level of characterization in *La Bête humaine*. Zola's novel is built around a quest for the author of a crime — the murder of Grandmorin and subsequently that of Séverine. However, symbolically, this quest is never fulfilled. The authors of both crimes are not discovered and their criminal acts are misattributed. Roubaud's confession is not believed, Jacques remains free and the innocent Cabuche is prosecuted in his place. Whilst the reader witnesses Jacques killing Séverine, Zola queries Jacques's status as the author of this crime. The decision to murder is not taken by Jacques, rather it is authored by the forces of his heredity, written in the tainted blood of his forebears. Zola blames Jacques's immediate ancestry: 'Et il [Jacques] en venait à penser qu'il payait pour les autres, les pères, les grands-pères, qui avaient bu, les générations d'ivrognes dont il était le sang gâté' (p. 1043). However, he also cites a more distant, untraceable heredity: 'Cela venait-il donc de si loin, [...] de la rancune amassée de mâle en mâle, depuis la première tromperie au fond des cavernes?' (p. 1044). Zola repeatedly depicts Jacques's moments of criminal authorship as moments of absence:

> [...] c'étaient, dans son être, de subites pertes d'équilibre, comme des cassures, des trous par lesquels son moi lui échappait, au milieu d'une sorte de grande fumée qui déformait tout. Il ne s'appartenait plus, il obéissait à ses muscles, à la bête enragée. (p. 1043)

Jacques's lack of criminal authorship in Zola's novel is powerfully expressed by means of references to his hands. Far from constituting a symbol of his agency, Jacques's hands underline his powerlessness: 'Tout se brouilla, ses mains révoltées, victorieuses de son effort à les cacher, se dénouèrent, s'échappèrent. Et il comprit si bien que, désormais, il n'était plus leur maître, et qu'elles allaient brutalement se satisfaire' (p. 1208). Jacques's hands ultimately do not belong to him, they obey the ghosts of his ancestors and he cannot restrain them:

> Et la terreur de ses mains les lui fit enfoncer davantage sous son corps, car il les sentait bien qui s'agitaient, révoltées, plus fortes que son vouloir. Est-ce qu'elles allaient cesser de lui appartenir? Des mains qui lui viendraient d'un autre, des mains léguées par quelque ancêtre, au temps où l'homme, dans les bois, étranglait les bêtes! (p. 1207)

For Zola, the decision to murder Séverine does not belong to Jacques. The authorship of the crime is shared by Jacques and the refracted influence of an ever-receding, and ultimately untraceable, series of ghostly ancestors.

Zola's 1890 novel about the author of a crime was adapted by the auteur Jean Renoir into a film of the same name, released in 1938. If the Vadim adaptation discussed in the previous chapter met largely with criticism and censure, Renoir's *La Bête humaine* is usually placed at the opposite end of the scale by critical opinion. According to *L'Encyclopédie du cinéma*, 'Il est certain que ce film est, de loin, la meilleure adaptation d'une œuvre d'Emile Zola — la plus fidèle — qui ait été portée à l'écran.'[4] Indeed, for André Bazin, Renoir's film improves on Zola's original text.[5] Penelope Gilliatt agrees, deeming the piece 'one of the very best Renoir films, adapted from Zola without the novel's rhetoric and, ironically, without its falsely "cinematic" scheme'.[6] Its acceptance in France is indicated by the fact that Renoir was asked by the Société Littéraire des Amis de Zola to lecture on his adaptation at the Sorbonne.[7] Renoir's adaptation did indeed make a number of changes to Zola's text, transposing the action to the France of the Popular Front. Technological advances, and his support for the political regime, led him to abandon the runaway train of Zola's dénouement, replacing it with Jacques's suicide and Pecqueux driving the train to safety. However, entering into a dialogue with Zola's text, Renoir reflects upon the key theme of authorship, exploring it both at the level of characterization and in relation to his own authorial identity.

Renoir explores the troubled nature of Jacques's criminal authorship as he interprets and adapts Zola's notions of heredity. Jacques (Jean Gabin) not only makes reference in dialogue to 'les générations d'ivrognes qui m'ont pourri le sang', but the film opens by scrolling down through a quotation created from an amalgamation of the novel's lines on heredity.[8] This quotation is surrounded by the dense smoke which Jacques, both in the novel and film, describes as overpowering him in his inherited homicidal rages.[9] With this quotation, Renoir's film acknowledges Zola as his textual ancestor, underlining the textual lifeblood which ties his work to that of Zola, just as heredity ties Jacques's authorship to the genetic texts of his ancestors. Moreover, Renoir accompanies this quotation with a musical motif that recurs whenever Jacques is reminded of or taken over by his *fêlure*, by the instincts of his ancestors. As John Anzalone puts it, 'the music we hear is the aural signature of Lantier's tragic heredity. Whenever it is heard again, violence or death are near'.[10] Jacques cannot escape the weight of his ancestral past and Renoir uses images of time to underline this. Roubaud surveys the body Jacques has murdered. Grandmorin's watch swings like a pendulum in his hand, a hand gradually severed by the edge of the shot, the watch italicized by the play of light on the metal. Characters dream of escaping the past. Jacques and Séverine indulge in thoughts of a future of forgetting. However, escape is impossible as Séverine makes clear in Renoir's film. Despite the hope for a fresh start or the clean slate promised by the Railwaymen's New Year ball, she claims 'devant nous maintenant c'est barré', 'demain sera comme hier'.[11] The past is a text which will constantly be repeated. Just as Zola isolated Jacques's hands from his body and his will, so Renoir's film, as part of an extended play on hands, will do likewise. The film opens with a set of hands metaphorically severed from their owner as the viewer watches Pecqueux's hands shovelling coal into the furnace. However, more importantly, Renoir's camera focuses on Jacques's digits to the exclusion of the rest of his body as he seizes the knife to murder Séverine. His digits act without his volition and Renoir, like Zola, shows that Jacques's present is authored by the past of his ancestors.

The instability of Jacques's identity has equivalents elsewhere in Zola's novel. Phasie looks at the passengers on the train, but she cannot count them or identify them as they fly by:

> Elle essayait de les compter, en moyenne, à tant par wagon: il y en avait trop, elle n'y parvenait pas. Souvent, elle croyait reconnaître des visages [...]. Mais l'éclair les emportait, elle n'était pas bien sûre de les avoir vus, toutes les faces se noyaient, se confondaient, comme semblables, disparaissant les unes dans les autres. Le torrent coulait, en ne laissant rien de lui. (p. 1032)

Identity proves no more fixed in Renoir's film. The adaptation opens with Roubaud asserting his identity and claiming 'je ne rougis pas de mon nom'. He will, however, subsequently discover the lie that is his life and become a shadow of his former self. Indeed, when Jacques attempts to kill him in the train yard, Renoir depicts Roubaud literally as a shadow on the wall.[12] Having been upright and enforced the law (he reminds passengers of railway regulations), Roubaud will infringe the law. He closes the film sprawled on the floor, stealing. Renoir, again playing on the imagery of hands will, for the second time in the film, sever Roubaud's digits with the edge of his shot, emphasizing the larcenous nature of his act as he steals from the hiding place beneath the floorboards.

Not only will Roubaud fall, but he will be replaced by Jacques. In Renoir's film, Roubaud waits for Séverine in the room, looking over the station, checking his watch, providing her with food. Later in the film, Jacques awaits her in the same space, with the same view, the same gestures and food. He takes Roubaud's literal and amorous space. The novel underlines the sense of replication at play:

> Elle [Séverine] ne répondit pas, reprise par le passé dans sa fièvre heureuse, revivant malgré elle les heures qu'elle avait vécues là, avec son mari. N'était-ce pas le déjeuner d'autrefois qui se continuait par ce gâteau, mangé sur la même table, au milieu des mêmes bruits? (p. 1192)

Jacques also usurps Roubaud's criminal space. Having witnessed Roubaud killing Grandmorin on the train, in the novel, Jacques replays a version of the scene in his mind, inserting himself in Roubaud's role: 'Une sueur l'inonda, il se vit le couteau au poing, frappant à la gorge Roubaud, comme celui-ci avait frappé le président' (p. 1235).[13] However, Jacques's replacement of Roubaud is no more fixed for, in Renoir's film, Henri Dauvergne will in part replace him in Séverine's affections and ultimately Pecqueux will replace him in a work situation, driving the train into post-filmic time. Indeed, Renoir's film deliberately blurs the boundaries of individual identity. Séverine plots Roubaud's death and, hearing steps on the stairs, she and Jacques prepare to kill him. Significantly the dialogue makes no use of Roubaud's name: 'Ça y est, c'est lui', 'Oui, c'est lui.' The camera cuts to follow the figure coming up the stairs, but, echoing the anonymity of the dialogue does not show the viewer his face. The irony of this scene is twofold when the identity of the man on the stairs is revealed to the audience immediately before Séverine's murder. Séverine is mistaken in relation to the identity of this man. It is not Roubaud, the man she thinks will kill her, though, had it been, she would have been saved. And, as the viewer realizes the identity of the man on the stairs, Séverine realizes the true identity of Jacques. She is murdered by the lover that she thinks she knows, but does not. In Renoir's film, identities are replaced and displaced as they are in Zola's novel.[14]

This exploration of the replacement and displacement of individuals, of the ghosts and memories of identity, takes place in a novel where the vocabulary of the spectral is frequent. Séverine is haunted by the memory of Grandmorin. He is 'ce vieux dont le spectre sanglant la hantait' (pp. 1145–46). The traces Grandmorin leaves behind have a similar effect on Roubaud. He fears touching his victim's watch and money in their hiding place: '[...] c'était comme un charnier, un trou d'épouvante et de mort, où des spectres l'attendaient' (p. 1138). Jacques believes that he sees the spectre of Flore after her death: '[...] il eut la sensation brusque qu'une autre figure blanche se dressait au pied du lit. Etait-ce donc un dédoublement de la morte? Puis, il reconnut Flore. Elle était revenue, pendant qu'il avait la fièvre, après l'accident' (p. 1299). The living are at times enveloped in comparably ghost-like terms. Roubaud is surprised by Séverine: 'Un moment, il ne la reconnut pas, crut sans doute à un spectre, en la voyant toute blanche avec ses regards d'épouvante' (p. 1159).[15] Even the landscape is not exempt from notions of haunting. Roubaud, contemplating the disintegration of his life, walks his rounds in the dark, 'soulagé lorsque le ciel blanchissait et tirait de l'ombre le grand fantôme pâle de la gare' (p. 1145). The novel, moreover, closes with a spectral image of the train: '[...] tous les appareils télégraphiques de la ligne tintaient, tous les cœurs battaient, à la nouvelle du train fantôme qu'on venait de voir passer à Rouen et à Sotteville' (p. 1331).

Notions of the spectral are not restricted to a narrative level in the novel *La Bête humaine*; rather they extend to Renoir's adaptation. Whilst Renoir's film omits the death of Flore and her ghostly return, it has its own ghost, that of Emile Zola. That the trace of the earlier source text inhabits an adaptation is not unusual. Indeed, in some form or other, it is a precondition of the adaptive process. However, Renoir not only acknowledges Zola's text in a very physical manner, he also, in specific scenes, underlines what he has altered, the text he has omitted. He thus makes present what is absent in his film, a present absence which finds perfect expression in the metaphor of the ghost. Zola's presence is everywhere apparent in Renoir's film. The adaptation opens with a fragment of Zola's novel, a physical reminder of Zola's text which is reinforced by Zola's portrait and the signature written by the invisible hand of the author himself. As Renoir played with the presence of text in his images in his previous Zola adaptation, *Nana*, he does something comparable in *La Bête humaine*. Text is secreted into the action. The shutters pulled down to prevent anyone witnessing the crime of Grandmorin's murder on the train, shutters which also block the scene from the gaze of the audience, mockingly bear the word 'réservé'. Jacques appears against a sign bearing the word 'fumeurs' and, as Tom Conley points out in his incisive reading of the film, his head initially obscures the 'f', hinting at the murderous '(h)umeurs' or heredity that drive him.[16] His head then covers the 'fu' of 'fumeurs', leaving 'meurs', a coded message warning of the murder taking place in the next compartment and those which will ensue. To Conley's insightful examples should be added the text of the poster on the wall as Jacques details the repairs needed by La Lison, text which alludes brilliantly to the ghost of Zola. The viewer glimpses on the poster the following warning for railway workers: 'Ne chargez pas le feu à l'entrée d'un tunnel.' The words are accompanied by an image of a mechanic and coalman losing control of the train. The message passes unnoticed in the film since Renoir changes Zola's original ending, replacing the scuffle on the runaway train with Jacques's suicide and Pecqueux driving the train to safety. However, through these hidden words Renoir alludes to the text of Zola, to the ending that is no longer there, to the ending that he has replaced. The film warns against precisely the dénouement of the novel — Pecqueux overloading the fire with coal at the entrance of a tunnel: 'Toutes les minutes, il ouvrait la porte, jetait du combustible sur la grille, en quantité déraisonnable. [...] Pecqueux rouvrit, s'acharna à remettre du charbon, comme s'il eût voulu faire sauter la machine' (pp. 1328–29). Renoir playfully follows this allusion to Zola's ending by dissolving the words of the poster into an image of Pecqueux shovelling coal *out* of La Lison's engine, teasingly underlining his reversal of the original ending. Thus, by means of the filmmaker's use of this poster, Zola's ending is present and absent in Renoir's adaptation. This poster, to use the terminology of Millicent Marcus, links Renoir's adaptation to Zola's novel and is an 'embedded allegor[y] of adaptation'.[17] Indeed, the ghost of the dénouement of Zola's text is evident in the very opening of Renoir's adaptation since it begins almost where Zola's novel closed, with a shot of Pecqueux's hands (again severed by the edge of the shot) shovelling coal into the mouth of a screaming furnace. A wheel-level shot of the moving train underlines its power, whilst a static shot allows the train to pull away from the camera, perhaps gesturing towards Zola's runaway train. The spectral ancestry of Zola's novel is everywhere present in Renoir's act of cinematic adaptation.

Whilst Zola's authorial ghost hovers over this adaptation of *La Bête humaine*, Renoir's presence as the author of this film is nonetheless discernible. Tom Conley, using the language of ancestry, situates him as a forefather in a series of cinematic auteurs: 'Certain auteurs, in the line of Jean Renoir, were seen producing elsewhere in many films one total, unfinished, conceptual Film'.[18] *La Bête humaine* features actors with whom Renoir had already worked and would work again (Gabin, Carette), makes use of Renoir's characteristic deep focus shots through windows and doors and, more significantly, refers the viewer to other sections of Renoir's authorial corpus, reinforcing his cinematic identity. Conley points out that *La Chienne* (1931) and *Boudu sauvé des eaux* (1932) form a reflective diptych. Michel Simon opens the film *Boudu* crying 'Chien! Chien!' These words,

> [...] add up to a filmic icon summarizing the visual dissolution of the masculine canine while recalling the title and ending shots of the feminine counterpart *La Chienne*, in which Legrand (also Michel Simon), a bank clerk and Sunday painter, becomes the tramp who is now [...] Boudu. A transubstantiation occurs before the narration is put in gear: the second film begins where the first, like the dog, has uncannily disappeared, or been left adrift in visual and audible memory.[19]

La Bête humaine taps into this reflective authorial structure. The murder scene when Jacques stabs Séverine is almost a replica of that which takes place in *La Chienne*. Both are filmed through the framing device of an open door. While both show the action of the stabbing, neither shows the body being stabbed. The action of both scenes is connected by the insertion of musical comment on the events ('Le Petit Cœur de Ninon' details a faithless female in its lyrics in *La Bête humaine* and street singers ironically sing of love and trust in *La Chienne* as Lulu is being stabbed by the man who loves her, a stabbing that will be blamed on the man she truly loves).[20] Likewise, Renoir's allusions to his earlier films, a self-citation akin to that used by Zola in the *Rougon-Macquart* series, find expression in the character of Cabuche whose fate mirrors that of Dédé in *La Chienne*: both are innocent parties accused of a crime, trapped in official corridors, interrogation rooms and the same pleas of innocence.

Renoir's authorial hold on *La Bête humaine* is strengthened by his cameo appearance as Cabuche. He refashions part of Zola's text in his own image. However, Zola's Cabuche, a quarryman, becomes a poacher in Renoir's version. Cabuche is only fleetingly associated with notions of poaching in Zola's novel. He states that the blood on his trousers, blood the police take to belong to the murder victim, comes from a rabbit he caught (p. 1102). The prevalence of the figure of the poacher in Renoir's work is clear, as underscored by characters in *La Fille de l'eau* (1925), Cabri in *La Marseillaise* (1938), Marceau in *La Règle du jeu* (1939), Tom Keefer in *Swamp Water* (1941), Sam Tucker in *The Southerner* (1945) and Renoir's play *Orvet*.[21] In the light of Michel de Certeau's definition of reading as poaching, it is my contention that this cameo role constitutes a wink to the authorial borrowing or poaching that has informed Renoir's authorial act. Certeau famously writes: '[...] les lecteurs sont des voyageurs; ils circulent sur les terres d'autrui, nomades braconnant à travers les champs qu'ils n'ont pas écrits, ravissant les biens d'Egypte pour en jouir'.[22] Such an argument is reinforced by the fact that Renoir chooses to reprise his cameo role as a poacher in *La Règle du jeu* when he appears as Octave. Carette (playing the part of Marceau) is the actual poacher of the piece, but whilst he longs to give up this life, Leo Braudy makes a convincing case for reading the failed musician Octave (Renoir), who lives on the wealth of those around him as a 'socialized poacher'.[23] In making clear his *braconnage* of Zola's text, Renoir indicates that, like Jacques, his authorship is, in some senses, undermined by the influence of its textual heredity, by the ancestry of the Zolian text from which he poaches. His film is neither fully his, not fully the work of another. His authorship is ghostly.

There are, however, ghosts other than those of Zola and Renoir haunting *La Bête humaine*. The ghosts of contemporary society can be detected in Renoir's film as the return of the repressed in the shape of Jacques's heredity parallels the return of the spectre of World War I as Europe teeters, in 1938, on the outbreak of World War II. The ghosts of history are, if anything, overshadowed by the ghost of the film's leading man, Jean Gabin. Whilst actors are habitually studied as passive icons modelled by the direction of a filmmaker, Patrick McGilligan, writing on James Cagney, makes a powerful case for a certain actors attaining an authorial role in a film:

> If an actor is responsible only for acting but is not involved in any of the artistic decisions of film-making, then it is accurate surely to refer to the actor as a semi-passive icon, a symbol that is manipulated by writers and directors. But actors who not only influence artistic decisions (casting, writing, directing etc.) but demand certain limitations on the basis of their screen personas, may justly be regarded as 'auteurs'.[24]

Gabin's acts in choosing scripts, buying the rights to novels if necessary, at times choosing co-stars and directors and using his status, financial and artistic, to ensure films were made, certainly place him in this category. François Truffaut cites Gabin as one of the artists with whom he would not work precisely because of their authorial status:

> Ce sont des acteurs trop dangereux qui décident du scénario ou le rectifient s'il ne leur plaît pas. Ils n'hésitent pas à imposer la distribution ou à refuser certains

> partenaires. Ils influent la mise en scène, exigent de gros plans. Ils n'hésitent pas à sacrifier l'intérêt du film à ce qu'ils appellent leur standing.[25]

Whilst Gabin's authorial role is in no way as strong as that of Zola or Renoir, the images of the film might nonetheless be said to be haunted by the traces of his identity. That Gabin has attained a mythical status in French cinema is clear. For Ginette Vincendeau this myth has its foundations in the 'type' Gabin played in a series of now classic films he made in the 1930s, the working-class hero with a good heart, harmed by destiny, forces beyond his control or a treacherous woman.[26] Gabin, in an interview with Didier Daix, pointed out the possibility of generalizing in relation to a section of his roles: 'Je ne veux surtout plus jouer les tueurs [...] les personnages que j'ai tournés n'étaient pas tous mauvais, mais c'étaient des gars marqués par le sort, des hommes au destin tragique'.[27] The prevalence of this mythical identity is such that it aroused critical comment as early as 1939. René Barjavel writes in critical terms of Gabin:

> On le reconnaît, quand il apparaît sur l'écran. On l'a déjà vu. On l'accueille comme un copain de régiment qu'on avait presque oublié. On se rappelle, en le revoyant, que c'était pas [*sic*] un mauvais gars. Il était beau gosse. Il avait du succès auprès des poules. [...] Il a pas [*sic*] très bien tourné. [...] Il a tué. Plusieurs fois. Sa vie, désormais, semble louvoyer, de déchéance en déchéance, entre les crimes et les suicides successifs. C'est pas [*sic*] un gars à fréquenter. [...] Ce qui est grave pour Gabin, c'est qu'il ne puisse s'évader de ce personnage.[28]

Gabin's stardom, even by 1938, is such that he brings the ghosts of previous films to *La Bête humaine*. Indeed, the ghosts of these performances, of this type haunt and perhaps even override the role of Jacques in Renoir's film. The protagonists of both Zola and Renoir are, however likeable, murderers with tainted blood flowing through their veins, criminals who harm society and allow the innocent Cabuche to be accused. However, so strong was Gabin's image as a working-class hero that, in 1989, to celebrate the bicentenary of the French Revolution and the French society created by it, Gabin, as Jacques Lantier, was asked to parade down the Champs Elysées in a wooden locomotive. The accumulated layers of Gabin's cinematic identity as a working-class hero overrode the identity of Jacques as created by Zola and Renoir. Zola's novel is not the only text to haunt the images of Renoir's film, it is also peopled by a spectral sense of the déjà vu, by the ghosts of the Gabin myth.[29]

Renoir's film might also be said to be haunted by the ghosts of earlier films, by the spectral memory of the train in cinematic history. The onset of film technology was, at times, viewed in a ghostly light. The Russian novelist Maxim Gorky, having seen projected moving images for the first time in July 1896, wrote: 'If you only knew how strange it is to be there' to witness 'not life, but its shadow [...] not motion but its soundless spectre'.[30] Mordaunt Hall, writing in the New York Times in April 1925 about *Madame sans gêne*, a piece depicting the French Revolution and age of Napoleon uses a similarly spectral vocabulary, suggesting that 'ghosts of the Napoleonic days seemed to come to life and tread once more the floors, staircases and lawns of the Chateaux of Fontainebleau and Compiegne'.[31] Both link films with notions of resurrection and haunting. In many respects, Renoir's opening shots of the train in *La Bête humaine* resurrect traces of the image of the train in cinema prior to his work. As Charles Musser points out: 'The railroad and the screen have had a special relationship, symbolized by the Lumières' famous *Train Entering a Station* (1895) and half a dozen other films'.[32] Phantom rides, films where the camera is mounted in front of a train engine, provided a popular spectacle for early filmgoers.[33] The words of the newspaper *The Era*, writing on the first phantom ride film *The Havershaw Tunnel* in 1897, might, with slight modifications, just as easily be applied to the opening railroad images of Renoir's film and specifically their forward-facing shots of the track:

> With a very slight stretch of the imagination he [the viewer] can fancy himself tearing along at a great speed on a cow-catcher, with the landscape simply leaping towards him. He sees the stretch of metals before him, just as if he were travelling with the train, which rushes into the tunnel, seen looming ahead long before the train enters the darkness, from which it emerges into a beautiful country, bathed in sunlight. A more exciting and sensational piece of realism has never been presented to an audience.[34]

Whilst railway films were frequently actuality-based pieces, actuality and fiction were soon merged in a hybrid fiction/actuality genre. Ferdinand Zecca, amongst other things one of the early adaptors of Zola, produced in 1901 a film entitled *Flirt en chemin de fer* in which a man tries to steal a kiss from an unwilling female passenger in the darkness of a train tunnel. Zecca makes the viewer a passenger on a train, offering them a window view of the passing countryside.[35] Renoir's much later railway film, *La Bête humaine* does likewise and might be seen to be inhabited by the ghostly memory of railway films, be they Phantom Rides or the plethora of actuality and/or fiction films based around the locus of the train.

Renoir's film thus contains a variety of traces of past works. So too, Henri Mitterand points out, does Zola's novel. Tracing the textual genealogy of *La Bête humaine*, Mitterand points out shades of a variety of other novels, works of theory, and contemporary crimes (the Fenayrou, Barrême and Poinsot cases as well, perhaps, as Jack the Ripper).[36] Zola's authorship, like that of his character Jacques, has a series of textual ancestors. The shadows of *Crime and Punishment*, for example, are pronounced. Zola read the translation of Dostoyevsky's work which appeared in French in 1885. Zola's protagonist brushes up against the central theory of Dostoyevsky's protagonist Raskolnikov, relating to the 'right to murder' that the strong have over the weak, when the novel refers to 'le droit au meurtre'. When contemplating killing Roubaud, Jacques's thoughts are phrased as a refutation of Dostoyevsky's earlier text:

> Tuer cet homme, mon Dieu! en avait-il le droit? Quand une mouche l'importunait, il la broyait d'une tape. [...] Mais cet homme, son semblable! Il dut reprendre tout son raisonnement, pour se prouver son droit au meurtre, le droit des forts que gênent les faibles, et qui les mangent. (p. 1236)

The reasoning is not enough to convince him and he does not kill on this basis.

However, if Zola's text looks back to the ghosts of past texts, it is also possible to discern the shadows of future works in Zola's novel. Whilst the previous chapter underlined the dangers of deeming Zola pre-cinematic since it affords a teleology to the processes of adaptation in this author's work which is misleading, the literary origins of structures that would subsequently become cinematic techniques are as visible in *La Bête humaine* as the previous chapter suggested they are in *La Curée*. As film cameras will subsequently move across the landscape to create establishing shots, the opening scene of the novel surveys the station from the fifth-floor room and Zola's narration pans from left to right, even tilting down to examine the viewpoint beneath this trajectory:

> En face [...] les maisons de la rue Rome se brouillaient, s'effaçaient, légères. A gauche, les marquises des Halles couvertes ouvraient leurs porches géants [...]; tandis que le pont de L'Europe, à droite, coupait de son étoile de fer la tranchée, que l'on voyait reparaître et filer au-delà, jusqu'au tunnel des Batignolles. Et, en bas de la fenêtre [...] les trois doubles voies qui sortaient du pont, se ramifiaient. (p. 997)

Zola's narration has the ability to zoom in and to pull back, providing us with a variety of visual shots. Close ups are frequent. Having panoramically surveyed the landscape, Zola zeroes in on a particular train, to the exclusion of all else: 'Mais toute son attention fut prise par le train de trois heures vingt-cinq, [...], empli déjà de ses voyageurs, et qui attendait sa machine. Il n'apercevait pas celle-ci' (p. 998). The literary fadeouts identified in *La Curée* have their equivalents in *La Bête humaine*. Having used the steam of his train to fade out the landscape at the end of one paragraph, Zola jumps forward in time, space and focus in the next: 'Immobile, la machine de l'express perdait par une soupape un grand jet de vapeur qui montait dans tout ce noir, où elle s'effiloquait en petites fumées, semant de larmes blanches le deuil sans bornes tendu au ciel.' The next paragraph begins, 'A six heures vingt, Roubaud et Séverine parurent' (p. 1022).

Notions of textual transformation lie at the core of Zola's novel. The pull of the future and the transformation it entails are clear themes underlined by descriptions of the train. In the final paragraph of the novel, Zola writes: 'Qu'importaient les victimes que la machine écrasait en chemin! N'allait-elle pas quand même à l'avenir, insoucieuse du sang répandu?' (p. 1331). Zola himself began to explore the transformation of his own text by adapting *La Bête humaine*, with Busnach, into a play. Whilst this play was never performed, it underlines the process of textual transformation to which Zola's novel has been subject almost from its inception. This process of textual transformation is one of the key narrative themes of *La Bête humaine*. Original texts are lost. Séverine's letter to Grandmorin goes missing. Similarly the letter settling the disputed ownership of the station apartment is lost. Madame Lebleu uses its absence to maintain possession of her apartment: '[...] il devait exister une lettre de son mari s'engageant à le rendre, si un nouveau sous-chef le réclamait. Comme on n'avait pas retrouvé la lettre encore, elle en niait l'existence' (p. 1225).[37] Significantly, the textual origin of Jacques's criminal authorship is itself fundamentally lost. Zola states repeatedly that Jacques acts in order to 'venger des offenses très anciennes, dont il aurait perdu l'exacte mémoire' (p. 1044 and p. 1152). Symbolically, his act leads the reader back in time and text to an origin that can no longer be found. Texts are also destroyed. Camy-Lamotte ultimately burns Séverine's letter (p. 1317). However, the ghost of the original text comes back to haunt the living and indeed Roubaud and Séverine's reaction to this letter is twice evoked in terms of haunting: 'Avait-on, à Paris, retrouvé les trois lignes d'écriture, ce billet maladroit dont la peur les hantait' (p. 1104). Zola writes: '[...] la pensée d'une preuve, à laquelle Roubaud n'avait pas songé d'abord, le hantait maintenant d'une peur continue: la lettre qu'il avait fait écrire à sa femme afin de décider Grandmorin à partir, cette lettre qu'on allait retrouver' (p. 1080). Original texts are associated with a sense of threat. Camy-Lamotte warns Séverine about the letter he conceals: 'Souvenez-vous que le dossier reste là, et qu'à la moindre faute, tout peut être repris' (p. 1126). Texts resurface. The lost letter comes back to life and is retold by Séverine in her confession to Jacques, despite his attempts to suppress it: 'C'était l'aveu qui revenait, fatal, inévitable. Et, cette fois, il en eut la nette conscience, rien au monde ne le retarderait' (p. 1195). Stories are recreated and altered in this novel, not always in the most faithful of manners. A mythical murderer is invented for the death of Grandmorin:

> [...] et une légende de police était en train de se former, romanesque: celle d'un assassin inconnu, insaisissable, un aventurier du crime, présent partout à la fois, que l'on chargeait de tous les meurtres et qui se dissipait en fumée, à la seule apparition des agents. (p. 1134)

The clerk adapts the text of the interviews, omitting anything inappropriate.[38] The investigator Denizet scripts 'une création véritable' to explain the murders, a creation with no basis in reality (p. 1307). In the pages of Zola's novel, authorship can be dual. Séverine writes a text dictated by Roubaud, whilst Roubaud earlier writes and signs a text dictated by his boss (p. 1004 and p. 1021). Our quest for an original author in the novel of Emile Zola leads us through a maze of texts lost, past and forgotten, just as it leads us forward through the process of displacement, replacement and adaptation.

The theme of textual transformation explored on a narrative level in Zola's novel, is enacted by the fate of the novel. Zola's novel about the replacement and displacement of texts and identities is itself replaced and displaced by Renoir's adaptation. However, Renoir's adaptation meets the same fate as it is transformed into Fritz Lang's *Human Desire* sixteen years later. Lang's adaptation in many ways reinforces Julie Sanders's observations about the 'filtration' effect of adaptations influencing further adaptations since the process of cross-fertilization is clear.[39] Lang discusses the production's Executive Producer in the following terms: 'Jerry Wald was very impressed with the Renoir film, in which there are a lot of trains going into tunnels — which Jerry thought was a sex symbol; I doubt that Renoir in 1938 ever thought about sex symbols, but anyway, Jerry thought so and he fell in love with trains.'[40] The influence of Renoir's film is tangible in Lang's adaptation and consequently its adaptive action is dual, reflecting and transforming as it does both Zola's text and its cinematic predecessor. Lang's involvement in cinematic adaptation was not fleeting. A significant number of his works are adaptations of earlier literary texts. He adapted not only literary works, but also remade films. When Lang reworked Renoir's *La Bête humaine*, he had already remade the French director's *La Chienne* (1931) — a film which became Lang's *Scarlet Street* (1945). Renoir's *La Chienne* was itself already an adaptation stemming from Georges de la Fouchardière's original novel *La Chienne*. Whilst the adaptation of earlier texts and films was not unusual for the era and environment in which Lang worked, the filmmaker seems to have been particularly engaged with the processes of adaptation, with the notions of replacement and displacement enacted by the pull of the future. He witnessed the transformation of his own work. Joseph Losey created a 1951 American remake of Lang's 1931 *M*, the story of a disturbed murderer of children. Moreover, Lang observed the unacknowledged appropriation of fragments of his own work in his lifetime. Lang describes his experience watching *Dillinger* (1945):

> Then came a whole sequence — about 300 or 500 feet — and suddenly I said, 'No, wait a moment — this was taken out of one of my pictures!' There was a bank hold up in *You Only Live Once* — the robbers used tear gas and wore gas masks — so you couldn't recognize the actors. The producers of *Dillinger* had bought this whole sequence from Walter Wanger and simply inserted it into their film [...] This scene was mentioned in the reviews, but nobody said it was mine. [...] The same thing happened to me when I saw a picture called *Buffalo Bill* [William Wellman, 1944], which had in it a lot of scenes I had shot for *Western Union*. So a producer sees a picture, goes to the company and says 'Look you're not releasing this film any more — I want to buy so and so much footage,' and he sticks it into his own picture.[41]

Unsurprisingly, in the light of his cinematic sources, Lang presents the process of adaptation, be it of films or novels, in a largely positive light. Lang claimed:

> By the way, I don't mind if somebody steals — I stole a lot of things in my life — and I wouldn't call it stealing; I think Stendhal said, 'It is permitted to take the good things where you find them.' Cecil DeMille took the kangaroo court from *M* and transposed it into a kangaroo court in a high school [*This Day and Age*, 1933], and I was very proud about it.[42]

Indeed, it could be argued that Lang plays with the process of transformation, teasingly inverting insignificant details to underline what he has changed in his remakes of *La Chienne* and *La Bête humaine*. In *La Chienne* Renoir has Lulu (the female protagonist) polish the fingernails of her lover and pimp, Dédé. Lang inverts this superficial detail, having Kitty (his version of Lulu) demand Chris (her helpless would-be lover) do her toenails. Comparably, in Renoir's *La Bête humaine*, Grandmorin greets Séverine with the words 'tu as maigri', whilst Owens (Lang's version of Grandmorin) greets Vicki (Lang's Séverine) with the phrase 'you've put on a little weight'.

Lang is, in many respects, a highly suitable candidate to adapt Zola's *La Bête humaine*. Zola's interest in the combined concepts of *race*, *milieu* and *moment* find equivalents in the broader body of Lang's work. A number of his works foreground his interest in notions of genetic inheritance and murder. The psychopathic killer in his early German work *M* speaks of his compulsion to murder:

> But can I... can I help it? Have I got this curse inside me? The fire? The voice? The pain? Again... again.. again I have to walk the streets. And I always feel that somebody is following me... it is me... it is myself... following... me.

His words echo, in part, the compulsion Zola's novel describes as driving Jacques in the form of heredity: 'Son unique pensée était d'aller tout droit, plus loin, toujours plus loin, pour se fuir, pour fuir l'autre, la bête enragée, qu'il sentait en lui' (p. 1046).[43] As Zola's Jacques is marked by the text of his genetic inheritance, so a number of Lang's films explore the plight of characters trapped by the literal marks with which they are imprinted. The murderer in *M* is twice caught by means of imprints: the identifying chalk letter printed on the back of his coat by the hand of the passer by and the traces of his letter found on the wood in his lodging.[44] Moreover, Zola's protagonist has much in common with the quintessential film noir hero, the filmic style with which Lang was frequently associated. Robert Singer makes a case for the association of film noir and Naturalism:

> If one accepts the premise that 'Fritz Lang's cinema is the cinema of the nightmare,' then those naturalist agencies operating in *Human Desire* (1954), the *noirish* adaptation of Zola's *La Bête humaine*, involving the remote environment of the railroad-town, the closed workers' society, corrupt lovers, violence, alcoholism, and the post-World War II historical milieu, actively link the noir aesthetic with naturalism.[45]

And Jeremy G. Butler's definition of the noir hero sums up the fate of Jacques in Zola's novel: 'The obsessive *noir* protagonist is drawn into a destiny he cannot escape; he is impelled toward his fate by exterior forces beyond his power and interior forces beyond his control'.[46]

If the phrase 'internal forces beyond his [the noir hero's] control' is compatible with Zola's notion of *race*, so 'exterior forces beyond his [the noir hero's] power', recalls the nineteenth-century novelist's concept of *milieu* — the external environment acting upon the characters. Zola's concept of milieu finds an equivalent in Lang's work as a whole. As Father Dolan puts it in *You Only Live Once* (1937) when Eddie Taylor (Henry Fonda) is pushed back to a life of crime despite himself, 'Every man — at birth — is endowed with the nobility of a king. But the stain of the world soon makes him forget even his own birthright.' Tom Gunning, one of the most persuasive readers of Lang's films, discusses the reflective, active nature of the environment in the director's work, alluding to 'a fatal environment which seems not only to reflect characters' anxieties, but to trigger a series of fateful coincidences'.[47] Charles Higham and Joel Greenberg, moreover, point out the privileged place trains hold as *milieu* in the iconography of film noir, 'clanking and swaying through storm-swept darkness, their arrival at remote stations signalled by the presence of mysterious raincoated figures, while in the narrow corridors, the antiseptic cramped compartments, assignations are made and, more often than not, a murder is planned'.[48] *Milieu* and its influence are as central to Lang's work as they are to Zola's novels.

As *moment* is key in Zola's texts, era enjoys a comparable importance in film noir, the movement with which Lang is at times associated. Zola's *La Bête humaine* offers a damning vision of the Second Empire, and as Karen Hollinger points out, the dark 'maladjusted' screens of film noir serve a similarly reflective function. They offer an image of 'the ideological contradictions, disequilibrium, and disturbing imbalance characteristic of the World War Two and post-war periods'.[49] As *race*, *milieu* and *moment* combine to fashion and entrap Zola's hero, so a sense of entrapment and inexorability inhabits many of Lang's films (and film noir more generally). Andrew

Sarris underlines the determinism of Lang's *Human Desire*.[50] Gunning teases out the way in which in Lang's film 'individuality and even desire always become subsumed into larger impersonal and often sinister systems', systems he terms the 'Destiny machine'.[51] Lang's own words reinforce such interpretations of his work: 'Yes, I think that is the main characteristic, the main theme that runs through all my pictures — this fight against destiny, against fate'.[52] Characters appear as trapped, as incapable of authoring their own destiny, in Lang's films as they do in the work of Zola.

Lang's noir credentials thus mark him out as a suitable adaptor for Zola's novel. However, reactions to the work as an adaptation of Zola's novel, unlike those in relation to Renoir's version, have been mixed. Russell Cousins assesses the film in the following terms:

> For the American viewer, Zola *à la* Hollywood becomes a moralistic crime writer where essentially decent characters eventually overcome temptation to live happily ever after, while wrongdoers are deservedly punished in a world which remains essentially a happily ordered place.[53]

Lang's adaptation makes numerous changes to the details of Zola's plot, changes so significant that, in the eyes of some critics, not even the ghost of Zola's original authorship subsists. Like Renoir, he transposes the action to his own contemporary era. Jacques, the murderer driven by heredity, becomes Jeff, the wholesome returning hero from the Korean war who falls for, but eventually resists, the murderous plots of the femme fatale, Vicki (Lang's version of Séverine). Instead of focusing on a hero driven to murder by the ghosts of his ancestors, Lang ignores notions of heredity, to focus instead on the disintegration of Carl (Lang's version of Roubaud). The reasons behind Lang's alterations are numerous. Some are practical. The topic of Zola's novel could not be easily adapted in Hollywood, for the Hays Code frowned on sex maniacs or epileptics in main roles. As Eisner points out, 'The American hero had to be sympathetic and normal, as a prerequisite of the American Dream'.[54] Lang's own words bear witness to his awareness of this necessity: 'Naturally, in an American movie, you cannot make the hero a sex killer. Impossible. So Glenn Ford has to play it, you know, like Li'l Abner coming back from Korea — hundred per cent red-blooded American with very natural sex feelings (if such a thing exists)'.[55] Lang also had to alter his reading of Zola's text in the light of opposition from his producer Jerry Wald. Lang reports Wald's reactions to his initial approach to the storyline: '"You both don't *understand* it. The *woman* is the Human Beast." What can you do against the producer? Hayes and I looked at each other and tried hard to convince him and then we made a compromise and again it became a triangle story'.[56] Lang is still, unmistakably, the author of this adaptation. He exercised a surprising amount of control over his films even within the constraints of the Hollywood studio system and produced, as Stephen Mamber points out, a set of works which clearly bear his signature: 'Throughout Lang's career in Hollywood, regardless of the adverse pressures upon him from the studios or the seemingly impersonal nature of some of his assignments, Lang has made films which are unmistakably individual'.[57] Lang's words reinforce such a notion. When asked in an interview whether a director can still exercise authorship over a film made in

Hollywood, he replies: 'In a certain way, yes. Many people tell me they could pick out a Lang picture immediately'.[58] Nevertheless, it is important to recognize that Lang's authorship bears the traces of other forces, the ghosts of other influences: the strictures of the Hays Code, the demands of studios and the film's producer.[59]

Despite these outside influences, Lang does reflect Zola's text. And, like Renoir, Lang's film dramatizes the ghostly nature of the adaptive process. As Renoir's film alludes to the text he has changed, affording a spectral presence to aspects of the novel which are absent, so in Lang's film, upon meeting Carl for the first time in the film, Jeff claims to know him already: 'Carl was with me the night of the big slide up the pass.' Carl adds: 'It was thirty below.' One wonders if this constitutes a glancing reference to Zola's depiction of the train crash in the snow, the train crash Lang's film excludes. Similarly, reference is made to Alec driving steam engines on these tracks, to the technological world preceding these trains, to the technological world inhabited by Zola's novel, but changed by Lang's film. However, Lang's principal reflection on the work of both Zola and Renoir lies in his exploration of authorship and its ghosts. Like both artists, Lang reflects on the ability of a character to author his/her own destiny. Authorship initially appears as haunted or as driven by the refracted influences of forces beyond the individual's control in Lang as it is in Zola's source novel. Much has been made of the notion of fate in Lang's work. Gunning points out: 'Destiny appears in Lang's films, not as a philosophy, but as a machine, whose mechanical nature in most of the films remains very literal.'[60] *Human Desire* initially appears to be the perfect embodiment of such a statement. The inexorability of some of Renoir's images, images perhaps epitomized by the interweaving tracks carrying characters to their destiny, finds an echo in Lang's film. Whilst Lang abandons all notions of heredity in his hero, he does depict Jeff as being as entrapped as his previous incarnations in the work of Renoir and Zola. In an archetypically noir shot, Jeff lies on his bed and the action of the light on the slats of the shutters casts bars on the space of his room, revealing his metaphorical prison. John Russell Taylor suggests that light is used psychologically in Lang and a study of the presentation of Vicki endorses such a statement.[61] Darkness is used to hem her in. Whilst she may often look out onto a world of daylight outside her home, the bars of her closed window separate her from it. She ventures out only in darkness and becomes increasingly associated with that darkness. When Jeff has to choose between Vicki and a life without her, between murder and innocence, the room, like a number of scenes in the film, is divided between darkness and light and Jeff stands on the threshold of both. The shadows that engulf Vicki are echoed by her words: 'It's too late. It's always too late'. However, images of imprisonment are most prominent in relation to Carl. The audience's first glimpse of him depicts him against a background of bars. The scene pulls Carl towards the confrontation which triggers the mechanism of his downfall, a pull symbolized by the shots of the tannoy loudspeaker. The camera focuses on the loudspeaker and the sign beside it, a sign which offers the hot-headed Carl advice: 'Safety first. Think.' However, with each of the increasingly insistent tannoy appeals for Carl to go to the yardmaster's office, where he will lose his temper, his job and ultimately his wife, the camera cuts closer to the shot of the tannoy, eventually cutting out the sign as Carl ignores its warning, triggering the fateful series of events. His head is cut off by the edge of the shot as he subsequently tries to strangle Vicki, a shot and an anger replicated by the film's dénouement when he succeeds in strangling her. His body is likewise severed by the edge of the shot and by the outlines of the train (he is seen through and below a train wagon) as Jeff tries to kill him. The scene subsequently shifts to show Carl stumbling in an extreme high-angled shot, a shot frequent in Lang's work and in film noir as a whole, a shot redolent of notions of entrapment. For Janey Place and Lowell Peterson, it is 'an oppressive and fatalistic angle that looks down upon its helpless victim to make it look like a rat in a maze'.[62] Personal authorship initially appears as problematic in Lang's film as it does in Zola's novel and Renoir's adaptation of it.

The pervasive sense of entrapment cultivated in the film is reinforced by Lang's play on symmetries and repetitions. Images, like spectres, return in slightly altered form in this adaptation which itself allows the altered return of both Zola's novel and Renoir's adaptation. The film opens and closes in the same space (the train cab) in a symmetrical play which will be discussed below. Carl and Vicki appear in a perfectly symmetrical shot as they argue in their home. Vicki stands in the kitchen door on the left of the shot, Carl in the open door of the right of the shot, their asymmetry as a couple emphasized as Vicki has her back to the camera and Carl faces it. The imbalance of the marriage is underlined by the almost perfect balance of the shot. The inexorability of certain of Lang's shots seems to drag characters to their fate. Jeff's head by the train dissolves into that of Carl as he burns the clothes in which he murdered Owens, symbolizing the way in which Jeff unwittingly becomes his silent accomplice as a result of his love for Vicki. Comparably, Vicki stands in the railway carriage watching her murderous husband (he has just killed Owens), clutching her neck, gesturing, unknowingly, to her own death, by strangulation, at the hands of this husband in a subsequent railway carriage at the film's close. Characters appear trapped in their fates in the narrative and haunting cinematic repetitions of Lang's film.

However, if the forces influencing personal authorship in Zola's novel and Renoir's adaptation are at times of an intangible, spectral nature, those controlling the events in Lang's film are, ultimately, given a very human form: Vicki, the femme fatale. As Renoir symbolized the action of Jacques's heredity in authoring his actions via the musical motif which occurred whenever he was taken over by his *fêlure*, so Vicki's influence has its own musical motif. When the audience first meets the character, sultry music plays on a record player within the scene. Whilst Carl turns this music off, it recurs extradiegetically to symbolize Vicki's influence in controlling characters' actions. It plays, for example, as Jeff tracks Carl in the train yard, persuaded to kill him by Vicki's machinations. Though Vicki does not appear in this scene, her musical signature makes clear her authorship of the action. Renoir's notions of heredity are replaced by the influence of the femme fatale.[63] Vicki stands with her stocking-clad legs on top of Carl, her dominance clear. Jeff's relationship with Vicki is marked by the sign of infraction. In their first rendezvous, a 'no smoking' sign appears on the wall behind them. Jeff smokes before it. The railway worker inadvertently prevents the two would-be lovers from kissing whilst on his rounds. The forces and rules of authority keep Jeff and Vicki apart. Vicki is structurally linked with notions of obfuscation and deceit. The lies of her mouth, revealed at the close of the film, are structurally signalled throughout the film. Vicki's face is concealed or masked in some way when she lies. Vicki stares out of the window as she glosses over her reasons for refusing to see Owens to her husband. As she subsequently lies to him about the sexual bargaining she used to get him his job back, her face is initially off screen, subsequently hidden as she looks in the wardrobe and her duplicity hinted at by the mirror — the double reflection points to the double layers of her words. As she pulls her dress over her head, undressing and hiding her face, her body metaphorically shows what her mouth lies about. The obfuscation and closed, dark spaces associated with Vicki are contrasted with the daylight linked with Alec's daughter. The film establishes the two females as inverse doubles, as the corrupt and the pure. Lang repeatedly links them. He cuts from Vicki at night to Alec's daughter calling Jeff for breakfast, cutting from Vicki's back walking away from the viewer to Alec's daughter walking towards the camera. The viewer sees Vicki climbing into the train as Alec's daughter climbs out of it. However, Alec's daughter is not Vicki's only double. Jean, the friend whose apartment Vicki borrows, offers the viewer a means to decode Vicki's machinations even before she admits them. Jean not only claims 'all women are alike, they've just got different faces so that the men can tell them apart', but her actions as she leaves to meet an older man with money, a man in whom she has only a financial interest, mirror exactly those of Vicki at the same moment (she is out with Owens).

Whilst Zola and Renoir depict Jacques as haunted by the ghosts of his ancestry, ghosts which undermine his authorship of his own destiny, Lang's film underlines Jeff's ability to author his own fate and assert his will freely. Thus, Lang ultimately offers a different vision of personal authorship at the level of plot from that offered either in Zola's novel or Renoir's adaptation. Much has been made of determinism and fate in Lang's films. Bogdanovich writes 'the fight against fate continues from *Der Müde Tod* (his first success in Germany) to *Beyond a Reasonable Doubt* (his last American picture)'.[64] However, fate takes a different form in *Human Desire* as character becomes destiny. Lang wrote in a letter to Eisner:

> I no longer believe in mystical fate. Every human being makes his own fate by the way in which he uses his experience (or does not use his experience), by the choice or rejection of events and situations he partakes in, by what he manages to achieve or not to achieve, for whatever reasons. No mystical fate, no God or whatever is responsible for his fate except himself. And this is why one cannot get away from what one has created for oneself.[65]

Jeff bears witness to such words, clearly establishing himself as author of his own fate. Despite the images of entrapment that surround Jeff in the middle section of the film, images such as the quintessentially noir shadow bars discussed earlier, two distinct paths are laid before the protagonist. These two paths are epitomized by the figures of Carl and Alec, both of whom are set up as potential doubles for Jeff. As has been discussed, an image of Jeff watching in the smoke of a train dissolves into a shot of Carl burning clothes, covering up the evidence of the murder he carried out. As Jeff visually becomes Carl on screen, he does so too metaphorically, as he, like Carl, lies to cover the evidence of the couple's guilt. Alec represents Jeff's other possible destiny. Jeff appears in a symmetrical shot where Alec and his wife double Jeff and Alec's daughter, the possible reflection of their destinies made clear. Jeff slips into neither destiny. Rather, he chooses that of Alec, a choice made clear by his precise echoing of the ghosts of Alec's words. Alec berates him in the railway cab for his illicit relationship with a married woman: 'It's no good. It ain't right.' Jeff subsequently uses traces of the same terms to confront Vicki in the flat: 'That's no good Vicki.' Jeff's personal authorship is underlined by his interaction with the train. The opening sequence depicts the train from all angles, but it also makes clear Jeff's mastery of the machine. A later shot of his severed hand, far from showing the protagonist's lack of authorship, cuts to show the mechanical effect of that movement, his control over the mechanism. Similarly, the opening sequence offers a clear and unobstructed view of the open track the train covers as it advances. This view will disappear in subsequent train journeys, replaced by framed shots, edged by the view of the cabin.[66] Lang metaphorically places a barrier between the camera and the open track, making clear that Jeff's freedom to act has been encroached upon by Vicki, the woman he has since met. The unobstructed shot of the train without the frame of the cabin only returns at the film's close when Jeff has broken off with Vicki and she, unbeknownst to him, has been killed. That an obstruction has been cleared from his life is metaphorically suggested by the work on the track carried out by the railwaymen to whom Jeff waves goodbye. He pulls his horn as Alec's daughter did earlier, linking himself to her, underlining that she and the life she represents are his choice. Jeff, unlike Jacques in either Zola's source novel or Renoir's adaptation, authors his own destiny and the female obstruction represented by the femme fatale Vicki is contained and destroyed. At the level of characterization, personal authorship proves less spectral in Lang's film than in either of the works it adapts.

However, like Renoir's, Lang's exploration of authorship is not confined to that of his characters. Lang uses his films to reflect upon his own authorial act, his own authorial presence, an exploration he does present in spectral terms. Whereas Renoir appeared directly in his films, Lang inserts himself surreptitiously into his own creative works. He claimed to have inserted traces of his own authorial act, close ups of his own hands in place of those of his characters throughout his filmic œuvre.[67] The shot of Jeff's hand, with its cause and effect logic in relation to the machinery of the train, could initially lead one to suspect that the inserted images of Lang's digits constitute a sign of mastery and authorship asserted by the director. However, Lang frames his approach to authorship in far more complex terms, in terms entirely in keeping with the ghostly approach of this chapter. Appearing as himself in Jean-Luc Godard's *Le Mépris* (1963), Lang, at Godard's behest, mouths a speech borrowing from a variety of sources. In the words of Tom Gunning:

> [...] this sequence of Godard's film [...] demonstrates the way a modern author (or a cinematic author: Godard as well as Lang) creates a text out of Barthes's 'fabric of quotations'. The film-maker functions less as a *scriptor* than a fashioner of palimpsests, texts written over other texts creating new meanings from the superimposition of old ones.[68]

Godard, introducing the famous shot from *M* where the chalked hand is about to be pressed onto the back of the coat of Hans Beckert, lays the following text over it: 'Seule la main qui efface peut écrire.' Hands in Lang's work bear witness to the way in which texts are fashioned using the traces of earlier authors, remaining ever haunted by their ghosts.

Lang's works may be said to be haunted on a number of levels. They are, as Gunning claims, filled with revenants:

> Indeed, we could claim that one of the master themes of Lang's films throughout his career (from *Der müde Tod* through *The Testament of Dr Mabuse* to *Fury*, *Woman in the Window* and *The Thousand Eyes of Dr Mabuse*) has been the difficulties of the return of the dead to the world of the living, the tragedy of revenants who remain in some way caught between two worlds.[69]

As Joe puts it in *Fury* (1936) when he returns to the brothers who thought him dead: 'You can't hurt a dead man and I'm dead. Everyone knows that, the whole country knows it.' Past authors do not just haunt characters in Lang's œuvre, they possess them. Lang's Dr Mabuse character, 'Lang's own *doppelgänger* as director and author who will haunt Lang for nearly the full extent of his career (from 1922 to his last film in 1960)', provides a striking example.[70] Mabuse dies in *The Testament of Dr Mabuse.* Professor Baum tries to decipher the apparently incomprehensible scribbles of the dead Mabuse; in so doing he not only becomes possessed by them, but also by their author. A superimposed image of Mabuse appears opposite Baum as he reads. It moves to merge with Baum, becoming him. Baum will subsequently become Mabuse's voice in the world of the living, transmitting his messages and authoring his actions.[71] Lang's film dramatizes very clearly the ghosts of authors past, showing the central place the resuscitation of their texts has in the framework of his corpus as a whole.

However, the pull of the future, the transformation to which texts will be subject, one of the central themes of this chapter, is also a theme enunciated in Lang's broader corpus as a consideration of *Spione/Spies* (1927–28) makes clear. As texts were lost, found and re-created in Zola's novel, in Lang's films they escape from their author and are copied into different media, re-transcribed, re-transmitted in a manner with interesting parallels for the adaptive process in which Lang participates in relation to *La Bête humaine.* In *Spies*, Lang depicts a man breaking pencils and tampering with writing booths. The film's hero then goes to the booths, and, unable to use those with the broken pencils, selects the booth seemingly left untouched, writing a message before leaving. Lang offers the viewer a shot of the cubicle's blotter, covered with illegible messages from untold hands. The hand of the anonymous man returns to lift this sheet of illegible scribbles, revealing a piece of carbon paper beneath it, a sheet bearing a clear copy of the hero's original text. This original is then, without its author's knowledge, stolen, read into a telephone, passing into different hands, beyond its original context and authorial control.[72] If Lang's films acknowledge the pull of authors past, they also underline the loss of re-transmission, the pull of the future and of transformation into subsequent media.

Lang's interest in Renoir lies specifically in notions of authorship, theft and retransmission, in the ghosts at the heart of the adaptive process. The Renoir films

Lang chooses to remake — *La Chienne* (1931), *La Bête humaine* (1938) — and the adaptations Lang himself makes of them — *Scarlet Street* (1945) and *Human Desire* (1954) — all centre on explorations of authorship, be it artistic or criminal. In *Scarlet Street*, the ghosts of Renoir's earlier film *La Chienne* are manifest. The heroine's flatmate and double, Milly (they share clothes, a flat, and previously shared a job), claims 'I ache like a dog', echoing the title Lang has changed. Lang's film centres on a bank clerk and Sunday-painter named Chris Cross. The viewer might be forgiven for taking Lang's protagonist as an authorial point of origin since his name suggests that x marks the spot, alluding to the cross that can be used in place of signatures.[73] However, Chris Cross underlines precisely the ghosts of transformation and alienation which lie at the heart of authorship. My use of the Lacanian term alienation is not accidental here, for Lang as a filmmaker was steeped in things psychoanalytic. His *The Woman in the Window* (1944) opens with his protagonist Professor Wanley giving a psychoanalytic lecture of sorts (key psychoanalytic terms appear on the blackboard). As a painter, Chris Cross copies past masters in order to train his eye, but his works are later appropriated, signed and sold to others by Kitty March, the woman he keeps, as she fabricates an authorial identity for herself with the help of her boyfriend Johnny. She passes off as her own not only his paintings, but his words, reproducing his statements on painting to the art critic Janeway in their entirety. She claims, like Chris, to 'put a line around what I feel when look at things', likens painting to 'falling in love', since 'every painting, if it's any good, is a love affair'. Chris's painting meets critical success bearing Kitty's name. He may admire his success in the reflected image of his art, but he cannot, like Lacan's specular self, possess it; it is forever alienated from him. According to Gunning, '*Scarlet Street* stands as possibly Lang's Hollywood masterpiece, partly because it offers his most complex view of the process of art-making and the identity of the artist/author'.[74] He suggests such evaluations of the artistic process are absent from Renoir's film. However, such a claim is put in question by the closing image of *La Chienne*. Whilst Lang's film ends with Chris Cross unable to paint or to kill himself, and haunted by the ghostly voices of Kitty and Johnny (he has murdered those who appropriated his authorship), Renoir's film, for all its gaiety, closes with an even more striking image of dispossessed, spectral authorship. A self-portrait by Legrand (Renoir's equivalent of Chris Cross), already stolen by Lulu and Dédé (Renoir's equivalent of Kitty and Johnny), is alienated still further from him as it is sold by an art dealer to a buyer. He neither sees nor recognizes what used to be his mirror reflection. The final image of the film depicts this haunted authorial identity which is at once his and not his pulling away from him in a car.

The theme of textual loss and transformation, of the ghostly traces of multiple authorship, is taken up on a narrative level in *Human Desire*. Texts circulate: Vicki's letter passes from her to Owens to Carl before coming back to her via Jeff. In each case the letter brings death — literal death in the cases of Owens and Vicki, metaphorical death in terms of Carl's life and Jeff's love for Vicki. The letter, like Jacques's genetic text in Zola's novel, has no original author. Vicki transcribes her husband's dictated words ('Write what I tell you to write') before misleadingly signing her name to this work authored by another. Speech proves similarly mobile as words become inhabited by the ghostly traces of other identities. Carl repeatedly coaches Vicki about what to say when she meets Owens to plead for her husband's job. As discussed earlier, Alec's words pass to the lips of Jeff as he proclaims 'That's no good Vicki'. Ironically, as their marriage crumbles, Vicki and Carl, the couple whose distance from each other has increasingly been emphasized in structural terms in the course of the film, are united in language. Both appeal to the lover leaving them 'I'll do anything you want', expressing their fear of solitude. Vicki even places Carl's language and conclusions in Jeff's mouth: 'Why don't you say it, Carl did, I'm no good.' Stories circulate and mutate in a manner even more underlined than that explored in Zola's novel. Vicki recounts five versions of her relations with Owens, incorporating various altered stories of the murder scene. Though related and containing similar details, each is different as the story mutates. The truth of its origin cannot be traced since the relationship exists in pre-textual time (both Vicki's reprisal of her relationship with Owens and his subsequent murder are kept away from the gaze of the viewer as doors are twice shut in the camera's face). Texts, be they written or spoken, in *Human Desire* shift and mutate, resonating with the spectral voices of other authors, as Zola's novel has shifted and mutated to form Lang's adaptation.

The successive incarnations of *La Bête humaine* are both peopled by a variety of authorial ghosts and explore the spectral nature of authorship itself as it shifts and mutates into new versions. Jacques is not fully author of his criminal act, for it is based on the receding ghosts of his ancestry. Zola too blurs the boundaries of his own authorship, pointing to the texts which he has borrowed from and transformed, as well as exploring the potential transformation of his authorial act into the medium of theatre. He foregrounds transformation as a narrative theme, creating a novel about replacement and displacement, which is itself replaced and displaced by Renoir's 1938 adaptation. Renoir not only renders Zola's text, but he echoes the nineteenth-century novelist's presentation of authorship as a haunted space. Renoir acknowledges the ghost of Zola even in the passages of text he has changed, making the original author both present and absent, and underlining the spectral status of his own authorial cinematic act. Renoir's text is neither fully his own, nor fully that of Zola. The authorial moments of Renoir and Zola subsequently become spectral traces in Lang's *Human Desire*. Lang's film turns away from notions of Jacques and his genetic inheritance, choosing instead to underline the character's successful authorship of his own destiny. *Human Desire* does however acknowledge and play with its own textual inheritance from both Zola and Renoir, incorporating this play into a wider problematization of notions of cinematic authorship in Lang's work, a problematization couched precisely in spectral terms. Lang's films play with the transformative powers of technology, the encryption and retransmission of messages, a play accompanied by an exploration of the shifting, mutating nature of identities and texts. This play on the replacement, displacement, transformation and authorial loss of original authorship under the influence of the pull of the future in some senses allegorizes the adaptive act. *La Bête humaine*, in all these forms, is a work peopled by the ghosts of texts past, as well as those still to come.

Notes to Chapter 5

1. This chapter stems, in part, from the following article: Kate Griffiths, 'The Ghost of the Author: Zola, Renoir and *La Bête humaine*', *Excavatio* 21: 1/2 (2006), 239–50. I am grateful to Anna Gural-Migdal for permission to reproduce aspects of the argument pursued in the article.
2. Three other cinematic adaptations inspired by Zola's novel exist: Leopoldo Carducci's *La Bête humaine* (Italy, 1918), Ludwig Wolff's *Die Bestie im Menschem* (Germany, 1920) and Daniel Tinayre's *La Bestia Humana* (Argentina, 1956).
3. Sanders, *Adaptation and Appropriation*, p. 24.
4. Roger Boussinot, *Encyclopédie du cinéma*, 2 vols (Paris: Bordas, 1980), I, 148.
5. 'Dans l'ensemble, on peut dire que Renoir a presque toujours amélioré le roman. Le milieu technique dans le film n'est pas inférieur à celui du livre, il le surclasse très souvent et la justification des personnages est bien meilleure', André Bazin, *Jean Renoir* (Paris: Ivrea, 2005), p. 63.
6. Penelope Gilliatt, *Jean Renoir: Essays, Conversations, Reviews* (New York: McGraw Hill, 1975), pp. 56–57.
7. See Michèle Lagny, 'The Fleeing Gaze: Jean Renoir's *La Bête humaine* (1938)', in *French Film: Texts and Contexts*, ed. by Susan Hayward and Ginette Vincendeau (London: Routledge, 1990), pp. 83–101.
8. 'A certaines heures, il la sentait bien cette fêlure héréditaire. Et il en venait à penser qu'il payait pour les autres... les pères, les grands-pères qui avaient bu... les générations d'ivrognes dont il était le sang gâté. Son crâne éclatait sous l'effort, dans cette angoisse d'un homme poussé à des actes où sa volonté n'était pour rien, et dont la cause en lui avait disparu' (Jean Renoir).
9. Zola describes Jacques moving and acting 'au milieu d'une sorte de grande fumée qui déformait tout' (p. 1043).
10. John Anzalone, 'Sound/Tracks: Zola, Renoir and *La Bête humaine*', *The French Review*, 62: 4 (1989), 583–89 (p. 586).
11. Martin O'Shaugnessy points out in relation to the dance, 'The choice of date is extremely ironic. Rather than signalling a new start, it shows characters whose future is shut off by their past', Martin O'Shaugnessy, *Jean Renoir* (Manchester: Manchester University Press, 2000), p. 143.
12. Renoir here is directly reflecting the shadows of Zola's text. Séverine alerts Jacques to Roubaud's presence in the novel: 'Tiens! son ombre qui passe sur le mur blanc!' (p. 1239).
13. As Jacques replaces Roubaud as murderer, Cabuche takes Jacques's space in the courtroom: 'Puis il [Jacques] sourit au second [Cabuche], l'innocent, dont il aurait dû occuper la place' (p. 1322).
14. Zola's novel utilizes precisely the vocabulary of replacement in relation to characters. Séverine appeals to Camy-Lamotte in relation to Grandmorin: 'Vous qui l'avez aimé, achevez sa bonne œuvre, remplacez-le auprès de moi' (p. 1110). Misard claims to Séverine: '[...] je suis à la disposition de Madame, et Madame peut compter que je la remplace ici comme un autre elle-même' (p. 1182).
15. Actual ghosts are comparatively rare in Zola's work. *Le Rêve* is a notable exception for it details a château haunted by the ghosts of generations of Hautecœur wives: 'Toutes revenaient, Ysabeau, Gudule, Yvonne, Austreberthe, toutes les Mortes heureuses, aimées de la mort qui leur avait épargné la vie [...] leur vol blanc emplissait le château' (Zola, *Les Rougon-Macquart*, IV: *Le Rêve* (1966), p. 866). However, metaphorical ghosts abound as living beings are described using the vocabulary of spectrality. See Kate Griffiths, 'Scribbling Ghosts: The Textual Spectres and Spectral Texts of Emile Zola', in *Possessions: Essays in French Literature, Cinema and Theory*, ed. by Julia Horn and Lynsey Russell-Watts (Bern: Peter Lang, 2003), pp. 51–65.
16. Tom Conley, *Film Hieroglyphs: Ruptures in Classical Cinema* (Minneapolis: University of Minnesota Press, 1991), pp. 145–47.
17. Marcus, *Filmmaking by the Book*, p. xi. Renoir's *La Bête humaine* forms a compelling French counterpart to Marcus's work, in an Italian context, on 'the adaptational techniques of a group of filmmakers who not only rely on literary sources, but who do so quite self-consciously, and who dramatize that self-consciousness throughout their work' (ibid., p. x). As Marcus persuasively points out, Pasolini, in adapting Boccaccio in *The Decameron* (1971), makes explicit

his controversial adaptive approach via a character engaged in an unsuccessful public reading of a Boccaccio text. In the face of his audience's displeasure, the teller throws away the book and announces 'Gentlemen, now I'll explain it Neopolitan style', to the crowd's delight. Marcus's words on this umbilical scene could just as easily refer to the umbilical poster in Renoir's film: 'This episode exemplifies what I would call an "allegory of adaptation" or an "umbilical scene" in which the film reveals the traces of its derivation from the parent text and discloses its interpretative strategy' (ibid., p. 140). Renoir is not alone, in a French context, in including such allegories of adaptation. Albert Lewin's *The Private Affairs of Bel-Ami* (1947) alters the ending of Maupassant's original work, but places testimony to that alteration in the mouth of one of its characters. See Floriane Place-Verghnes '"Il fallait brûler Maupassant": du danger d'adapter *Bel-Ami*', *Bulletin Flaubert–Maupassant*, 12 (2003), 61–84.

18. Conley, *Film Hieroglyphs*, p. xxi.
19. Ibid., p. xxix.
20. The street singers sing the following lines: 'Sois bonne, ô ma belle inconnue, / toi pour qui j'ai si souvent chanté, / ton aumône est la bienvenue, / fais-moi la charité.' They echo Legrand's hopes for kindness in Lulu and his failure, to date, to recognize her true identity. For details of the role of music in Renoir's films, see Dominique Nasta, 'Fonctions de la musique dans les films de Renoir', in *Jean Renoir: nouvelles approches*, ed. by Frank Curot (Montpellier: Université Paul Valéry, 1995), pp. 239–54.
21. Jean Renoir, *Orvet* (Paris: Gallimard, 1955).
22. Michel de Certeau, *L'Invention du quotidien* (Paris: Gallimard, 1990), p. 251.
23. Braudy, *Jean Renoir: The World of his Films*, p. 175. Braudy interestingly suggests that form mirrors content, interpreting Renoir's camera style in general precisely in terms of poaching: 'Renoir's camera is far from invisible. It is a kind of poaching camera, making its own paths through the world of his films. The early French films broke out into nature but preserved the woodenness of composition by frame, whatever the subject. Renoir's camera, on the other hand, can move into and out of a scene, exploring beyond the surface and withdrawing to show that there is more world than the frame can momentarily delimit' (ibid., p. 44).
24. Patrick McGilligan, *Cagney: The Actor as Auteur* (South Brunswick/New York: A. S. Barnes, 1975), p. 199.
25. *Arts*, 720, 29 April 1959, cited in Claude Gauteur and Ginette Vincendeau, *Jean Gabin: anatomie d'un mythe* (Paris: Nouveau Monde, 2006), p. 58.
26. Gauteur and Vincendeau, *Jean Gabin*, p. 126.
27. *Ce Matin–Le Pays*, 30 November 1949, cited in Gauteur and Vincendeau, *Jean Gabin*, p. 82.
28. René Barjavel, *Le Merle blanc* 249, 7 January 1939. Also cited in Gauteur and Vincendeau, *Jean Gabin*, p. 44.
29. The actress playing Flore (Blanchette Brunoy) could also be said to have something of a ghostly fate in Renoir's œuvre as a whole since her role in relation to the actor playing Jacques (Gabin) is reincarnated several times in different filmic contexts. In *La Bête humaine*, *Le Baron de l'écluse* (1960) and *La Marie du port* (1950) Brunoy reprises her role as a woman doomed to love and be spurned by a character played by Gabin.
30. I. M. Pacatus (pseudonym for Maxim Gorky), *Nizhegorodski Listok* (4 July 1896), cited in translated form in Grieveson and Krämer, eds, *The Silent Cinema Reader*, p. 1.
31. *New York Times* (18 April 1925), 19, 1. Also cited in Grieveson and Krämer, eds, *The Silent Cinema Reader*, p. 4.
32. Charles Musser, 'Moving Towards Fictional Narratives: Story Films Become the Dominant Product, 1903–1904', in Grieveson and Krämer, eds, *The Silent Cinema Reader*, pp. 87–102 (p. 93).
33. For further detail, see Frank Gray, 'The Kiss in the Tunnel (1899), G. A. Smith and the Emergence of the Edited Film in England', in Grieveson and Krämer, eds, *The Silent Cinema Reader*, pp. 51–62.
34. *The Era*, 30 October 1897. Also cited in Gray, 'The Kiss in the Tunnel', p. 55.
35. For further details, see Musser, 'Moving Towards Fictional Narratives', p. 94.
36. Cited in Zola, *La Bête humaine*, p. 1716.
37. Textual loss is something of a broad theme in Zola's work. The narrator of *Contes à Ninon*,

referring to the transcription of his story to paper, conceives of such an act as a dangerous one: 'Hélas! je crains de me préparer ici de grands chagrins. C'est violer le secret de nos tendresses que de confier nos causeries au vent qui passe, et les amants indiscrets sont punis en ce monde'. Zola, *Œuvres complètes*, IX: *Contes et nouvelles* (1968), p. 31. Similarly, the wind carries away the words of Angélique and her love in *Le Rêve* (p. 879). As Lacan, referring to textual dispersal in the gaze of the viewing/reading other, claims that 'une lettre c'est justement une parole qui vole [...] S'il peut y avoir une lettre volée, c'est qu'une lettre est une feuille volante', Zola's work contains images of the wind carrying away words (Jacques Lacan, *Le Séminaire de Jacques Lacan. Livre 2*, p. 232). Pascal in *Le Docteur Pascal*, conceives of his work in the following terms: 'De toute cette passion solitaire, il n'était né que des livres, du papier noirci que le vent emporterait sans doute'. Zola, *Les Rougon-Macquart*, V: *Le Docteur Pascal* (1967), p. 1047.

38. The clerk's texts are 'si bien épluchés des mots inutiles et compromettants' (p. 1093).
39. Sanders, *Adaptation and Appropriation*, p. 24.
40. Lang cited in Peter Bogdanovich, *Fritz Lang in America* (London: Studio Vista, 1967), p. 92.
41. Bogdanovich, *Fritz Lang in America*, pp. 96–97.
42. Ibid., p. 105.
43. Lang's own words on the protagonist in *M* (Hans Beckert) could also be applied to Zola's depiction of Jacques. He stated, in a 1947 interview entitled 'Why I am interested in Murder': 'I have tried to approach the murderer imaginatively to show him as a human being possessed of some demon that has driven him beyond the ordinary borderlines of human behaviour, and not the least part of whose tragedy is that by murder he never resolves his conflicts' (Lang cited in Lotte Eisner, *Fritz Lang* (New York: Da Capo Press, 1986), p. 111).
44. According to Tom Gunning, 'In both *The Death of Siegfried* and *M* the mark of fatality is inscribed on the characters' clothing, transforming them into unconscious bearers of the plot's progress, inscribed with an alphabet they cannot read, but whose consequences the audience realises.' (Tom Gunning, *The Films of Fritz Lang* (London: British Film Institute, 2000), p. 37.)
45. Robert Singer, '"At the Still Point": Framing the Naturalist Moment', in Gural-Migdal and Singer, eds, *Zola and Film*, pp. 194–206 (p. 200).
46. Jeremy G. Butler, '*Miami Vice: The Legacy of Film Noir*', in *Film Noir Reader*, ed. by Alain Silver and James Ursini (New York: Limelight Editions, 1996), pp. 289–305 (p. 290).
47. Gunning, *The Films of Fritz Lang*, p. 301.
48. Charles Higham and Joel Greenberg, '*Noir* Cinema', in Silver and Ursini, eds, *Film Noir Reader*, pp. 27–35 (p. 27).
49. Karen Hollinger, '*Film Noir*, Voice-Over, and the Femme Fatale', in Silver and Ursini, eds, *Film Noir Reader*, pp. 243–60 (p. 244).
50. 'As Renoir is humanism, Lang is determinism. As Renoir is concerned with the plight of his characters, Lang is obsessed with the structure of the trap.' Andrew Sarris, 'Films', *The Village Voice*, 7 December 1967. Also cited in Eisner, *Fritz Lang*, p. 339.
51. Gunning, *The Films of Fritz Lang*, p. xii.
52. Lang cited in Bogdanovich, *Fritz Lang in America*, p. 35.
53. Cousins, 'Was Judas a Woman?', pp. 115–16.
54. Eisner, *Fritz Lang*, pp. 338–39.
55. Lang cited in Bogdanovich, *Fritz Lang in America*, p. 92.
56. Ibid., pp. 95–96.
57. Stephen Mamber, 'The American Films of Fritz Lang', *Daily Bruin*, 15 October 1969. Also cited in Eisner, *Fritz Lang*, p. 159.
58. Lang cited in Bogdanovich, *Fritz Lang in America*, p. 96.
59. The signature of the producer can be detected in one specific scene transition. As has already been suggested, Jerry Wald was impressed by what he saw as the sexual imagery of trains and tunnels in Renoir's film, an imagery by which Lang was far from convinced. Significantly, as Vicki and Jeff travel to their illicit rendezvous in Jean's flat in the city, the scene closes with the train entering a tunnel and the subsequent scene opens with a post-coital situation in the flat.
60. Gunning, *The Films of Fritz Lang*, p. 10.
61. 'Light is never in Lang used merely decoratively, atmospherically, but always psychologically to

convey emotional states.' John Russell Taylor, 'The Nine Lives of Dr Mabuse', *Sight and Sound*, Winter 1961–62. Also cited in Eisner, *Fritz Lang*, p. 390.

62. Janey Place and Lowell Peterson, 'Some Visual Motifs of *Film Noir*', in Silver and Ursini, eds, *Film Noir Reader*, pp. 65–76 (p. 68).
63. James Damico describes the archetypical Noir femme fatale, offering a definition that fits Vicki: 'Either because he is fated to do so or by chance, or because he has been hired for a job specifically associated with her, a man whose experience of life has left him sanguine and often bitter meets a not-innocent woman of similar outlook to whom he is sexually and fatally attracted. Through this attraction, either because the woman induces him to it, or because it is the natural result of their relationship, the man comes to cheat, attempt to murder, or actually murder a second man to whom the woman is unhappily or unwillingly attached [...], an act which often leads to the woman's betrayal of the protagonist, but which in any event brings about the sometimes metaphoric, but usually literal destruction of the woman, the man to whom she is attached, and frequently the protagonist himself'. James Damico, '*Film Noir*: A Modest Proposal', in Silver and Ursini, eds, *Film Noir Reader*, pp. 95–105 (p. 103).
64. Bogdanovich, *Fritz Lang in America*, pp. 6–7.
65. Lang cited in Eisner, *Fritz Lang*, p. 147.
66. Much has been made of the barriers and framing devices used in film noir to underline notions of entrapment in relation to characters. Place and Peterson, writing on general traits of film noir claim: 'Claustrophobic framing devices such as doors, windows, stairways, metal bed frames, or simply shadows separate the character from other characters [...]. And objects seem to push their way into the foreground of the frame to assume more power than the people' (Place and Peterson, 'Some Visual Motifs of *Film Noir*', p. 68).
67. Gunning writes: 'whereas Hitchcock's appearances emphasized his highly recognizable figure, Lang's appearances remain anonymous. He appears not as a face, or a caricature silhouette, but in close-ups of hands, standing in for actors playing characters in his films. Although we cannot identify with certainty which of the close-ups of hands in Lang's films (and there are many of them) actually show his own hand (presuming his anecdote is true), it is not unlikely that it is actually Lang's hand which is marked with chalk in *M*'. Gunning, *The Films of Fritz Lang*, p. 2. Moreover, Eisner identifies the whistle in *M*, the whistle of the deranged child killer as belonging to Lang: 'During the shooting, Lorre confessed that he could not whistle; it would have to be dubbed into the sound track. Others tried, including Thea von Harbou and the film's editor, but the results were somehow not exactly what was needed. Finally, Lang himself did the whistle. For once his being non-musical served him well: the off-key, tuneless whistle exactly fitted the unbalanced character of the murderer.' (Eisner, *Fritz Lang*, p. 124).
68. Gunning, *The Films of Fritz Lang*, p. 6.
69. Ibid., p. 38.
70. Ibid., p. 96.
71. Ibid, p. 150.
72. Ibid., p. 140.
73. Critics have offered alternative interpretations of Lang's punning use of his protagonist's name. 'For most of the film, the name Chris Cross has evoked the idea of exchange, particularly all the exchanges from which Chris is excluded, the exchange of paintings without his name being involved, his inability to exchange his wife for Kitty, in spite of his deception of Homer Higgins.' (Gunning, *The Films of Fritz Lang*, p. 334.)
74. Ibid., p. 324.

CONCLUSION

Cinematic adaptations, more often than not, get a bad press. At best they are viewed as faithful copies of a textual original, at worst, inferior copies, betrayals of that textual original. However, this book has aimed to show that the terms of this debate, the concepts of textual original and a singular subsequent copy, are not always sufficient to encompass the complexity of the relationship of some of Zola's texts with certain of the cinematic versions subsequently made of them. As an author, Zola destabilizes notions of origin in and through a number of his texts.

Zola explores the problematic personal origins of specific characters. In *L'Œuvre*, painted copy replaces the original model from which it was created as Christine's portrait takes her space in reality, a space which it always already occupied. The copy precedes and supersedes Christine, rather than merely depicting her. Nana, a heroine so imitated in the novel bearing her name, reveals herself not as a point of origin but as a copy as she constantly performs a plethora of parts, mythical identities and stereotypes on stage and off. In *La Bête humaine*, Jacques's actions cannot be traced to his own identity and will as a point of origin, but are rather indebted to or adapted from the genetic texts of an ever-receding series of ancestors.

Through certain of his texts, Zola probes notions of literary origin. *La Curée* explores its own status as a dubious adaptation of Racine's *Phèdre*. As Racine's play is a text which not only adapts previous adaptations, but gestures back to the mutating labyrinthine myth of Phaedra which lies somewhere behind them, so Zola's novel explores a series of superimposed texts not only in his heroine's mind but also via his own authorial intertexts. Nor is *La Curée* the only one of Zola's novels which explores the author's relationship with the texts lying behind some of his pages. *La Terre*, a novel precisely about the act of inheritance, explores, albeit in a manner far more indirect than the textual relations of *La Curée*, its own textual inheritance from another eminently traceable text: Shakespeare's *King Lear*. Zola borrows both from other texts and from other genres, exploring the porous boundary between the written word and the world and methods of art in *L'Œuvre*. He claims to translate both the methods of certain artists and the reality of their artistic *milieu*. However, in keeping with Zola's questioning of origins, the original reality which *L'Œuvre* seeks to translate is one which cannot ultimately be accessed.

If Zola at times adapts earlier texts and realities in his novels, adaptations of those novels might be considered as adaptations of adaptations, copies of what are already copies. As this monograph has demonstrated, specific cinematic adaptations of Zola's texts move to explore their status as adaptations, evaluating their own authorial act. Jean Renoir's silent adaptation of *Nana* evaluates its status as a truncation of

Zola's text, gesturing towards what it cannot show, be it for reasons of length or acceptability. An increased level of self-reflexivity may be detected in Renoir's subsequent adaptation of *La Bête humaine* as the director explores his position as an artistic poacher of Zola's text. Renoir signals, more explicitly this time, what he has changed. In making present the dénouement he has removed, Renoir inserts the ghost of Zola's authorial identity in his cinematic images. Like Renoir, Edouard Molinaro dramatizes the limitations of his adaptation of Zola's work. In inserting a scene which both acknowledges and crops the theatrical context of Zola's original, Molinaro in *Nadia Coupeau, dite Nana*, asks his viewer to consider the filmmaker's adaptive act. Nor are Renoir and Molinaro the sole directors to explore their own adaptive act in relation to Zola; they are joined by Roger Vadim. This New Wave director's version of *La Curée*, though frequently maligned, intriguingly examines its own status as a warped reflection of Zola's text via the image of a kaleidoscopic mirror. Moreover, as Zola explored authorship as a palimpsest in *La Curée*, so Vadim does likewise, teasingly inserting a variety of competing intertexts whose receding origins he encourages his viewer to trace. He adapts both Zola's novel and a number of the texts behind it. In contrast, Fritz Lang, in *Human Desire*, adapts both Zola's novel and the images of certain of the adaptations made from it. These filmmakers thus enter into something of a dialogue with the Zola novels they adapt, a dialogue about the nature of authorship and origin. As Zola assesses the potential, limitations and borrowed origins of his own authorship, so a number of the filmmakers adapting him do likewise.

Whilst the introduction to this work gestured towards the sheer scope of adaptations which Zola's texts have spawned, my conclusion will close by focusing once more on the most recent staging of an adaptation of his works: Marianne Elliott's 2006/07 production at the National Theatre London of Nicholas Wright's adaptation of Zola's own theatrical adaptation of the novel *Thérèse Raquin*. The layers of adaptation behind this adaptation combat the linear, one-way dialectic of copy and original, a dialectic this book has sought to question in relation to Zola and his work. In a manner wholly consistent with my exploration of Zola's authorship, Wright and Elliott's adaptation plays with the porous interface between genres. It weaves itself with threads and intertexts drawn from a variety of media.

Various layers of authorship inform Wright's adaptation. According to the printed edition's legal material, 'Nicholas Wright has asserted his right to be identified as the author of this work'.[1] Yet, Wright's subsequent preface points to Zola as the textual owner of the work: 'The play is his [Zola's].'[2] Wright situates himself as restoring Zola to himself, claiming: 'Zola's ruthlessness in forcing his first important novel into theatrical form ("a Procustean bed" as he called it) was sometimes harsher than it needed to be [...]. So some details of the novel have been restored.'[3] However, origins in the novel lying behind these various layers of adaptation and re-adaptation are themselves as problematic as those in the texts studied in the course of this volume.

At the level of characterization, the origins of Thérèse are shrouded in mystery. Madame Raquin's brother, a character about whom the reader knows very little, deposits Thérèse as a child in his aunt's arms in a passage with significantly few names: 'Sa sœur l'interrogea à peine sur cette fille qu'il lui donnait. Elle sut vaguement que la chère petite était née à Oran, et qu'elle avait pour mère une femme indigène d'une grande beauté' (p. 620). Madame Raquin's brother, the sole means to clarify this mystery, dies soon after and thereafter Thérèse can only sense, but not verify, the inherited text of her genetic origin: 'On m'a dit que ma mère était fille d'un chef de tribu, en Afrique; j'ai souvent songé à elle, j'ai compris que je lui appartenais par le sang et les instincts' (p. 549).

Zola's novel itself inherits from a variety of previous texts, adapting them to create itself. Russell Cousins points out the complex textual origins of the novel. *Thérèse Raquin* is a reworking by Zola of a short story he had published in *Le Figaro* on 24 December 1866, 'Un mariage d'amour'.[4] However, this story itself stems, by Zola's own admission, from *La Vénus de Gordes*, serialized in the same paper, written by Adolphe Belot and Ernest Daudet. Introducing 'Un mariage d'amour', Zola signals the texts from which he has created his work as well as the novel which he will subsequently create from it:

> Le roman que publie *Le Figaro* et qui obtient un si légitime succès d'émotion me rappelle une terrible histoire de passion et de souffrance. Je vais la conter en quelques mots, me réservant d'écrire un jour le volume qu'elle demanderait.[5]

Cousins explores certain of the adaptations, theatrical and cinematic, triggered by Zola's novel, citing Marcel Maurette's 1947 version and Raymond Rouleau's 1981 stage adaptation and Marcel Carné's 1953 film adaptation amongst others. These acts of adaptation mirror in part the acts of adaptation leading to the creation of the novel itself. As Cousins puts it, 'If in the twentieth century other writers have created alternative versions of Zola's fiction, whether for the stage or for the screen, they are continuing in that tradition to which the author himself subscribed.'[6]

As questions of adaptation are key to the genesis of Zola's text in both its novelistic and theatrical incarnations, so too Elliott's production of Wright's play explores its status as an adaptation woven with a variety of influences from different genres. The performance draws upon the structures of art and cinema. Elliott's production is first and foremost a work of the theatre and its theatrical inheritance stems not only from Zola's adaptation of *Thérèse Raquin* but from the novel itself, a novel which explores notions of theatre both at the level of content and structure. The theme of performance lies at the heart of the plot as Thérèse is repeatedly depicted as a consummate actress. Initially she plays the role of obedient servant, directed by Madame Raquin. The narrative claims: 'Thérèse [...] était obligée de jouer un rôle. Elle le jouait à la perfection, grâce à l'hypocrisie savante que lui avait donné son éducation' (p. 620). Zola depicts her as a 'bonne comédienne' (p. 553). Russell Cousins points out the theatrical structures woven into the novel's scenery. As Madame Raquin attempts with her hand to write her denunciation of the murderers, her digits appear as if in a spotlight: 'Thérèse [...] regardait la main de sa tante, blafarde sous la lumière crue de la lampe, comme une main vengeresse' (p. 638). The closing image of the dead lovers appears in a similarly theatrical light: 'Les cadavres restèrent toute la nuit sur le carreau de la salle à manger, tordus, vautrés, éclairés de lueurs jaunâtres par les clartés de la lampe que l'abat-jour jetait sur eux' (p. 667).[7]

Wright's adaptation does foreground Zola's theme of the theatrical. Thérèse and Laurent, all passion between them dead, on their wedding night act in a vain attempt to reignite it. They repeat the words from their earlier romantic rendezvous before Thérèse breaks off: 'What's the good of acting? We can't even convince ourselves'.[8] However, Wright and Elliott's theatrical piece is also clearly influenced by art. Charles Spencer, bemoaning the lack of sensuality between the performance's hero and heroine (played by Charlotte Emmerson and Ben Daniels), writes: 'The sexiest scene, in fact, is when we voyeuristically watch a solitary Emmerson silently washing herself in an image nicked straight from a Degas painting.'[9] Turned away from the audience, Thérèse washes herself naked from the waist up at the start of Act II, metaphorically cleansing herself of the sin of Camille's murder. The image, framed like a picture by the entrance to this room within a room, appears behind a gauzy screen, adding an impressionist feel, wholly consonant with Zola's artistic interests, to this evocative tableau. Via this addition to Zola's text, Emmerson and Wright emphasize the intertextual fabric of their piece. However, this addition also echoes the artistic bent of Zola's source novel. Zola presents himself as an artist in his post-publication preface to the novel: 'Je me suis trouvé dans le cas de ces peintres qui copient des nudités', claiming to think 'uniquement à mettre cette femme sur sa toile dans la vérité de ses formes et de ses colorations'.[10] Moreover, in the novel, Camille's portrait not only proves key to the action, but the language of artistry and the techniques of painting infiltrate Zola's narrative. Camille's portrait seeps beyond the edges of its canvas infiltrating the novel as a whole as it not only depicts Camille, but instead Camille becomes the artistic copy made of him, his drowned body coming to mirror the portrait previously painted of him: 'Le portrait était ignoble, d'un gris sale, avec de larges plaques violacées. [...] Et le visage de Camille ressemblait à la face verdâtre d'un noyé; le dessin grimaçant convulsionnait les traits' (p. 546). Laurent will later mistake this portrait for the ghost of Camille as he appeared in the morgue:

> L'effroi lui faisait voir le tableau tel qu'il était, ignoble, mal bâti, boueux, montrant sur un fond noir une face grimaçante de cadavre. Son œuvre l'étonnait et l'écrasait par sa laideur atroce; il y avait surtout les deux yeux blancs flottant dans les orbites molles et jaunâtres qui lui rappelaient exactement les yeux pourris du noyé de la Morgue. (p. 610)

However, Wright and Elliott's adaptation not only references its intertextual relationship with art contemporaneous with Zola, it also borrows compellingly, albeit anachronistically in a Zolian context, from the techniques of modern cinema. As Camille shakes the box of dominoes above his head to begin what will be his last game, the theatrical action advances in a series of jerky freeze frames as characters hold frozen positions before being swallowed by darkness and re-appearing milliseconds later, their movements a few degrees further advanced. The violence of these pseudo freeze-frame shots and their unsettling impact perhaps replaces that of the murder the performance does not show, the murder which takes place implicitly in the ellipsis between one act and the next. These theatrical jump cuts are used again in the production's depiction of the first night of the lover's marriage. Zola's novel makes clear that the lives of Thérèse and Laurent disintegrate, referencing the ashes of their passion and life: 'Tous deux s'avouaient avec terreur que leur passion était morte, qu'ils avaient tué leurs désirs en tuant Camille. Le feu se mourait doucement; un grand braisier rose luisait sur les cendres' (p. 610). However, Elliott references this disintegration by borrowing the techniques of cinema. Laurent and Thérèse appear in a series of frozen stances, sewn together discontinuously (the shots do not flow into each other) in a manner which not only, as Matt Woolf puts it, reveals 'the now-married lovers in all their psychic grief', but also deliberately disrupts the flow of the theatrical performance.[11] This cinematic borrowing jars the audience's theatrical experience, abruptly pointing the audience to the insertion of another medium: film.[12]

Elliott's production, with its borrowings from a variety of texts and media underlines the way in which, in a Zolian context, adaptation is not always a linear, one-way process from A to B, the simple transformation of an original novel into a different form which loses and betrays some of that original. A selection of Zola's novels destabilizes notions of origin on a variety of levels. At the level of characterization, characters have origins which cannot always be fixed. At the level of plot, works of art do not always allow access to the real originals to which they point. At the level of his own authorship, Zola engages with the palimpsest that is his own text, with the variety of works and media informing his authorship. To adapt certain Zola texts is, in some senses, to adapt works which ask the reader to engage with questions of authorship, originality and adaptation. A variety of the cinematic adaptations studied in the course of this volume engage precisely with such questions, creating self-reflexive films which dramatize and assess the very act of their own adaptation.

Notes to the Conclusion

1. *Thérèse Raquin: A Play by Emile Zola dramatized by Nicholas Wright* (London: Nick Herne Books, 2006).
2. Ibid., p. x.
3. Ibid., p. x.
4. Cousins, *Zola: Thérèse Raquin*, p. 9.
5. Ibid., p. 9.
6. Ibid., p. 84. Moreover, Claude Schumacher situates the novel as tapping into the labyrinthine series of myths surrounding the Phèdre intertext this book has explored in reading *La Curée*. Commenting on Thérèse's fascination with Laurent's neck and smell, Schumacher writes: 'The connotation is unmistakeable: Thérèse, like Phaedra's mother Pasiphea, is unnaturally attracted to the beast and, should she succumb, a tragedy would inevitably ensue', Claude Schumacher, *Zola: Thérèse Raquin* (Glasgow: University of Glasgow French and German Publications, 1990), p. 16. He continues, 'Zola was fascinated by Racine's tragedy and the fate of Phèdre is not irrelevant in our reading of Thérèse's destiny: a similar sexual curse destroys them both' (ibid., p. 55).
7. For an analysis of the novel's narrative structure and its interaction with classical tragedy, see Cousins, *Zola: Thérèse Raquin*, pp. 40–50.
8. *Thérèse Raquin: A Play by Emile Zola dramatized by Nicholas Wright*, p. 54.
9. Charles Spencer, 'Dim Shadows of Zola's Hellish Vision', *Daily Telegraph*, 15 November 2006.
10. Cited in Zola, *Œuvres complètes*, I: *Premiers romans*, p. 520.
11. Matt Woolf, 'Thérèse Raquin', <http://london.broadway.com/story/id/3004722> [accessed 25 July 2007].

12. Claude Schumacher sees the novel itself in cinematic terms at points. Describing the way in which the novel revolves around Thérèse's bed, he likens the journey to this bed as an 'extended travelling shot.' (Schumacher, *Zola: Thérèse Raquin*, p. 53.)

BIBLIOGRAPHY

ANTOINE, ANDRÉ, *Mes Souvenirs sur le Théâtre Libre* (Paris: Arthème Fayard, 1921)

ANZALONE, JOHN, 'Sound/Tracks: Zola, Renoir and *La Bête humaine*', *The French Review* 62: 4 (1989), 583–89

AUBERY, PIERRE, 'Zola peintre et la littérature', in GUIEU AND HILTON, eds, *Emile Zola and the Arts*, pp. 1–8

BAGULEY, DAVID, 'Histoire et mythe dans *Son Excellence Eugène Rougon*', *Cahiers naturalistes*, 56 (1982), 46–60

——'Le Réalisme grotesque et mythique de *La Terre*', *Cahiers naturalistes*, 61 (1987), 5–14

——'Zola, The Novelist(s)', in LETHBRIDGE AND KEEFE, eds, *Zola and the Craft of Fiction*, pp. 15–27

——*Napoleon III and His Regime: An Extravaganza* (Baton Rouge: Louisiana State University Press, 2000)

——'*Riduttore, Traditore?* On Screening Zola', *Excavatio*, 21 (2006), 198–212

——ED., *La Curée de Zola ou 'La Vie à outrance'* (Paris: Sedes, 1987)

BAKKER, B. H., ed., *Emile Zola: Correspondance*, 10 vols (Montréal: Les Presses de l'Université de Montréal; Paris: CNRS, 1978–95)

BARRETT, MARIE-THÉRÈSE, '*Le Ventre de Paris*, Claude Lantier and Realist Themes of Food and Markets in Seventeenth- and Nineteenth-Century Paintings', in GUIEU AND HILTON, eds, *Emile Zola and the Arts*, pp. 47–54

BARTHES, ROLAND, *Mythologies* (Paris: Seuil, 1957)

BASILIO, KELLY, 'Naturalisme zolien et impressionnisme: le rôle de la métonymie', *Cahiers naturalistes*, 66 (1992), 83–90

BAZIN, ANDRÉ, *Jean Renoir* (Paris: Ivrea, 2005)

BECKER, COLETTE 'Illusion et réalité: la métaphore du théâtre dans *La Curée*', in BAGULEY, ed., *La Curée de Zola*, pp. 119–28

BEIZER, JANET, 'Uncovering *Nana*: The Courtesan's New Clothes', *L'Esprit créateur*, 25 (1985), 45–56

BELLALOU, GAËL, '*Nadia Coupeau, dite Nana*: A Modern Adaptation of Zola's Eponymous Work', *Bulletin of the Emile Zola Society*, 30 (2004), 16–22

BERTHIER, PHILIPPE, 'Hôtel Saccard: état des lieux', in BAGULEY, ed., *La Curée de Zola*, pp. 107–18

BEST, JANET, *Expérimentation et adaptation: essai sur la méthode naturaliste d'Emile Zola* (Paris: José Corti, 1986)

——'Espace de la perversion et perversion de l'espace: la génération du récit dans *La Curée*', *Cahiers naturalistes*, 63 (1989), 109–15

BILLINGTON, MICHAEL, 'Thérèse Raquin', *Guardian*, 15 November 2006, <arts.guardian.co.uk> [accessed 24 July 2007]

BLANCHOT, MAURICE, *La Part du feu* (Paris: Gallimard, 1949)

BLOOM, HAROLD, *The Anxiety of Influence: A Theory of Poetry* (Oxford: Oxford University Press, 1973)

BLUESTONE, GEORGE, *Novels into Film* (Berkeley/London: University of California Press, 1957)

BOGDANOVICH, PETER, *Fritz Lang in America* (London: Studio Vista, 1967)
BORIE, JEAN, *Zola et les mythes* (Paris: Seuil, 1971)
BOUSSINOT, ROGER, *Encyclopédie du cinéma*, 2 vols (Paris: Bordas, 1980)
BRADY, PATRICK, *L'Œuvre de Emile Zola: roman sur les arts, manifeste, autobiographie, roman à clef* (Geneva: Droz, 1967)
BRAUDY, LEO, *Jean Renoir: The World of His Films* (London: Robson, 1977)
BRIGGS-LYNCH, ELIZABETH, 'Manet's *Nana*: The Connection with Zola's *L'Assommoir* and *Nana*', in GUIEU and HILTON, eds, *Emile Zola and the Arts*, pp. 9–14
BROOKS, PETER, *Body Work: Objects of Desire in Modern Narrative* (Cambridge, MA: Harvard University Press, 1993)
BUSQUE, ALICE-ANNE, 'Le Regard-caméra d'Emile Zola dans *Thérèse Raquin*', in WARREN, ed., *Zola et le cinéma*, pp. 177–94
BUTLER, JEREMY G., '*Miami Vice*: *The Legacy of Film Noir*', in SILVER AND URSINI, eds, *Film Noir Reader*, pp. 289–305
BUTLER, RONNIE, *Zola: La Terre* (London: Grant & Cutler, 1984)
CAPITANIO, SARAH, 'L'Hypertextualité chez Zola: le cas de *La Curée*', *Cahiers naturalistes*, 68 (1994), 49–62
CARTER, LAWSON A., *Zola and the Theater* (New Haven, CT: Yale University Press; Paris: Presses Universitaires de France, 1963)
CERTEAU, MICHEL DE, *L'Invention du quotidien* (Paris: Gallimard, 1990)
CHOTHIA, JEAN, *André Antoine* (Cambridge: Cambridge University Press, 1991)
CLARK, ROGER, *Zola: Nana* (London: Grant & Cutler, 2004)
COLLIER, PETER, 'Valéry and Rodin: Orpheus Returning', in COLLIER AND LETHBRIDGE, eds, *Artistic Relations*, pp. 278–90
——, and ROBERT LETHBRIDGE, eds, *Artistic Relations: Literature and the Visual Arts in Nineteenth-Century France* (New Haven, CT: Yale University Press, 1994)
CONLEY, TOM, *Film Hieroglyphs: Ruptures in Classical Cinema* (Minneapolis: University of Minnesota Press, 1991)
COUSINS, RUSSELL, *Zola: Thérèse Raquin* (London: Grant & Cutler, 1992)
——'Refracting Zola; The Cinematic Prisms of René Clément and Roger Vadim' *Bulletin of the Emile Zola Society*, 7 (1994), 14–22
——'Zola and the Cinema: Early Screen Versions of *Germinal*', in POLLARD, ed., *Emile Zola Centenary Colloquium, 1893–1993*, pp. 113–26
——'Adapting Zola for TV: The Example of Jacques Rouffio's *L'Argent*', *Excavatio*, 12 (1999), 153–61
——'Was Judas a Woman? Re-inventing Zola for the Cinema', in THOMPSON, ed., *New Approaches to Zola*, pp. 111–20
——'Antoine's Version of *La Terre*: An Experiment in Naturalist Cinema', in GURAL-MIGDAL and SINGER, eds, *Zola and Film*, pp. 15–26
CUROT, FRANK, ed., *Jean Renoir: Nouvelles approches* (Montpellier: Université Paul Valéry, 1995)
DAMICO, JAMES, '*Film Noir*: A Modest Proposal', in SILVER and URSINI, eds, *Film Noir Reader*, pp. 95–105
DARROW, MARGARET H., *Revolution in the House: Family, Class, and Inheritance in Southern France, 1775–1825* (Princeton, NJ: Princeton University Press, 1989)
DAVIS, COLIN, *Haunted Subjects: Deconstruction, Psychoanalysis and the Return of the Dead* (Basingstoke: Palgrave Macmillan, 2007)
DERRIDA, JACQUES, *Mal d'archive* (Paris: Galilée, 1995)
DESFOUGÈRES, ANNE-MARIE, '*La Curée*: roman et dramaturgie classique', in BAGULEY, ed., *La Curée de Zola*, pp. 5–14
DEZALAY, AUGUSTE, '"La Nouvelle Phèdre" de Zola ou les mésaventures d'un personnage tragique', *Travaux de linguistique et de littérature*, 9: 2 (1971), 121–34

——*L'Opéra des Rougon-Macquart: essai de rythmologie romanesque* (Paris: Klincksieck, 1983)
——'Déstruction et sacrilège chez Zola', in BAGULEY, ed., *La Curée de Zola*, pp. 195–201
DOUSTEYSSIER-KHOZE, CATHERINE, *Zola et la littérature naturaliste en parodies* (Paris: Eurédit, 2004)
DUFFY, LARRY, *Le Grand Transit Moderne: Mobility, Modernity and French Naturalist Fiction* (Amsterdam/New York: Rodopi, 2005)
EISENSTEIN, S. M., 'Literature and Cinema: Reply to a Questionnaire', in *S. M. Eisenstein. Selected Works, Volume One: Writings, 1922–1934*, ed. and trans. by Richard Taylor (London: British Film Institute, 1988), pp. 95–99
EISNER, LOTTE, *Fritz Lang* (New York: Da Capo Press, 1986)
ELLIOTT, KAMILLA, *Rethinking the Novel/Film Debate* (Cambridge/New York: Cambridge University Press, 2003)
FERNANDEZ-ZOÏLA, ADOLFO, 'Le Système écriture-peinture et le figural dans *L'Œuvre*', *Cahiers naturalistes*, 66 (1992), 91–103
FRYDLAND, MAURICE, *Roger Vadim* (Paris: Seghers, 1963)
GAUTEUR, CLAUDE and GINETTE VINCENDEAU, *Jean Gabin: anatomie d'un mythe* (Paris: Nouveau Monde, 2006)
GENETTE, GÉRARD, *Palimpsestes: la littérature au second degré* (Paris: Seuil, 1982)
GÉRARD, ALBERT S., 'Zola's *La Curée* and Racine's *Phèdre*', in *Narrative Ironies*, ed. by Raymond A. Prier and Gerald Gillespie (Amsterdam/Atlanta: Rodopi, 1997), pp. 207–22
GIDDINGS, ROBERT, and ERICA SHEEN, eds, *The Classic Novel: From Page to Screen* (Manchester: Manchester University Press, 2000)
GILLIATT, PENELOPE, *Jean Renoir: Essays, Conversations, Reviews* (New York: McGraw Hill, 1975)
GOLSAN, KATHERINE, 'From Theater to Cinema: Jean Renoir's Adaptation of *Nana*', in GURAL-MIGDAL AND SINGER, eds, *Zola and Film*, pp. 62–68
GOODKIN, RICHARD E., ed., *Autour de Racine: Studies in Intertextuality* (New Haven, CT: Yale University Press, 1989)
GRAND-CARTERET, JOHN, *Zola en images* (Paris: Juven, 1908)
GRAY, FRANK, 'The Kiss in the Tunnel (1899), G. A. Smith and the Emergence of the Edited Film in England', in GRIEVESON and KRÄMER, eds, *The Silent Cinema Reader*, pp. 51–62
GRIEVESON, LEE, and PETER KRÄMER, eds, *The Silent Cinema Reader* (London/New York: Routledge, 2004)
GRIFFITHS, KATE, 'Scribbling Ghosts: The Textual Spectres and Spectral Texts of Emile Zola', in HORN AND RUSSELL-WATTS, eds, *Possessions*, pp. 51–65
——'Hunt the Author: Zola, Vadim and *La Curée*', *Studies in European Cinema* 2: 1 (2005), 7–17
——'Descartes and Lacan: Print and the Subject of Citation', *New Zealand Journal of French Studies*, 27 (2006), 16–28
——'The Ghost of the Author: Zola, Renoir and *La Bête humaine*', *Excavatio*, 21: 1/2 (2006), 239–50
GUIEU, JEAN-MAX, *Le Théâtre Lyrique d'Emile Zola* (Paris: Fischbacher, 1983)
——, and ALISON HILTON, eds, *Emile Zola and the Arts* (Washington, DC: Georgetown University Press, 1988)
GUNNING, TOM, *The Films of Fritz Lang* (London: British Film Institute, 2000)
——'From the Opium Den to the Theatre of Morality: Moral Discourse and the Film Process in Early American Cinema', in GRIEVESON and KRÄMER, eds, *The Silent Cinema Reader*, pp. 145–54
GURAL-MIGDAL, ANNA, and ROBERT SINGER, eds, *Zola and Film: Essays in the Art of Adaptation* (Jefferson, NC: McFarland, 2005)
HARKNESS, NIGEL, *Men of their Words: The Poetics of Masculinity in George Sand's Fiction* (Oxford: Legenda, 2007)

HARROW, SUSAN, *La Curée* (Glasgow: University of Glasgow French and German Publications, 1998)

HARVEY, LAWRENCE E., 'The Cycle Myth in *La Terre* of Zola', *Philological Quarterly*, 38 (1959), 89–95

HAYWARD, SUSAN, and GINETTE VINCENDEAU, eds, *French Film: Texts and Contexts* (London: Routledge, 1990)

HERTZ, HENRI, 'Emile Zola, témoin de la vérité', *Europe*, 30 (1952), 83–84

HIGHAM, CHARLES, and JOEL GREENBERG, '*Noir* Cinema', in SILVER and URSINI, eds, *Film Noir Reader*, pp. 27–35

HOLLINGER, KAREN, '*Film Noir*, Voice-Over, and the Femme Fatale', in SILVER and URSINI, eds, *Film Noir Reader*, pp. 243–60

HORN, JULIA, and LYNSEY RUSSELL-WATTS, eds, *Possessions: Essays in French Literature, Cinema and Theory* (Bern: Peter Lang, 2003)

HOWARD, HEATHER, 'Staging the Courtesan: Taking Zola's Nana to the Movies', in GURAL-MIGDAL and SINGER, eds, *Zola and Film*, pp. 45–61

IRIGARAY, LUCE, *Speculum: de l'autre femme* (Paris: Minuit, 1974)

JEAN, JOAN DE, 'Sappho, c'est moi, selon Racine: Coming of Age in Neo-Classical Theater' in GOODKIN, ed., *Autour de Racine*, pp. 3–20

JULLIEN, DOMINIQUE, 'Intertextuality as Labyrinth: The Presence of Racine in Michel Butor's *L'Emploi du temps*', in GOODKIN, ed., *Autour de Racine*, pp. 108–24

KLOSS, WILLIAM, 'Zola and the Old Masters', in GUIEU and HILTON, eds, *Emile Zola and the Arts*, pp. 35–45

KUBLER, CORINNE, 'Intertextualités zoliennes', *Cahiers naturalistes*, 63 (1989), 169–81

LACAN, JACQUES, *Ecrits* (Paris: Seuil, 1966)

—— *Le Séminaire. Livre 2* (Paris: Seuil, 1978)

—— *Le Séminaire. Livre 3* (Paris: Seuil, 1981)

LAGNY, MICHÈLE, 'The Fleeing Gaze: Jean Renoir's *La Bête humaine* (1938)', in HAYWARD and VINCENDEAU, eds, *French Film*, pp. 83–101

LECOMTE-HILMY, ANNE, 'L'Artiste de tempérament chez Zola et devant le public: essai d'analyse lexicologique et sémiologique', in GUIEU and HILTON, eds, *Emile Zola and the Arts*, pp. 85–99

LEDUC-ADINE, JEAN-PIERRE, 'Paris et l'ordre spatial dans *L'Œuvre*', in GUIEU and HILTON, eds, *Emile Zola and the Arts*, pp. 165–75

LEGOUIS, EMILE, '*La Terre* de Zola et *Le Roi Lear*', *Révue de la littérature comparée*, 27 (1953), 417–27

LEMARIÉ, YANNICK, '*Nana*, un film de Dorothy Arzner', *Cahiers naturalistes*, 75 (2001), 243–54

LETHBRIDGE, ROBERT, 'Zola et Haussmann: une expropriation littéraire', in BAGULEY, ed., *La Curée de Zola*, pp. 85–96

—— 'Manet's Textual Frames', in COLLIER and LETHBRIDGE, eds, *Artistic Relations*, pp. 144–58

—— 'La Pot-bouille des genres: adultération et originalité chez Zola', *Cahiers naturalistes*, 74 (2000), 17–32

——, and TERRY KEEFE, eds, *Zola and the Craft of Fiction* (Leicester: Leicester University Press, 1990)

LÉVI-STRAUSS, CLAUDE, *Mythologiques. Le Cru et le cuit* (Paris: Plon, 1964)

LEVITAN, WILLIAM, 'Seneca in Racine' in GOODKIN, ed., *Autour de Racine*, pp. 185–210

MCFARLANE, BRIAN, *Novel to Film: An Introduction to the Theory of Adaptation* (Oxford: Clarendon Press, 1996)

MCGILLIGAN, PATRICK, *Cagney: The Actor as Auteur* (South Brunswick/New York: A. S. Barnes, 1975)

MARCUS, MILLICENT, *Filmmaking by the Book: Italian Cinema and Literary Adaptation* (Baltimore/London: Johns Hopkins University Press, 1993)

MARDORE, MICHEL, *Roger Vadim* (Paris: Premier Plan, 1959)
MITTERAND, HENRI, 'Le Musée dans le texte', *Cahiers naturalistes*, 66 (1992), 13–22
MUSSER, CHARLES, 'Moving Towards Fictional Narratives: Story Films Become the Dominant Product, 1903–1904', in GRIEVESON AND KRÄMER, eds, *The Silent Cinema Reader*, pp. 87–102
NELSON, BRIAN, '*Nana*: Uses of the Female Body', *Australian Journal of French Studies*, 38 (2001), 407–29
NIESS, ROBERT J., *Zola, Cézanne and Manet: A Study of L'Œuvre* (Ann Arbor: University of Michigan Press, 1968)
O'SHAUGNESSY, MARTIN, *Jean Renoir* (Manchester: Manchester University Press, 2000)
PAGÈS DU TARN, *La Nouvelle Phèdre* (Paris: Gustave Havard, 1858)
PALACIO, JEAN DE, '*La Curée*: Histoire naturelle et sociale, ou agglomérat de mythes', in BAGULEY, ed., *La Curée de Zola*, pp. 171–77
PETREY, SANDY, 'Anna-Nana-Nana: identité sexuelle, écriture naturaliste, lectures lesbiennes', *Cahiers naturalistes*, 69 (1995), 69–80
PLACE, JANEY, and LOWELL PETERSON, 'Some Visual Motifs of *Film Noir*', in SILVER and URSINI, eds, *Film Noir Reader*, pp. 65–76
PLACE-VERGHNES, FLORIANE, '"Il fallait brûler Maupassant": du danger d'adapter *Bel-Ami*', *Bulletin Flaubert–Maupassant*, 12 (2003), 61–84
POLLARD, PATRICK, ed., *Emile Zola Centenary Colloquium, 1893–1993* (London: Emile Zola Society, 1995)
POOLE, ADRIAN, *Shakespeare and the Victorians* (London: Thomson Learning/Arden Shakespeare, 2004)
PRENDERGAST, CHRISTOPHER, 'Le Panorama, la peinture et la faim: le début du *Ventre de Paris*', *Cahiers naturalistes*, 67 (1993), 65–71
RACINE, JEAN, *Phèdre* (Paris: Larousse, 1990)
REFF, THÉODORE, 'Manet's Portrait of Zola', *Burlington Magazine*, 117 (1975), 35–44
RENOIR, JEAN, *Orvet* (Paris: Gallimard, 1955)
——, and PIERRE LESTRINGUEZ, *Scénario: Nana*, (Paris: Arte Editions, 2004)
REWALD, JOHN, *The History of Impressionism* (New York: Moma, 1961)
RICKS, CHRISTOPHER, *Allusion to the Poets* (Oxford: Oxford University Press, 2002)
ROBERT, GUY, *La Terre d'Emile Zola: étude historique et critique* (Paris: Les Belles Lettres, 1952)
——*Emile Zola: principes et caractères généraux de son œuvre* (Paris: Belles Lettres, 1952)
ROY-REVERZY, ELÉONORE, 'Nana, ou l'inexistence: d'une écriture allégorique', *Cahiers naturalistes*, 73 (1999), 167–80
SANDERS, JULIE, *Adaptation and Appropriation* (London/New York: Routledge, 2006)
SCHOR, NAOMI, 'Mythe des origines, origines des mythes: *La Fortune des Rougon*', *Cahiers naturalistes*, 52 (1978), 124–34
——*Zola's Crowds* (Baltimore/London: Johns Hopkins University Press, 1978)
SCHUMACHER, CLAUDE, *Zola: Thérèse Raquin* (Glasgow: University of Glasgow French and German Publications, 1990)
SHAKESPEARE, WILLIAM, *King Lear*, ed. by Elspeth Bain, Jonathan Morris and Rob Smith (Cambridge: Cambridge University Press, 1996)
——*Antony and Cleopatra*, ed. by Richard Madelaine (Cambridge: Cambridge University Press, 1998)
——*King Richard II*, ed. by Andrew Gurr (Cambridge: Cambridge University Press, 2003)
SILVER, ALAIN, and JAMES URSINI, eds, *Film Noir Reader* (New York: Limelight Editions, 1996)
SINGER, ROBERT, 'Introduction', in GURAL-MIGDAL AND SINGER, eds, *Zola and Film*, pp. 5–14

——'"At the Still Point": Framing the Naturalist Moment', in GURAL-MIGDAL and SINGER, eds, *Zola and Film*, pp. 194–206

SMITH, DIANE, and ROBERT SINGER, 'A Drunkard's Representation: The Appropriation of Naturalism in D. W. Griffith's Biograph Films', *Griffithiana*, 65 (1999), 96–125

SPENCER, CHARLES, 'Dim Shadows of Zola's Hellish Vision', *Daily Telegraph*, 15 November 2006, <www.telegraph.co.uk> [accessed 24 July 2007]

THIBAULT, JEAN-FRANÇOIS, 'La Peinture en marche: académisme et modernité chez Claude Lantier', in GUIEU and HILTON, eds, *Emile Zola and the Arts*, pp. 25–33

THOMPSON, HANNAH, ed., *New Approaches to Zola* (London: Emile Zola Society, 2003)

——*Naturalism Redressed: Identity and Clothing in the Novels of Emile Zola* (Oxford: Legenda, 2004)

VADIM, ROGER, *Memoirs of the Devil*, trans. by Peter Beglan (New York/London: Harcourt Brace Jovanovich, 1976)

VAN HOOFF, DOMINIQUE, 'Emile Zola et l'Impressionnisme ou la révolution positiviste en peinture', *Excavatio*, 1 (1992), 73–83

WAGNER, GEOFFREY, *The Novel and the Cinema* (London: Tantivity Press, 1975)

WARREN, PAUL, ed., *Zola et le cinema* (Sainte-Foy: Les Presses de l'Université Laval; Paris: Presses de la Sorbonne Nouvelle, 1995)

WILLIAMS, TONY, 'Eisenstein and Zola: Naturalism, Cinema and Mythography', in GURAL-MIGDAL and SINGER, eds, *Zola and Film*, pp. 27–44

WILSON KNIGHT, G., *The Wheel of Fire: Interpretations of Shakespearian Tragedy* (London: Methuen, 1949)

WOODSON WADDELL, HOLLY, 'The Naked Truth: Renée and the Myth of Phaedra in *La Curée*', *Excavatio*, 18 (2003), 143–56

WOOLF, MATT, 'Thérèse Raquin', http://london.broadway.com/story/id/3004722 [accessed 25 July 2007]

WRIGHT, NICHOLAS, *Thérèse Raquin: A Play by Emile Zola dramatized by Nicholas Wright* (London: Nick Herne Books, 2006)

ZOLA, EMILE, *Les Rougon-Macquart*, ed. by Henri Mitterand, 5 vols (Paris: Gallimard, 1960–67)

——*Œuvres complètes*, ed. by Henri Mitterand, 15 vols (Paris: Cercle du Livre Précieux, 1966–69)

——*Ecrits sur l'art*, ed. by Jean-Pierre Leduc-Adine (Paris: Gallimard, 1991)

——*Correspondance*, ed. by B. H. Bakker, 10 vols (Montréal: Les Presses de l'Université de Montréal; Paris: CNRS, 1978–95)

INDEX